HOUDINI

ON

MAGIC

EDITED BY WALTER B. GIBSON & MORRIS N. YOUNG

1897

DOVER PUBLICATIONS, INC.

Houdini just after effecting his release from a strait-jacket while suspended from a high building. Note the strength of the ankle supports and the guy rope used to prevent his body from swaying.

The editors are grateful to Harcourt Brace and Co. for permission to reprint material from "Houdini's Escapes" by Walter B. Gibson, copyright 1930 by Bernard M. L. Ernst and from "Houdini's Magic" by Walter B. Gibson, copyright 1932 by Bernard M. L. Ernst. The editors also express their gratitude to John J. McManus for use of illustrations from his magic collection.

Library of Congress Catalog Card Number 53-13518

Manufactured in the United States of America

Dover Publications, Inc.
180 Varick Street
New York 14, N.Y.

CONTENTS

12441

INTRODUCTION

From my first casual meeting with Houdini, some ten years prior to his death, our acquaintance developed progressively into a friendship based upon our common interest in magic, both technical and historical. While Houdini was continuing a career that had already gained him fame, I was establishing myself as a professional writer — some of my work covering magic and kindred subjects, which of course caught Houdini's attention.

As a result, Houdini enlisted my services for literary projects which he considered essential to his future plans. I was thoroughly acquainted with Houdini's early writings and widely versed in magical lore and methods. Hence the association, even in its earlier and intermittent stages, gave me an insight of Houdini, both as a person and a performer.

Our conferences were held in such places as the upstairs study of Houdini's New York home, in the back-room of Martinka's shop on Sixth Avenue, then a meeting place for magicians, or in taxicabs, when Houdini was riding to a train and had free moments to go over notes. Occasionally, we strolled down Sixth Avenue in the shadow of the old "el" and stopped in the office of the Hippodrome to continue our discussions of magic.

Houdini had been a regular attraction at the Hippodrome so he was always welcome there. I saw several of his performances there, including his under water escape performed in the famous pool that was featured on the Hippodrome stage. Not long ago, a new building was erected on the site of the old Hippodrome. In excavating for the foundation, the metal supports of the old "apron" stage came into sight and from a building opposite, I was able to trace the outline of the tank where Houdini had been submerged twice a day.

Though only yesterday in my memory, it seemed somehow to belong to a long-forgotten age which, in a sense, is a true appraisal. In the rapid whirl of modern progress, the equivalent of centuries has passed so far as the public's acceptance of the seemingly miraculous is concerned. Houdini actually sprang to fame during the horse-and-buggy era. His name was known in practically every American home before the word "Ford" meant anything more than the shallow part of a river where Houdini did overboard jumps, shackled with handcuffs, from the deep end of a pier

One of Houdini's sensational "challenges", for example, was an escape from a twisted mesh of Weed Tire Chains, soon after they were introduced In pictures of his early outdoor escapes, we frequently see police in "plug" helmets, holding back the crowds attired in bustles and blazers. Yet as late as the 1930's, anywhere from Portland, Maine, to St. Paul, Minnesota, you were always meeting someone who would point to a river and say, ungrammatically: "There's the bridge Houdini jumped off of." As a bridge jumper, Houdini relegated Steve Brodie to a strictly amateur status; what was more, Houdini did it handcuffed.

It resolves to this: Houdini, as a mystifier, belonged to the line of Pinetti, Anderson, Heller, and their ilk who had flourished during the century before him. To support this comparison, it should be noted that Pinetti, aside from being a master of bombast, was the first great escape artist, performing such feats in his full evening show. Anderson, showman as well as magician, appeared also as an actor and billed his show in extravagant circus-fashion. Houdini followed the same pattern. Heller literally stunned theatre audiences with the challenge of his new "Second Sight" act which Houdini matched later by coupling his jail breaks with his challenge handcuff act.

In contrast, Houdini had none of the suavity and polish of Robert-Houdin from whom he adapted his name, or the Great Herrmanns: Carl, Alexander, and Leon; nor even of Thurston, his contemporary on the American stage whose big magic show Houdini tried to rival at the close of his own career. It was not that Houdini lacked the smooth qualities that the public associates with master magicians; he could probably have developed them, for he had an amazing ability at acquiring whatever he felt he needed for success. But the two styles, that of the bold challenger as contrasted to that of the debonair deceptionist, just did not mix.

What Houdini did was something more remarkable in that he sprang from the status of a stunt performer to a recognized authority in his field, presenting his performances with an impressive dignity and winning fame on the lecture platform as well as on the stage. It is claimed that as a showman, he outdid Barnum — logical enough considering that Barnum had a whole museum to ballyhoo while Houdini's only "living authority" was himself.

In fact, Houdini's greatest problem was beating out the flames of his early publicity in order to rise to a higher category. This can be appreciated only by persons who witnessed Houdini's rise as I did, for I had heard much about him, seen his billings, and been present at his performances long before I met him personally. The public, always looking for a catch-phrase to explain wonders which actually baffle them, gradually found a convenient answer for Houdini's escapes.

"The man is a contortionist," someone would say. "He can slip handcuffs from his wrists and throw his shoulders out of joint so he can wriggle out of anything."

The fact that Houdini was chunky and of powerful physique was disregarded by the people who advanced that theory. His outdoor strait-jacket escape, performed in full view, spread this false concept. It had reached such general acceptance that when Houdini's press agent, Arthur B. Chase, coined the verb "houdinize" for the 1920 edition of Funk & Wagnall's standard dictionary, it was defined: "To release or extricate oneself from (confinement, bonds or the like) as by wriggling out."

True, Houdini did wriggle out of ropes, sheets, and similar bonds, but they represented only a modicum of his repertoire. How he could have wriggled from a nailed-up packing box, a padlocked milk-can filled with water, or his "upside-down" torture cell, was an unanswered question, yet those were the escapes that Houdini advertised most heavily and upon which his success depended.

A brief summary of Houdini's career will clarify much of his success story. Born Erich Weiss, in Appleton, Wisconsin, on April 6, 1874, Houdini was the son of Dr. Mayer Samuel Weiss, a rabbi of extremely modest means who later moved to New York City. Young Erich ran away with a circus, but later came home, and in his late 'teens was appearing as a magician at Coney Island with a partner under the billing of the "Houdini Brothers".

Houdini had coined that name to symbolize "Like Houdin", whose magical autobiography had impressed him. Erich had three different partners in the "Houdini Brothers" act, the last of the trio being his own brother, Theo, who later became known professionally as Hardeen. The brother act broke up when Erich married his wife Beatrice and as "Harry and Bessie Houdini", they went on tour, featuring the "Substitution Trunk Trick" which had been the big bang with the Houdini Brothers.

Far from being a success, Houdini met with many vicissitudes during his early career. He related some of these to me when he played Keith's Theatre in Philadelphia during the early 1920's. We were chatting in back of the theatre when Houdini looked around, made sure no one was close enough to hear him, and said, confidentially:

"Don't breathe a word of this now, but save it for some time when it won't matter, like years from now. You've seen the act that Bessie and I are doing here. It's the same act we worked in dime museums, nine times a day, for eighteen dollars a week. Now, we're doing two a day and getting eighteen hundred. If the management knew, they might want us to change it."

That act included the "Needle Trick", in which Houdini placed a quantity of needles and a length of thread into his mouth, apparently swallowed them, then brought out the needles threaded; and the "Substitution Trunk", in which Houdini and Bessie changed places instantaneously, in and out of a sealed bag inside a locked trunk.

What literally increased Houdini's commodity value a hundredfold was the fame gained through his handcuff act. At the turn of the century, there had been a terrific demand for vaudeville in England, and magic was particularly favored. T. Nelson Downs, with his coin act; Howard Thurston, as a card manipulator; Billy Robinson, Herrmann's old stage manager, masquerading as a "Chinese Mandarin Magician" under the adopted name of Chung Ling Soo; Horace Goldin, with his "rapid-fire" act of stage illusions, were but a few of the performers who came from America to cash in on the British bonanza.

Houdini had been working up his "challenge handcuff act" and came to London with it. Escape acts were already known in England and regarded as a mediocre form of entertainment. But Houdini crashed the public prints by escaping from a jail cell at Scotland Yard, and he became an immediate sensation. Houdini recognized the link between publicity and success, for he both zealously and jealously fought off the competition of rivals in

England and on the Continent. Some were performers who had already been doing escapes, but Houdini took the attitude that all were imitators. He was following the policy that many great mystifiers had adopted before him; that of instilling the public with the notion that he was something quite unique. Oddly, Houdini exploded that myth himself by booking his brother Theo as Hardeen, with a duplicate act to fill the engagements he could not handle. But the idea soon prevailed that Houdini and Hardeen were actually rivals. So when Houdini introduced a new escape act, Hardeen frequently toured with the old one, thus closing the field to competition.

It must not be supposed that Houdini translated artistry solely in terms of business. His craving for knowledge in every phase of magic transcended all bounds. Without a doubt, he applied many rules learned from his research into the lives and methods of his predecessors. Between shows, he was constantly haunting old book-shops and other places where playbills could be found, spending large sums in the accumulation of the vast collection which is now in the Congressional Library at Washington.

Houdini's intense sincerity in such research was demonstrated by his penchant for restoring the neglected graves of forgotten magicians, both in Europe and America. He delved into the careers of his forerunners and wrote copiously of their accomplishments and achievements, even at the expense of his one-time idol, Robert-Houdin, whose autobiography, Houdini finally decided, had been grossly exaggerated.

The result was a controversy that still rages as a teapot tempest in some magical circles. This is puzzling as an intelligent reading of Robert-Houdin's autobiography reveals self-evident fictions. Though Houdini was over-bitter in his criticism, his authority on the subject remains undisputed. A canard has been circulated that Houdini later regretted having written his *Unmasking of Robert-Houdin*, but I happened to be with Houdini when he autographed a whole shelf of those volumes in Hornmann's Magic Shop in New York. In my many conversations with Houdini on magical history, I never knew him to depart one whit from his statements regarding Robert-Houdin.

Much of that material appeared originally in Houdini's "Conjurer's Monthly" from which it was later compiled and partly rewritten. In choosing historical subjects for this present volume,

Houdini on Magic, the same source has been used, but Houdini's writings have been carefully preserved in the original form. The same applies to historical data from other sources. It has been kept untrammeled, as it were, so the reader may appreciate Houdini's full sentiments even at the occasional expense of literary quality.

It was Houdini's custom frequently to dictate such material, giving it a freshness and sincerity wherein even the sidelights are of interest. Probably no better appraisal of the "old time" magicians could be given than through these whole-hearted descriptions by a modern practitioner of their art who had studied their careers in the light of his own and told what he had to tell in a direct and plausible style.

This, in turn, furnishes many passing glimpses into Houdini's own character and personality. I can vouch for the fact that the comments are in keeping with his style and close to Houdini's spoken word. This applies to such material as the excerpts from *The Right Way to Do Wrong*, taken from Houdini's earlier writings, as well as data on *Handcuff Escapes*.

Under *Rope Ties*, however, we find material that was more carefully written and at a later period; how far it was revised is a question. It is valuable as it deals with Houdini's methods. This applies even more to some of the material taken from my own two volumes, *Houdini's Escapes* and *Houdini's Magic*. Some facts regarding these would not be amiss at this point.

At the time of Houdini's death, I was preparing three volumes on simple magic which were to appear under Houdini's name and to be sold both with his show and in bookstores. These were to be the forerunners of more ambitious titles covering many phases of magic. For one thing, Houdini furnished me with anecdotes from his career which had never appeared in print, and I had planned, through further interviews, to obtain a full volume of these.

But Houdini's death intervened, and none of the partly-completed books was published. However, through Houdini's attorney, Bernard M. L. Ernst, I was furnished with a large amount of material that Houdini had laid away through the years, specifically stating that some day it should be published. It was from these notes that I compiled the two volumes which appeared as *Houdini's Escapes* and *Houdini's Magic*.

Most of the escape material was in the form of rough notes, some written on steamship stationery and therefore traceable as to exact time by checking with Houdini's trips between America and Europe. A fair percentage of these escapes were covered in detail in Houdini's own language, so in describing the escapes, I quoted him quite freely.

In choosing some of those escapes for this volume, I have used those which could be transcribed back to Houdini's own terms. I added some quotes by new reference to original notes and in some places, I have filled gaps with obvious statements that approximate Houdini's own. This material is quite as close to Houdini's original as much of the edited copy in the average book would be. In some instances, by rearranging sentences, the original wording was kept intact.

Remember, however, that Houdini wrote these as rough notes, not as final copy, so that the style differs from the things he dictated. In preparing *Houdini's Magic*, however, I had the benefit of a certain amount of final copy. Whether it was Houdini's original with revisions, or material obtained from other sources, the notes did not specify. But since it was definitely intended to appear under Houdini's name, I have taken some of that material, and included it here in *Houdini on Magic*.

In all technical works on magic, it is customary to adopt certain styles in describing and explaining tricks, thus causing a marked departure from the author's normal mode of expression. This was quite true of Houdini's books on magic, as indeed it has been with my own technical writings. Moreover, any of Houdini's books that might have been heavily revised or "ghosted" outright, would be the volumes explaining tricks. Drawn from Houdini's knowledge of magic, they were intended as informative works, not as personalized expressions. Houdini, very practical in matters magical, was apt to jot down details of new tricks exactly as he heard them described.

It will not be digressing to inject a personal note on this score. Houdini and I spent many hours with Carl Brema of Philadelphia, whose name as a maker of magic has become legendary in its own right. One of Brema's creations was the improved "Hindu Wand" trick, now sold by the thousands, but then a strict novelty. In fact, Houdini had never seen the full routine until I appeared as one of the local guest magicians on his stage at the Chestnut Street Opera House in Philadelphia. The wands so wowed the audience that Houdini wanted a special set for himself. Brema made them up, and I spent an hour in Houdini's dressing room, going through

every move with Houdini while we dictated each detail to his secretary. Several years later, when I was going through the notes
for *Houdini's Magic*, I found that very routine for the "Hindu
Wands" typed in finished form. I cite this to show the difficulty
in determining precise origins where descriptions of certain tricks
are concerned.

Houdini used to leave a taxicab with the meter running outside
of Brema's and forget all about it until a bill of several hours had
piled up. This shows how intensely he was intrigued by all that
pertained to magic. On one occasion, I took him to a magicians'
meeting in my car, which that season was a Ford Model T coupe
with a front seat of only two-person width and with the door-
catches inconveniently placed behind a person's elbow. When he
tried to twist around and work the catch, Houdini found it stuck
and in all seriousness, he demanded, "Say — how do you get out
of this thing?" It wasn't until I had reached across and pulled the
knob for him that he began laughing, because he, of all people,
couldn't get out of a Ford coupe.

Though Houdini's escapes will always remain intriguing to
the public because of the tremendous publicity attached to them,
Houdini was not too secretive regarding his methods. He explained
many secrets when they began to become known, or he had replaced
them with something better. This was good business in that it les-
sened the value of such escapes when they were appropriated by
Houdini's rivals.

But in the final analysis, Houdini's great claim to permanent
fame lay in his crusade against fraudulent mediums and other
charlatans who preyed upon the public. Fearless of hazard or
threat, he worked ceaselessly in the exposure and suppression of
such fakery. The publicity he gained was tremendous, but it did
not compensate for the risk he encountered. Today, many people
have forgotten what an important factor spiritism had become in
American life shortly after World War I when Sir Arthur Conan
Doyle and other famous personages were conducting an all-out
campaign in its behalf. It is now considered much as a crank
phenomenon as was proved by its merely spasmodic revival after
World War II.

The eclipse of fake spookery may be credited almost entirely
to Houdini's crusade against such chicanery as he left no doubt in

practical minds as to its underlying fallacies. This is all the more to Houdini's credit, because he, more than any other person, was in a position to capitalize on such fakery had he so desired. Proof of this is found in the fact that many believers in the occult still affirm that Houdini was actually a medium but would not admit it. One psychic "authority" stated that Houdini dematerialized himself in order to escape from his Water Torture Cell and later rematerialized himself outside the contrivance. It was to spike such absurdities as this that Houdini was willing to let so many of his secrets be explained.

Always a challenger, Houdini was ready to match any claim that bordered on the supernatural. His feud with Rahman Bey, the Oriental mystic, was a case in point. When Rahman Bey allowed himself to be "buried alive" at the bottom of the Hudson River, Houdini did not banter words about it. He constructed a casket of his own and demonstrated that he could stay under water just as long as the Egyptian fakir.

His challenge to Margery the medium was another instance of Houdini's ceaseless struggle against superstition. In order to show the full breadth of Houdini's interests, material relating to fake mediums and other frauds has been included in the present volume. This emphasizes all the more that Houdini's tricks were testimony to human ingenuity not dependent upon any supernatural ability.

In all, this book, with its abundance of Houdini's own writings, shows how clearly magic, as practised by Houdini, was and is explainable by one faculty only: that of human accomplishment.

WBG

HOUDINI ON HANDCUFFS AND RESTRAINTS

Whatever Houdini's hopes, ambitions, or claims in the twin fields of Magic and Mystery, his name was built upon his skill at releasing himself from handcuffs, particularly in the Challenge Act where the cuffs were supplied by strangers. At almost the outset of his career, Houdini extended the challenge to jail escapes and gained himself reams of publicity in dozens of cities. As a result, the public associated Houdini's handcuff challenges with his famous jail escapes. To these, Houdini soon added the straitjacket escape, which he later performed as a publicity stunt while hanging head down above a crowd.

Of this trio, however, the handcuffs came first. So strongly was this built in the public mind that for a time, Houdini advertised himself as "Harry Handcuff Houdini" and though he branched out into other types of escapes and challenges, some far more sensational than the handcuff act, the fame of his early career not only left an indelible imprint upon his later work, but actually shaped it. Always, Houdini was more the showman than the magician because from him audiences expected something more akin to miracles than tricks.

Houdini's writings on handcuffs, jail escapes, and straitjackets are therefore of primary interest. To some readers it will come as a surprise to learn that Houdini exposed some handcuff secrets, considering that his career depended on them. It might also be assumed that he reserved such writings until he was through with the secrets concerned. Quite to the contrary, these represent some

1

of his earliest literary efforts, published while he was still actively engaged in baffling the public with the very artifices he discloses.

Houdini's purpose was twofold: He wanted to establish himself as the pioneer of the Challenge Act and at the same time worry his imitators by giving away the more common devices upon which they depended. Frequently, along with crediting himself with certain inventions, Houdini disclaimed inferior methods as though he would never have stooped to their use. So even Houdini's exposures carry the implication that his own work approached the supernormal.

However, his coverage of the subject was too conclusive to leave any doubts in an analytical mind. The simple answer is that when Houdini reserved methods for his own use, it was not necessarily because they were superior, but because they were less known than those which he did explain. About the only thing conclusively proved was that the exposure of such mysteries only increased public interest in witnessing their performance, for Houdini and his rivals kept merrily on their way regardless of their mutual recriminations and retaliations.

Houdini's comments on these subjects are interesting from the historical as well as the explanatory standpoint. The present selection of such secrets goes beyond his early writings and includes some special methods and inventions that he developed later. Inasmuch as locks and handcuffs in themselves constitute a highly technical subject, it has been deemed advisable to stress the human element as much as the mechanical side in this volume.

While there is no doubt as to the accuracy of many facts presented by Houdini, it is obvious that he was prejudiced against the rivals he styled "imitators" and was therefore inclined to ignore data in their favor. His own brief tracing of the handcuff act and its sources, found in the following pages, makes it clear that it was anybody's property. Whatever the extent of Houdini's innovations, it could only be expected that other performers would accept the popular trend and devote their talents to such fields.

Houdini's early statements are therefore open to some amendment. He speaks disparagingly of a performer named Brindemour, whom he practically brands a failure. Ten years after Houdini made that statement, Brindemour was playing high class vaudeville circuits with an excellent handcuff act that was very favorably received. I personally witnessed Brindemour's show and regard him as one of the most polished mystifiers of the American stage.

Less than six years ago, I talked with Cunning, another handcuff expert criticised by Houdini, and confirmed the fact that he successfully outmaneuvered Houdini in the course of a public challenge. This discounts Houdini's earlier comment that Cunning was a "would-be" mystifier. Like Houdini, Brindemour and Cunning have gone from this earthly stage, so it is only fitting that their passing controversies should be laid to peaceful rest.

WBG

LIGHT ON THE SUBJECT OF JAIL BREAKING
AS DONE BY MY IMITATORS

I am induced to take this step for the manifest reason that the public of both hemispheres may, through ignorance of the real truth, give credence to the mendacious boasts and braggadocio of the horde of imitators who have sprung into existence with mushroom rapidity of growth, and equal flimsiness of vital fibre, and who, with amazing effrontery and pernicious falsity, seek to claim and hold the credit and honor, such as they may be, that belong to me.

It is in the same spirit and for the same cogent reason, I execute my present duty of duly setting forth my right to the title which I hold and the absolute pilfering of name, fame, and the other emoluments of success by those others who advertise and rate themselves as "Handcuff Kings," "Jail Breakers," etc,. *ad libitum, ad nauseum.*

That I have a horde of imitators may not be as well known as it will be to those who have the patience and the sense of fairness sufficiently developed to lead them to read this article through to its conclusion.

Therefore, it will not be considered unbecoming of me to set forth here the details of my conception, execution, and performance of the Challenge Handcuff and Escape Act as presented by me at this time in the principal vaudeville and music hall theatres of Europe and America. And I trust also that I will not be deemed guilty of undue egotism, or of having an attack of "exaggerated ego," to borrow a popular term growing out of the Thaw trial, if I assert that this act has proved to be the greatest drawing card and longest lived sensation that has ever been offered in the annals of the stage. This has been demonstrated by the record-breaking attendance in every theatre in which I have given the act, either in part or whole, and also by the duration of my term of engagement in the principal theatres among those in which I have been booked.

"Art is long and life is short," says the ancient poet.

The stage and its people, in the light of history, make this a verity.

As examples, take the famous Davenport Brothers, also the "Georgia Magnet," also the "Bullet Proof Man," etc. For the benefit of those who have not heard of the latter sensational attraction — which was indeed a great novelty for a limited time — I will explain that the man was a German who claimed to possess a coat that was impervious to bullets. He would don this coat and allow any one to shoot a bullet of any calibre at him. Alas! One day a marksman shot him below the coat, in the groin, and he eventually died from the wounds inflicted. His last request was that his beloved invention be buried with him. This, however, was not granted, for it was thought due to the world that such an invention should be made known. The coat, on being ripped open, was found stuffed or padded with powdered glass.

Returning to the subject of my own career, I assert here with all the positiveness I can command that I am the originator of the Challenge Handcuff Act, which consists in the artist's inviting any person in his audience to submit handcuffs of his own from which the performer must release himself. And it is proper that I should add at this point that I do not claim to have conceived and originated the simple handcuff trick. Every novice in this line knows that it has been done for many years, or so far back, as the lawyers say, "that memory runneth not to the contrary."

French historians of the stage show that as far back as early 1700, La Tude performed it. Pinetti did chain releases in 1780, and other modern magicians have had it in their programs ever since 1825. The Sr. Bologna, instructor of John Henry Anderson,

made a small trick out of it. Anderson placed it among his repertoire the second time he came to America in 1861 and when
exposing the Davenport Brothers, he made quite a feature of it.
In fact, I have an old monthly of 1870 in which a handcuff trick
is explained in an article exposing spirit mediums.

Dr. Redmond, who, I hear, is still very much alive in England,
made quite a reputation as a rope expert and handcuff manipulator
in 1872-3, and I have several interesting bills of his performances.

Few give me credit, but had I been able to copyright my new
tricks, they would all have to pay me a royalty.

But, as such cannot be done, the only thing I ask of the numerous imitators is to give credit where credit is due.

No one, to my knowledge, performs my tests according to my
method except my brother Theo Hardeen, as they ALL resort
to fakery and collusion in presenting to the public that which
they wish to have thought is exactly as Houdini performs his
challenges.

The following challenges have been performed by myself, some
of which are very interesting. Release in full view of the audience
from straitjackets used on murderous insane; the nailed up in
packing case escape; the packing case built on the stage; the paper
bag; the willow hamper; the hamper swung in the air; the steel
unprepared cage or basket; riveted into a steel water boiler; hung
to a ladder in mid-air; nailed to a door; escape from unprepared
glass box; out of a large football; release from a large mail pouch;
escape from a roll top desk; escape from a zinc-lined piano box,
etc., etc. In fact during long engagements, I have accepted a different challenge for every performance.

In order to stop all controversy concerning this jail breaking
affair, I shall publish the methods that have been used by some
of those who will stop at nothing in order to willfully deceive the
public.

First of all, there is a young man who calls himself Brindemour
who, according to all I can learn, claims to be the originator of
jail breaking and has accused me of stealing the material from
him. He has even gone so far as to say that I assisted him. Why,
in 1896 I visited Woonsocket, R. I. with a show and made quite
a hit with the handcuff act. There I met a photographer whose
name was George W. Brown. He made himself known to me and

informed me that he was an amateur magician, and that at certain periods of the year he gave performances for friends and lodges. His great hit was to impersonate a ballet girl.

He showed me pictures of himself in ballet costume and seemed to be proud that he could impersonate the female sex so perfectly. That was in 1896. About a year later, after purchasing a bunch of handcuff keys, this Brown called himself Brindemour. He gave a trial show at Keith's Providence house for Manager Lovenberg and failed to make good. His great stunt then was to make the church bells ring, which is accomplished with a confederate and was Sig. Blitz's standby. At any rate, the Great Brindemour, failing to make good, followed me into Philadelphia and started in to expose his handcuff act. He did this in Providence, also Philadelphia, and made a dismal failure. The effect of his work showed him that he was on the wrong track, and eventually he did not expose the few fake tricks that he had and went into it without the exposures.

He pursued the same old groove until I returned to America, when he deliberately copied all of my challenges as best he could. I wondered how he did his jail breaking stunts, as I knew that he could no more pick a lock than the Czar of Russia will give the Russian newspapers the right of free press. Recently I have ascertained the facts as to several of his escapes, or rather their "mysterious means," and I will give the reader the benefit of my investigations. At the same time I invite the closest investigation of anything that I have ever done. While filling an engagement at Albaugh's Theatre, Baltimore, Brindemour escaped from the cells at police headquarters under the following circumstances: A reporter on the *Baltimore News,* by name of "Clint" MacCabe, called on Harry Schanberger, who is engaged in an official position at police headquarters (this incident was told me personally by Harry Schanberger and in the presence of witnesses). MacCabe, after a chat with Harry Schanberger, borrowed the set of keys from Schanberger, telling him that he wanted to give them to Brindemour, so that he could give a press performance and make the people believe that Brindemour had escaped "on the square."

Schanberger loaned MacCabe the two keys, and naturally Brindemour escaped from the police headquarters cells, using the genuine keys that belong to the Police Department.

AND HE DARES TO CALL HIMSELF THE POLICE MYSTIFIER!

In mind I can almost hear the spirit of poor Chas. Bertram say, "Isn't that wonderful?" The strange thing about this affair is that in Baltimore, another alleged jail breaker met his quietus for the time being.

He is Cunning, who also labors under the delusion that he is the original world's greatest. I quote from the *Baltimore News,* and it will be seen how much "talent" this gentleman possesses. Extract from the *Baltimore News,* Thursday, February 8, 1906:

CUNNING'S GAME EXPOSED

Cunning, the hitherto mysterious opener of handcuffs and shackles, who is exhibiting at the Monumental Theatre this week, was found out today by Acting Turnkey John Lanahan at the Central Station and had to abandon the feat that he had promised to do of escaping from a locked cell.

Before being locked in the cell, Cunning went into the latter, pretending to examine it and secretly placed a key upon a ledge, but Lanahan discovered the key just as Cunning was about to be locked in, and when told of the discovery, the wizard said, "You've got me," admitted that he could not open the cell without a key, and abandoned the exhibition.

The real truth of this jail break is that Mr. Joe Kernan went to the police captain and borrowed the keys and handed them to Cunning. The turnkey, Lanahan, not being in the "know," discovered the palpable "planting" of the keys and ran with them to the captain. In this way the "stunt" was unexpectedly exposed.

Personally, I think it ought to be a prison offense for any official to loan his keys to these would-be and so-called mystifiers, and if managers wish to lend themselves willfully to deceive their audience, the quicker they find out that they are treading the wrong path the better for them, too. You can take any stagehand, and in five minutes make just as good a jail breaker as the many that are now trading on my name.

Another "gross" misrepresenter is a youth named Grosse. This man, or rather youth, claims that he can open time lock safes and all the complicated locks of the world, stating that handcuffs are mere play to him. Why, he can't even pick his teeth, and if he were put to a test with a lock picker, I doubt that he could even throw back a one tumbler lock. Yes, he would have trouble to pull back a common latch.

No doubt some of the police that are entangled with some of these jail breakers will grow hot under the collar at me for showing this thing up, but as long as these fellows are pretending to do my work, and as long as they stoop to do it in this manner, just so long will I publish the real facts as soon as I find them out.

In conclusion, I wish to state that I defy any manager or police official to come forward and prove that I, by any underhanded means or conniving methods, have stooped or lowered my manhood to ask them willfully to deceive the public by such base misrepresentations.

THE STRAITJACKET RELEASE

The word straitjacket alone conjures up to the mind pictures of violent maniacs and thoughts that tend to gruesome channels.

The origin of the presentation of this release on the stage occurred to me during the season of 1894–5 while touring the Canadian provinces where I went to fulfill an engagement with Marco, the magician (now James Dooley of Hartford, Conn.). The company fared disastrously, because a man had assumed the name of Marco and the preceding season toured through the same territory giving so poor a show that the audiences went away complaining. When the real Marco company arrived, they sparingly patronized us, but as they left, we could hear remarks all over to the effect that "this is not the same Marco we had here last time." The name of the bogus Marco was, I believe, Skinner, and the people said it was actually one well earned and appropriate for the kind of show he presented to them.

Our show closed in Halifax, Nova Scotia, and I thereupon determined to proceed by myself and give the whole show. While in St. Johns, I met a Dr. Steeves, who then was in charge of a large insane asylum, and received an invitation from him to visit his institution, which I accepted. After showing me the various wards, he eventually showed me the padded cells, in one of which,

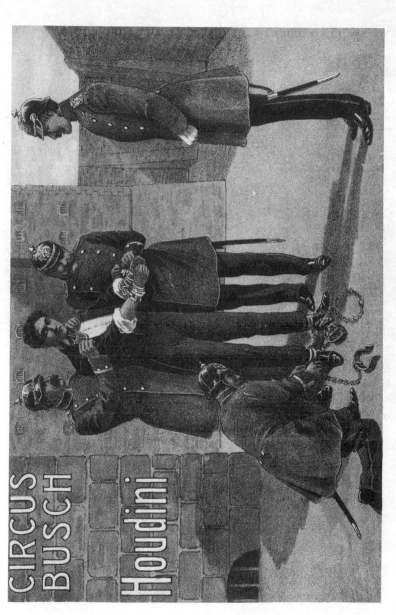

Houdini escaping from the German police under challenging conditions. This billing was used during his tour of Germany during his early rise to fame at the beginning of the century.

From the John J. McManus Collection.

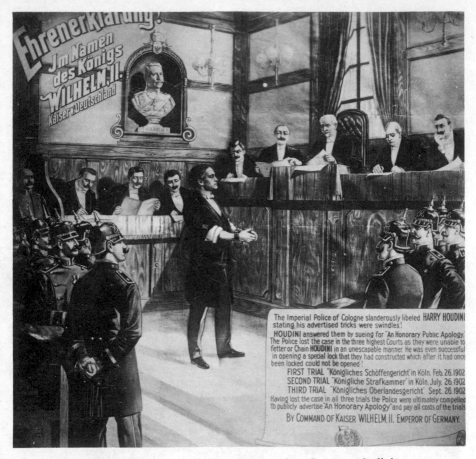

Houdini's demonstration before the German judiciary.

through the small bars of the cell door, I saw a maniac struggling on the canvas padded floor, rolling about and straining each and every muscle in a vain attempt to get his hands over his head and striving in every conceivable manner to free himself from his canvas restraint which I later on learned was called a straitjacket.

Entranced, I watched the efforts of this man, whose struggle caused the beads of perspiration to roll off him, and from where I stood, I noted that were he able to dislocate his arms at the shoulder joint, he would have been able to cause his restraint to become slack in certain parts allowing him to free his arms. But as it was that the straps were drawn tight, the more he struggled, the tighter his restraint encircled him, and eventually he lay exhausted, panting, and powerless to move.

Previous to this incident I had seen and used various restraints such as insane restraint muffs, belts, bed-straps, etc., but this was the first time I saw a straitjacket, and it left so vivid an impression on my mind that I hardly slept that night, and in such moments as I slept, I saw nothing but straitjackets, maniacs, and padded cells! In the wakeful part of the night, I wondered what the effect would be to an audience to have them see a man placed in a straitjacket and watch him force himself free therefrom.

The very next morning I obtained permission to try to escape from one, and during one entire week, I practised steadily and then presented it on the stage and made my escape therefrom behind a curtain. I pursued this method for some time, but as it was so often repeated to me that people seeing me emerge from the cabinet after my release with hair disheveled, countenance covered with perspiration, trousers covered with dust, and ofttimes even my clothes being torn, remarked, "Oh, he is faking it, it did not take all that effort to make his escape," that eventually I determined to show to the audience exactly what means I resorted to to effect my release and so did the straitjacket release in full view of everybody.

The two accompanying illustrations show a front view and a back view of strapping on a straitjacket such as is used on the murderous insane. It is made of strong brown canvas or sail cloth and has a deep leather collar and leather cuffs; these cuffs are sewn up at the ends, making a sort of bag into which each arm is placed; the seams are covered with leather bands attached to which are leather straps and steel buckles which, when strapped upon a person, fit and buckle up in back. The sleeves of this jacket are made so long that when the arms of the wearer are placed in them and folded across the chest, the leather cuffs of the sleeves, to which are attached straps and buckles, meet at the back of the body, one overlapping the other. The opening of the straitjacket is at the back where several straps and buckles are sewn which are fastened at the back.

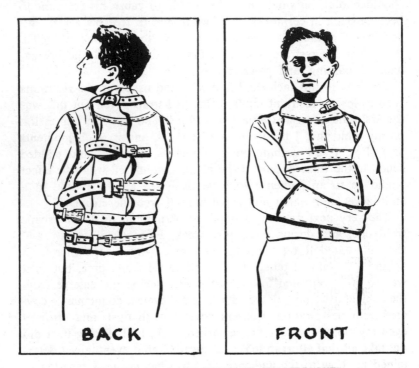

BACK   FRONT

FRONT AND BACK VIEW OF STRAITJACKET

The first step necessary to free yourself is to place the elbow, which has the continuous band *under* the opposite elbow, on some solid foundation, and by sheer strength, to exert sufficient force at this elbow so as to force it gradually toward the head, and by further persistent straining, you eventually force the head under the *lower arm*, which results in bringing both of the encased arms in front of the body. (It is very important that these instructions be followed closely step by step; and when placing the arms across the chest, sufficient care must be observed simply to place one arm on top of the other and not have them interlocked.)

Once having freed your arms to such an extent as to get them in front of your body, you can now undo the buckles of the straps of the cuffs with your teeth, after which you open the buckles at the back with your hands which are still encased in the canvas sleeves, and then you remove the straitjacket from your body.

There are various kinds of straitjacket made from different materials, some being entirely made of leather; and, of course, the more inflexible the material, the more difficult is your release and the longer the time required.

In 1901, Count Schwerin, then chief of police of Hanover, Germany, had his warders place me in a straitjacket from which it took me one hour and twenty-nine minutes to effect my release. The pain, torture, agony, and misery of that struggle will forever live in my mind.

There is a peregrinating imposter in Germany who escapes from a straitjacket from which any child could make its escape. He has it made of pliable white canvas with very long sleeves and short body, though when strapped on him, it seems as if he were firmly secured. In making his escape, he goes through fantastic gyrations and eventually wriggles out of his fastenings.

The American imitators, as a rule, improvise a straitjacket that they can pull over their heads. Of course, these latter two are trick straitjackets and should not be confounded with the genuine ones.

SKELETON KEYS SOMETIMES CALLED MASTER
KEYS FOR WARD LOCKS

Such keys are made for opening a set or series of locks each of which has a different make of key so that one key will not open another lock in the set, yet, the holder of the master or skeleton key will open all. In old locks with fixed wards, this was done by making the wards of a slightly different form and yet such that the skeleton would pass them all.

It is always possible to find the shape of the wards by merely putting in a blank key covered with wax and pressing it against them. When this was done, it was by no means necessary to cut out the key in the complicated form of ward as shown here, because no part of that key does any work except the edge B C farthest from the pipe A, and so a key in the shape of the next one would do just as well; and a small collection of skeleton keys, as they are called, of a few different patterns were all the stock in trade that a lock picker required.

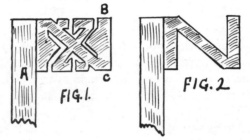

FIG. 1 SHOWS THE ORIGINAL KEY USED BY THE PURCHASER OF THE LOCK. FIG. 2 SHOWS THE SKELETON KEY REQUIRED TO OPEN THE SAME LOCK.

In the accompanying illustrations, some wardlock pickers most in use are shown. There is one which is adjustable. The bits fit into holes in the shank of the key and are secured by screws, so that you can regulate them to whatever size you require for the lock you wish to open.

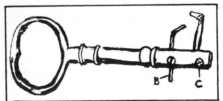

ADJUSTABLE WARDLOCK PICKER.

Another illustration shows some simple yet very useful lock pickers, and while a number of them look very. much like each other, they are of different sizes so as to lift the tumblers and throw back the bolt. The four marked X are the ones I used in my celebrated lawsuit at Cologne, and with which I picked hundreds of three and four lever locks almost as quickly as they could be opened with a key, for I practiced every day and night for three months on these particular locks.

The lock used in Germany on the regulation transportation

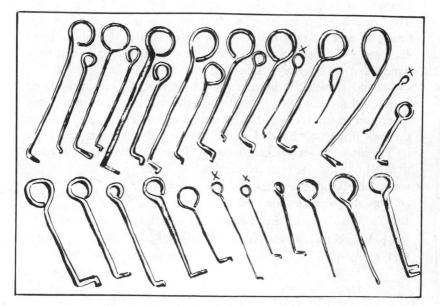

AN ASSORTMENT OF LOCK-PICKERS FOR OPENING SIMPLE TWO AND THREE LEVER LOCKS.

chain is of a peculiar 3 or 4 lever pattern. The post in the keyhole prohibits a strong pick from entering , so I made several different shaped lock pickers from piano wire.

This was thin and very stiff, for I knew in order to win my lawsuit I would have to open any lock that was placed before me, and started in to practice. The best practice I could obtain was to procure a position as a repair locksmith in a small shop. In Berlin I knew a locksmith, Mueller, who has a shop on Mittle Strasse, and he was more than willing that I should work for nothing, and I commenced repairing locks for him. He soon discovered that his 35 years of experience as a locksmith was nothing as compared to my trick in opening locks, and he soon had a thriving trade for his young man to open locks. In order that I should know the exact heights of the various locks used on the police chains, he ordered a great gross, and soon exchanged them for another great gross of other patterns, etc. In that way I would pass 6 to 10 hours daily picking locks and soon, with the assistance of the four marked picks, I could open any lock that contained the 5 or 6 Chubb levers. The "gate ways" were never made close, as is the case in the very fine lever locks, so it became a very simple matter for me to open each and every lock which was made on that principle, and very handy that experience was in court.

I found I could facilitate matters by taking an ordinary elastic garter and fastening it to the clasp of the padlock and looping the other end to my foot so that by stretching the elastic and holding the lock in the left hand, I would have a pull on the clasp. Now by inserting the lockpicker, I could lift one lever after the other until all were of the proper height, when the elastic, like a faithful servant at the proper time pulled the clasp back, which freed from the bolt, and thereby caused the lock to open.

ELASTIC ATTACHED TO CLASP
OF PADLOCK TO FACILITATE
OPENING.

Just at this juncture, it is not out of place to describe the German transport chain which is used by the German police almost exclusively for transporting prisoners.

THE WAY THE TRANSPORT CHAIN SHOULD BE FASTENED TO THE WRISTS.

The chain has two rings, one for each hand, one being located at the end of the chain and the other in the center. One lock is utilized for securing both hands. In the illustration, you will note that the chain entwines both wrists which rest one above the other.

PULLING THE FIRST HAND OUT BY SHEER STRENGTH, USING THE TEETH AS AN AIDE.

After the chain has been fastened on your wrist as in the illustration, the first movement is to bring each arm lengthwise on the other, the fingers of both hands pointing toward the opposite elbows, and by sheer force of strength, you extricate yourself from the chain one hand at a time.

FREEING THE OTHER HAND WITH THE AID OF THE ONE THAT WAS FIRST SLIPPED OUT OF THE CHAIN.

LOCK PICKING IMPLEMENTS

This illustration shows sundry little pieces of wire picks, also a powerful combination pliers and wire cutter (C). When you open or close this pair of pliers, the lower pins or rivets, as shown in the illustration, travel in slots in two planes of steel in the upper part of the handle and so enable a person to cut very thick wire as easily as paper. In this illustration, there is also a piece of malleable steel wire (D), which, with the aid of the pliers, can be twisted or bent into any shape and snipped off to any required length. This is always useful for immediately making such special lockpickers as are required.

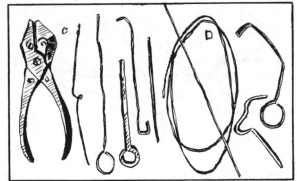

VARIOUS PIECES OF WIRE, PICKS, AND POWERFUL COMBINATION PLIERS AND WIRE CUTTER.

The next illustration shows lockpickers, which will give you an idea as to how the wards are placed in the French locks.

In no country have I found so many expensive locks in use as in France; almost every door is equipped with a six-lever Chubbs or Bramah lock. Crooks would have an exceptionally hard time to pick such locks, so they resort to the quicker and easier method of forcing the doors with heavy chisels.

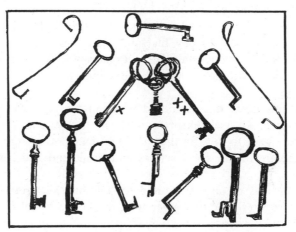

LOCK-PICKERS FOR FRENCH LOCKS.

The lockpickers or keys marked XX and X were taken from a French murderer whose specialty was robbing churches.

He was a daring criminal and was caught by the merest accident. He had laid plans for a cool and premeditated murder of one of the Geldbrief Träger in Berlin, which class of postmen carry only money sent by mail and sometimes are entrusted with large sums.

This man, Olschansky, sent through the mail to himself 100 *Mark* (about $25) having previously hired a small room in a street where the house was almost empty of lodgers.

The room was on the top floor, and when the postman arrived Monday morning, he found Olschansky awaiting him, and to all intents and purposes, Olschansky was just seated at his morning lunch (which all Germany partakes of about 10 o'clock) consisting of bottled beer and sandwiches.

Olschansky offered the postman a bottle of beer, but gave him no glass. He was then compelled to drink out of the bottle, and as the bottle was raised to his lips, Olschansky raised a heavy board and drove the bottle down the postman's throat, stifling him, and then immediately struck him over the temple and kept on hitting the stunned man until he had beaten the life out of his body.

He took all the mony from the leather bag carried by the postman, locked the door, and left the building.

But he forgot to pay the beer man, and instead off going about his business, he went to pay his bill, as he was an honest man. This man noticed blood stains on Olschansky's shirt cuff.

Olschansky paid him with a 20-*Mark* gold piece, and this was his undoing.

In the afternoon the murdered postman was discovered, and the beer man, Gastschenkwirth, reported to the police that 20 marks were paid to him by the man who had not enough money the day before to pay for his food and drink and had asked for credit.

A search was at once instituted for Olschansky, and with the system of registering each lodger with the police by all hotel and boarding house keepers, Olschansky was found, and in his possession were the two keys herewith illustrated.

I happened to be at the Police Presidium next morning and spoke to Olschansky, who looked more like a caged wolf than a man and had very little to say.

But two weeks later, when found guilty, he had plenty to say and informed the police of the various churches he had robbed, how he obtained keys for the doors, and showed he was a far more dangerous criminal than was at first suspected.

After he had been executed, I asked for the keys that had been found in his possession and obtained them. I have found that they will open almost every church door in Germany where they do not use padlocks, and the key marked X seems to be a kind of master key to the spurious Bramah locks.

The next illustration shows a set of master keys useful on the English Rim lock. Previous to the year 1778, when Baron invented the now well-known tumbler lock, the majority of locks used in

England were of such a nature that at the present date they would
be called "jokes."

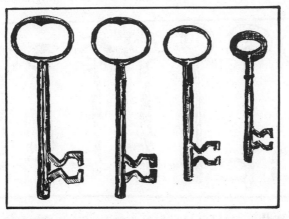

MASTER KEYS USEFUL ON ENGLISH RIM LOCKS.

With the illustrated sets of pickers, there are thousands, yes,
tens of thousands of locks in England that can easily be opened.
Naturally it will take some practice which, when once acquired,
is seldom lost.

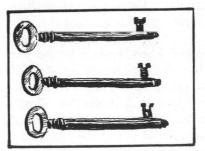

MASTER KEYS FOR AN AMERICAN LOCK IN USE IN GREAT BRITAIN.

Another illustration shows some master keys for an American
lock greatly in use in Great Britain. A majority of office doors are
fitted with this master-fitting key.

Here are different size master keys for the common ward locks. Note how they vary in size, and with the seven illustrated, few locks of the ward lock construction would be impregnable.

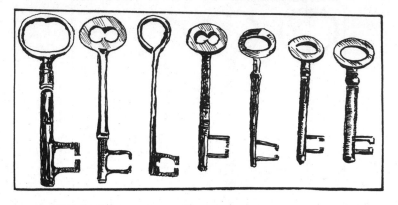

VARIOUS MASTER KEYS FOR COMMON WARD LOCKS.

The handcuff manipulator who imagines that he can go abroad with a few false handcuff keys and make a success has only to give it a trial, and he will find out to his sorrow that an unskilled performer will not be tolerated very long. The Germans, particularly, are like a flame in the pan, a quick flash and then oblivion!

Once in Dortmund, Germany, the landlord of the hotel at which I was stopping came and asked if I would do him a great favor.

A guest who had hired a room by the year was gone for a business trip to Nürnberg and would not be back for several months.

This guest had taken the key of the room with him, and as there happened to be a rush at the hotel, Mr. Thrifty Landlord wished to make double revenue by letting this room to a transient guest.

Of course I was not aware of the fact, and to oblige the landlord at his request, I opened the lock of the door. As he wanted a key to the door, I went to a hardware store and purchased a blank key which I intended to cut to fit this lock.

Being an old-fashioned hotel, it had no master keys, and I really went to a lot of trouble to oblige my host.

The next morning I read a three-column article headed: "Houdini exposed. Buys up all the keys in town, and no wonder he opens all doors." Then the bright editor told a very interesting story of how he happened to be in the shop and saw Houdini looking over all the blanks and buying several thousands of them; when in reality, I bought one blank, for which I paid five cents (about 20 *Pfennige*). Ever since that time, I shun hardware shops as I would a pest house.

OPENING SEALED HANDCUFFS

If you wish to have handcuffs sealed, it would be well to try and have a pair rather large so as to slip the hands. You can then easily open the cuff by giving it a sharp blow with the keyhole downwards. Strike the cuff where the hinge and keyhole are on

HOW TO HIT THE CUFF TO OPEN IT.

the heel of your shoe or against the floor, and it will spring open.
I once used a plate of lead fastened onto drawers at the leg above
the knee, sewn in to prevent its slipping away. This was bent to
the shape of the leg so that it was not perceived. I struck the cuff
where the plate of lead was fixed. This method, however, was
rather uncertain. On reference to this illustration, you will see how
and where I hit the cuff to open it.

THE PLUG EIGHT HANDCUFF

Herewith is presented the Plug Eight Handcuff. This is an
extraordinary broad one, used in South Africa during the Boer
war, and they say the cuff is used on the Kaffir diamond thieves.
No matter how heavy the manacle may be, the locking arrangement is generally the same. This cuff is made by Hiatt of Birmingham, Froggott of Boardsley, and the one time handcuff maker,
Fields. Strange, but almost all of the English cuffs are made in
Birmingham or its vicinity.

THE "PLUG EIGHT"
SHOWING CUFF OPEN,
CLOSED, KEY, AND
STEEL PLUG.

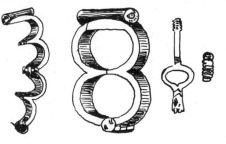

You will notice that when it is open, it resembles a double W
and when closed, it resembles the figure eight; after it is locked,
you insert a small steel plug into the circular keyhole, and from
this steel core or plug, I have named the cuff "Plug Eight". In
fact I have named every single cuff in the world today. And all

of my imitators have taken my "Tales" and names bodily **and** without pretense of knowing why the cuff is so called

You will note that the key to the Plug Eight has two teeth at one end: this is the end that unscrews the "Steel Plug". After this "plug" has been removed, you take the other end of the key and insert it into the key hole and unlock the cuff by turning the key in various directions. Some are female cuffs, which turn from left to right, whilst others are the regulation right to left "unlocking cuff". It is very easy to make a master for these cuffs as all work on the same principle.

The easiest cuff to work with is the English Regulation as illustrated here

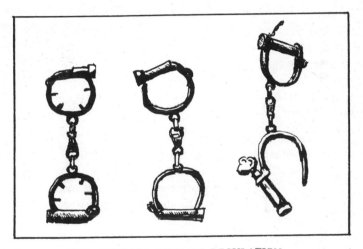

THE COMMON ENGLISH REGULATION.

Having provided yourself with a set of these manacles, you get duplicate keys for same. With one solitary exception, all these cuffs have spring locks and are manipulated by screwing the key in to open, but they close on pressure with a snap. The exception is what is styled "Plug 8".

For performance: You must adopt the best method suitable to you for concealing your duplicate key. Either in some get-at-able pocket or in a shoe, drapery of cabinet, etc. You may have difficulty in getting handcuffs from your audience, so you must prepare for this emergency by having some of your own secretly "planted" beforehand by your assistant with some confederates in audience.

As each come on, you examine the irons and satisfy yourself they are of the regulation pattern as it is from regulation handcuffs alone you guarantee to free yourself.

Having examined the cuffs, you allow your committee to lock them on you, all present being satisfied you are securely locked. You enter your cabinet and, obtaining possession of your duplicate key, you simply unlock cuff and again conceal key. There are, however, some cuffs larger than others, and in this case, you slip one hand from cuff; then it is easy to procure your key and open both.

MOSCOW ESCAPE

During my engagement at the "Establishment Yard" in Moscow, Russia, several officers stepped upon the stage to act as a committee, and one of them was very arrogant and would insist on standing in the center of the stage, thereby obstructing the view of the audience. In my politest Russian, I asked him to step aside, but instead of so doing, he demanded how I, a common menial, dared even address him. I honestly did not know what he meant and again asked him to step aside and this time omitting "Please". The officer became enraged and planted himself right down in the midst of the footlights, refused to budge, and commanded me to go on with the performance.

By this time, I knew that he was someone of high rank from the way the rest of the folks about bowed, scraped, and fawned to him; so I thought that the best thing I could do was to inform the audience that unless this officer stood aside I would refuse to go on with the show.

Police strapping Houdini in a regulation strait-jacket preparatory to his escape from the restraint

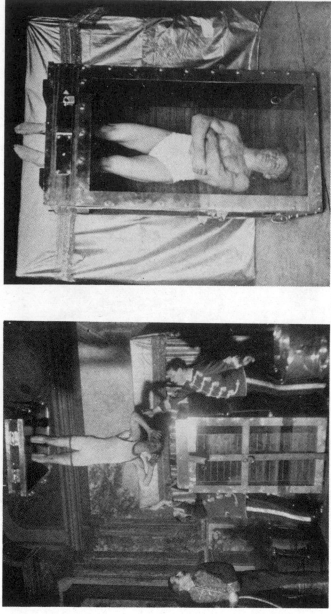

Two stages of the famous "Water Torture Cell", Houdini's greatest escape act for many years. His feet locked in stocks, Houdini was lowered into the water-filled interior and the top was padlocked by a metal grille. His escape was effected while the cell was covered by a curtained cabinet. The cell front had interior metal bars, ostensibly as protection in case the glass broke and the water rushed out. Actually, Houdini gripped these bars with his hands, to work his head and shoulders to the top. There, doubled up, he sprang the secret release of the stocks composing the top and slid the rear half, drawer-fashion, from its frame, automatically releasing his ankles and providing sufficient space to emerge from the cell top.

The officer only grinned, so I had the cabinet carried down stage so that if the curtain was rung down, it could only come down to the top of my cabinet, and the siege started! There were many officials of high rank in the audience, and soon they started to protest to think that the show had been cut off. Eventually the manager was sent for, and he explained things to me as best he could, but I remained obstinate and insisted that unless this officer stood aside, I would not go on with the show.

It was explained to me that people working for a living, and especially performers, are not looked upon in a favorable light as the majority of Russian men act simply as guides for their acts and generally employ all kinds of women to sing in their troupes, and instead of being paid a salary by the theatrical managers, they have to pay for the privilege of having their troupes work the cabinets. Their cabinets are on the order of the Western wine rooms, only on a very much higher scale.

In Russia, the well-to-do folks come to dine in the cabinets, and if they do not wish to see an act on the stage or have missed a turn, they pay to have the act go through its performance in the cabinet.

The audience in the "Establishment Yard" was now aroused to a fever pitch, and it was only on my explaining to an officer that in America I was rated as a millionaire, that he profusely apologized to the audience and to me and stepped aside. This officer was the means of obtaining a performance for me at the Palace Kleinmichel where I appeared several times in the presence of the Grand Duke Sergius (who was assassinated several years ago), and we became quite friendly. During one of my entertainments, the Grand Duchess assisted me in the role of Second Sight Artist. All this helped to make a name for me in Russia which will not be forgotten for some time to come. Naturally, this caused a great deal of jealousy amongst the Russian magicians, and one after the other started to run down my performance. Robert Lenz claimed that he did the trunk trick thirty years ago, and because his wife was so much fatter, larger, and more awkward than Madame Houdini, he claimed that his trick was superior. He started in to do a lot of exposing, and one bright morning I arose and found all over the streets of Moscow bright red posters reading, "Roberta, the Celebrated Exposer, will show you how to escape from all handcuffs, and from all locks."

I awaited his opening and then saw his show. Of all the false representations and schemes for obtaining money under false pretense, "Roberta, the Celebrated" took the bun, biscuit and bake shop.

He did not even know what a handcuff key looked like, and his entire exposure consisted in removing a rivet from all his manacles, which had been specially prepared for the purpose.

In this illustration you will note that the Neck-cuff or Collar is open at the hinge, and the "False" rivet is shaped like a screw; this is also shown on the handcuff.

On the cuff the dotted lines "A" show where the rivet is held, and the false screw or rivet is screwed down tight with a good pair of pliers, so that with the bare hands or fingers no one can unscrew the bolt.

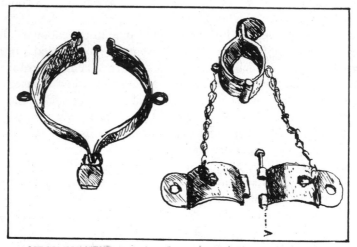

NECK-CUFF AND HANDCUFF SHOWING FALSE RIVET.

Naturally you can allow anyone to bring along as many locks as they desire, and you can make your escape. All you have to do is to take out your pliers, unscrew the bolt, and close it up again. With this arrangement you can build a large cross or gallows and allow the committee to lock you with as many locks and chains as they wish to bring along, but be sure that they run the chains through the staple or place prepared to hold the locks. The collar which I invented and used years ago, when being compelled to give two or three performances, was one that fooled even the best magicians in the world. It was made of light metal, and the fake part of it could not be moved either with the fingers or an instrument. The secret was in the hinge, as I had a steel pin placed in the rivet (which was hollow), and this pin could only be removed by using a strong horseshoe magnet which would pull it up to the top and allow the hinge to open. This method defies detection, and I can honestly recommend it to anyone wishing to make a good set of "fake" handcuffs or make what is known as a "Spirit Collar."

COLOGNE POLICE LIBEL SUIT

The police of Germany are very strict in matters of false billing or misrepresenting exhibitions to the public, and so when the Cologne police claimed that I was travelling about misrepresenting, and that my performance was "swindle", and when Schutzmann Werner Graff published a false story in the *Rheinische Zeitung*, which put me in a very bad light, as a man of honor I could not overlook the insult.

Claiming that I had been slandered, I asked for an apology and a retraction of the false stories which all the press of Germany had copied, but I was simply laughed at for my trouble.

I engaged the best lawyer of Cologne, Herr Rechtsanwalt Dr. Schreiber, Louisenstrasse 17, and commenced suit.

The first trial occurred in Cologne, February 19, 1902. I charged that Schutzmann Werner Graff had publicly slandered me, whereupon, as answer, Herr Graff told the judge and jury that he was willing to prove that I was misrepresenting, and that he could chain me so that I could not release myself. I permitted myself to be chained by Herr Transport Police Lott, and to show how easy it was, in the presence of the judge and jury, released myself.

After a four day trial, I won the lawsuit, and the Cologne police were fined and were to apologize to me publicly, "in the name of the Kaiser".

Instead of so doing, they took it to the higher court, "Strafkammer". At this trial they had specially manufactured a lock which was made by Master Mechanic Kroch, which when once locked, could not be opened, not even with the use of the key.

The police asked that I show my ability to open this lock after it had been locked.

I accepted the challenge and walked into the room selected by the jury where I could work unhindered, and in four minutes reentered the court room and handed the judges the prepared lock *unopened*.

Again I won the lawsuit, and again it was appealed, but this time to the highest court in Germany, "Oberlandesgericht", and there the learned judges again gave me the verdict from which there was no appeal.

THE SPIRIT COLLAR

Along with handcuffs and leg irons, there are special types of metal collars made to lock about a person's neck and from which escape is seemingly impossible. The most unusual of these is the "Spirit Collar" which is made in the shape of an ice pick, with a center rivet which can be examined before and after the escape.

This device is placed about the neck, and the handles are locked, bringing the points of the ice pick close together. These points have small caps on them as a protection against their jabbing your neck, and the space between is so slight that it appears impossible to remove the collar without unlocking it. In fact, the lock can be sealed up, but still the collar is removed from the neck, and the seals are found unbroken.

The secret is that a certain part of the neck is very thin. If you put one point of the collar under your chin near your ear, you can force it way into your neck, and you will be able to work the collar from your neck. This is done in a series of stages, carrying the point past the jugular vein, the caps of course preventing injury at that stage.

By gaining as much distance as possible between the points, the escape is facilitated, and you actually accomplish it without tampering with the lock or the collar in any way whatever. This gives the escape the effect of a "spirit test" presumably accomplished by some unseen aid.

THE CHAMPION LOCK CUFF

This is a splendid freak cuff, a very formidable device, yet escape from it is easy. However, it can be thoroughly examined by a committee without the slightest chance of anyone's detecting its secret. It can be introduced as a special challenge cuff and will look the part.

It is made on the style of the Russian Cuffs, like those in Scotland Yard, which gives it a very genuine appearance. There are two bands to receive your wrists; these are placed on a rod by means of holes through the bands. One end of the bar terminates in a bolt. Any lock can be hung through a hole in the other end of the bar and still escape is possible.

One form of this device depends upon a special bar which unscrews in the center. This can be a round bar with an eccentric bump which enables the hands to unscrew the bar. You can also have the holes in the hand loops square or of some eccentric form. In this case, the long bar is also made square, which allows the hands to unscrew it and take it apart.

Another method is to have the bolt-head unscrew. It fits into a key, which consists of a plate with a square hole, fixed in the cabinet. You use this to hold the bar steady while the bolt-head is being taken off.

This can be made into a very sensational looking cuff by making use of a very heavy piece of steel for the bar. It should be as weighty as possible and to show that the bands are not slipped, it is wise to have a pair of ratchet cuffs on the wrists at the same time.

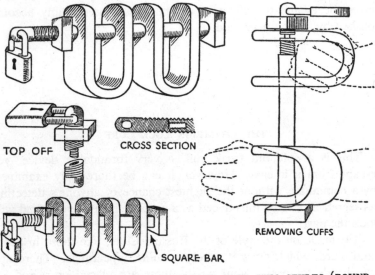

TOP OFF   CROSS SECTION

REMOVING CUFFS

SQUARE BAR

OPERATION OF THE CHAMPION LOCK CUFF. TWO STYLES (ROUND BAR AND SQUARE BAR) ARE SHOWN

HOUDINI ON ROPE MAGIC

Knowledge of Rope Ties is fundamental with the escape artist. Some of Houdini's earliest publicity sheets and broadsides show him bound inextricably in ropes, ready to attempt a release. In fact, ropes were used by escape kings long before handcuffs came into vogue as a theatrical item. But in the old days, the "act" was presented with a different twist.

The Davenport Brothers, who flourished from the 1860's on, allowed themselves to be tied in a cabinet along with a lot of bells and tambourines, which soon began to ring and bang away as proof of "spirit" manifestations. When the cabinet was opened, the Davenports were found as solidly tied as at the start.

The famous magician, Harry Kellar, who once traveled with the Davenports, featured a Rope Tie in all his entertainments, showing that he could duplicate the feats of the noted brothers without spirit aid. Such workers had to be unusually adept as they not only released themselves but worked their hands back into the ropes. However, they could specify the manner in which they were to be tied, a privilege which the escape artist often lacks.

It stands to reason that anyone who can escape from handcuffs should be willing to attempt a rope escape. What is more, there are many people who "know the ropes" better than they do handcuffs — boy scouts and sailors, for example. Such challengers are too numerous for any escape artist to dodge, so he has just one answer: He must learn rope ties to stay in business.

That is no hardship, for it is worth the trouble. Once he has become adept at ties, the escape specialist can use them in many other ways. He can be tied up in trunks or boxes from which he plans to escape, thus enhancing his act. He can demonstrate "spook" tricks and other feats of rope magic, all of which have entertainment value. In addition to the so-called "spirit ties" which are really "in and out" releases, there are many clever conceits, such as the mysterious appearance or evanishments of knots, that pass as pseudopsychic phenomena.

Houdini made a thorough study of these along with rope escapes. In later years, he exposed these "spook tricks" with other fraudulent phenomena during his regular magical performances. Meanwhile, Houdini had written copiously on Rope Magic, adding his own pet methods — particularly those of escapes — to the more general effects. His treatment of the subject forms a valuable compendium which would be difficult to surpass, extending much farther into the strictly magical field than the domain of the escape artist.

Many of these tricks, culled from Houdini's writings and notes, were the sort that he personally presented on the stage. Where knot tricks were concerned, Houdini frequently demonstrated them with huge silk handkerchiefs which offered a more colorful display than ropes. Essentially, however, many of the tricks were the same whether handkerchiefs or ropes were used.

This section on Rope Magic will therefore prove as invaluable to the working magician as to the aspiring escape artist or the student of psychic phenomena, as it includes many of the tested tricks that have mystified appreciative audiences before Houdini's time and ever since.

WBG

KNOW YOUR ROPES

Rope ties have one distinct advantage over all other forms of escape; namely, no possible suspicion is attached to the ropes themselves. In many cases where locks, chains, handcuffs, trunks, pillories, and the like are used, the apparatus is more or less under suspicion, but where ordinary ropes or tapes are the only means employed, the performer gets all the credit for the escape. Where tapes can bo oubstituted, it is generally best to use them as they create even less mistrust than ropes.

The best rope for general purposes is Silver Lake Sash Cord. In some cases the new cord is the better, but in others it will be necessary to work it till it becomes pliable; just how far to carry the softening process differs with different ties, but a little experience will determine this point.

The first thing for the performer to ascertain is whether any member of the committee has followed the sea or is for any reason familiar with knots. If such a one is found, he should be used for tests where difficult knots and secure binding does not interfere with the effect. By all means, when possible, get a physician on the committee, as it always creates a good impression to have him examine the hands, wrists, arms and shoulders, and have him report to the audience that there is no way of contracting the bones and muscles so as to slip out of the knots.

The program should be so arranged that each effect will appear a little more difficult than the preceding one, finishing with something showy and apparently difficult. The clothesline tie is particularly good for an effective finale.

Don't lose confidence in an effect because it has been presented many times before. An old trick in "good hands" is always new. Just see to it that yours are "good hands".

Don't allow yourself to "go stale" on your act. Keep up your enthusiasm! There is nothing more contagious than exuberant enthusiasm, and it is sure to "get" an audience.

A SIMPLE RELEASE

This is perhaps the oldest known to the conjuring profession, the effect being to release the hands when they are tied behind the back in the ordinary way.

Although simple, it is by no means easy and will require considerable practice in order to escape in the limited time allowed by impatient audiences, but it is a very necessary part of the escape artist's education and should be thoroughly mastered.

It is accomplished by bending the body forward and working the arms down over the hips until the hands are just behind the knees. This will seem impossible at the first trial, but keep at it and you will get the knack after a while. When the hands are in position back of the knees, sit down on the floor and cross the legs, the left above the right, work the left arm down over the left knee and withdraw the left foot and then the right from the looped arms. This brings the knotted wrists in front of the body, and the knots may then be untied with the teeth.

For this tie new sash cord should be used, for two reasons: first, because it is impossible to tie very tight knots with it, and second, because its smooth surface facilitates the slipping over the hips.

THREE EFFECTS WITH THE HANDCUFF TIE

For the following effects, use about four yards of light cord or tape. I prefer tape about ¾ inches wide.

Invite someone to step on the stage and examine the tape. Have him tie one end around your left wrist, not too tight. You let him hold the other end of the rope and stand close to the front of the stage.

Now make a small coil in the tape a few inches from your left wrist. Push a loop through the coil and tighten the coil to form a fake knot. Do this openly, calling attention to the knot, which you hold in the fingers of your left hand.

Turn and walk up stage. With your back to the audience drop the fake knot from the left hand. With the right, quickly make a loop in the tape a foot from the left wrist. Pass the loop under the tape surrounding the left wrist, give it a half turn and pass it over the hand as shown, then down under the wrist tape again and a real knot will be formed. Pull the tape tight and you will automatically dispose of the fake knot.

Now let the gentleman examine the knot, and to his surprise

he finds that he cannot untie it without releasing his end of the rope. Say to him: "Perhaps you didn't see just how it was done.

THE HANDCUFF TIE.

Let me try it once more. This time we will have both wrists tied."

Have the tape cut a yard from the left wrist and the end tied around the right. "Now you see there can be no deception as I am practically handcuffed and to make it more interesting. I would like to borrow a finger ring."

The ring having been procured, it is slipped over a loop in the tape, as shown. You then ask your assistant to face the audience and hold his hands in such a position that all can see that he does not have a hand in the tying. Consume a couple of minutes in getting him properly placed and then stand at his side and ask him

to count, one-two-three. At the word three, separate the hands
and show the ring securely tied in the center of the tape.

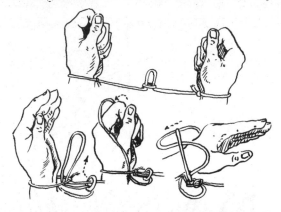

This tie is made as follows: While placing the gentleman's face
to the audience, stand behind him, so that your hands will be concealed by his body, which will give you sufficient time to make the
necessary moves, which will require only a moment. While the
hands are concealed, pass the loop under the band on the left
wrist, as shown, then over the hand and back under the band. Hold
the knotted ring and several loops of the tape in your left hand as
you step to the side of the gentleman, and at the word of three, let
all drop, and the ring will be found to be properly knotted.

After the assistant acknowledges that he cannot remove the
ring without cutting the tape or untying the knots, say to him: "Is
it possible that even now you don't know how it is done? Well,
well, well! However, I have known similar cases before, so I will
give you one more chance, and this time I will use a ring big
enough for you to see. Is this one big enough? Examine it please;
Solid ring? No opening? No? You did not examine it closely; I
find an opening almost big enough to put my fist through. You
saw the ring, but didn't see the hole, because the ring part is bigger
than the hole, but we all know that the whole is bigger than any
part, so, while the ring is bigger than the hole, the whole is bigger
than the ring, and, the whole is bigger than the hole, and still you
didn't see it." While speaking, put the loop of tape through the
ring, same as in the case of the finger ring, and hold the ring and
loop in the left hand, and continue, "Was that too much for you?
Pardon me, I should have asked you to sit down." Go up stage and

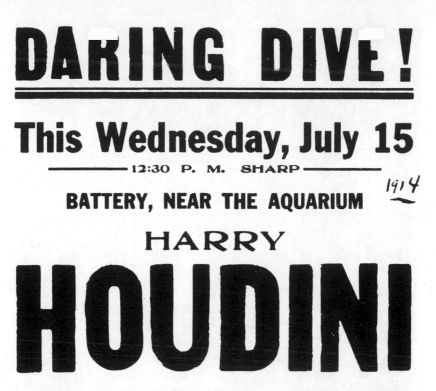

DARING DIVE!

This Wednesday, July 15

———— 12:30 P. M. SHARP ————

1914

BATTERY, NEAR THE AQUARIUM

HARRY

HOUDINI

Now Appearing at Hammerstein's Victoria Theatre and Roof Garden

Securely handcuffed and leg ironed will be placed in a heavy packing case, which will be nailed and roped, then encircled by steel bands, firmly nailed. Two hundred pounds of iron weights will then be lashed to this box containing HOUDINI. The box will then be THROWN INTO THE RIVER. Houdini will undertake to release himself whilst submerged under water.

The Most Marvelous Feat Ever Attempted in This or Any Other Age.

Wednesday, Rain or Shine

One of the many printed challenges issued by Houdini during his early career. This is but a sample of the vast variety of Houdini "throwouts" that have now become collectors' items. They were issued in many lands and languages.

Packing box containing Houdini, handcuffed and shackled, is lowered into the water, in 1914. Houdini, of course, released himself from the irons while the box was being nailed shut and roped for its overboard trip. Escape from the box depends on a trick panel in one end. Held by only two nails, it pivots inward when a hidden catch or wedge is sprung. An ordinary packing box, if constructed to specifications, can be faked very quickly by the performer's assistants, either back stage or en route to the river.

bring down chair that stands at back and have the gentleman sit at the center near the front. Then say. "Now I am going to do this one right under your nose." Step behind him and put your arms over his head and bring them down by his sides, which will bring your hands in front of him, and, as you promised, "right under his nose". Make two or three motions, as if tying a knot, then draw the hands apart and the ring will be found to be linked on the tape. Remove the arms and allow the gentleman to rise, saying: "There, you certainly must have caught it that time. Take the ring off, please. You can't? Well, sir, I am sorry to say that I find your case quite hopeless, so I must ask you to cut the tape and free both the rings. Thank you very much. Will you please return the borrowed ring to its owner?"

For this effect two rings exactly alike are necessary. The rings may be of metal, glass, or celluloid, the last being preferable on account of lightness, and they must be large enough to slip easily over the head and forearm. At the beginning, one of these rings is "loaded" on the left arm near the elbow, and kept in place by rolling up the sleeve preparatory to the several ties. The rest hardly needs to be explained. As you go up stage to get the chair, the original ring is slipped under the vest and the other brought down and held in the same way as the first; then by letting go, it drops down to the center of the slackened tape.

THE THUMB TIE

Methods of escape from apparently securely tied thumbs are easily traced back to the days of Pinetti, 1784, and future research may give them even greater antiquity; the tie in which two cords are used, however, as it first attracted attention when introduced into this country by the Japanese Ten Ichi Troupe, has become known as the "Ten Ichi Thumb Tie." With the single exception of the Kellar tie, no other has caused as much discussion or brought out as many imitations. Many clever performers have duplicated the effect, but none seems to have been able to prepare the hand-made, fibre paper cords as used by the Japs, and, therefore, no one has thus far exactly reproduced the original method although the effect remained the same to the eyes of the public.

The sudden popularity of the trick created a demand for the secret, and many manufacturers of magical apparatus put out various forms of metal fakes, false thumbs, etc., by means of which they claimed that the effect could be duplicated, but all of these were promptly discarded, and today only sleight-of-hand and showmanship are made use of in this "tie".

The usual form of presentation follows closely that of the Ten Ichis, that is, the thumbs are tied by a committee, and the performer takes a position fifteen or twenty feet away. The committee then throws a number of solid hoops toward him, which pass between his hands and onto his arms. The knots are instantly examined and found to be unchanged. Other tests of the same nature follow; such as, linking the arms with those of a committeeman whose hands are clasped, linking through the backs of chairs, around an upright pole, and the like.

THE THUMB TIE.

The first method which I shall describe is the one that is most commonly used and the one that probably approaches most closely the Ten Ichi method. For this, two fairly stiff cords about one-eighth inch in thickness, and respectively sixteen and twenty inches in length are used. Some performers use cords wound with Japanese paper, but this is worse than useless, as any smooth woven cord will answer the purpose and does not give the impression of preparation.

After the cords have been examined, the larger one is wound twice around the thumbs, which are presented as shown here, the cords drawn as tightly as possible and knotted on the top, as shown.

THE TYING OF THE SHORTER CORD.

During the tying, the thumbs should be held somewhat closer together at the tips than shown in the cut. The shorter cord should be passed between the thumbs and twice around the other at right angles, tying this on the top also, thus forming a sort of figure eight, as shown, with a thumb through each loop, and the remaining ends may be tied together if the committee desires. Now by moving the tips of the thumbs farther apart, like opening a scissors, it will be found that the right thumb can be instantly withdrawn and returned to its loop.

When waiting for the hoops to be thrown the hands should be held flat, palm to palm, the fingers pointing upward. In this position, the thumbs cannot be plainly seen, so that the right thumb may be withdrawn before the hoop is thrown. Then catch the hoop between the hands, pass it into the arm, return the thumb to the loop, and bring the tips together as before and step quickly forward to have the knots examined. All these take but an instant if they have been properly practiced.

THE CLOTHESLINE TIE

This is a very showy tie, and is well adapted to close a rope act.

About fifty or sixty feet of sash cord is used, and the statement that it is a seventy-five foot clothesline is never disputed.

The whole secret lies in the fact that it is quite impossible to tie a man while in a standing position, with such a length of rope, so that he cannot squirm out of it with comparative ease, if the tying BEGINS AT ONE END OF THE ROPE and finishes at the other.

At the beginning of the test, you should hold the rope coiled in the hand, and the first move is to uncoil the rope and have it inspected by the committee. Then explain that there seem to be a few still skeptical, and for that reason you will give the committee "plenty of rope" and let them tie you in any manner they please. During this speech, you again coil the rope, at the same time explaining to the committee quietly that in this form it will be more easily handled, passed through the knots, etc., the object of this being to force them to begin tying at one end. Some performers have a slip-knot already tied in the end of the rope, but this is not necessary, and is rather suggestive of preparation.

It is the experience of all who have used this tie that the first few knots are carefully tied, but after a time, it will be found that the rope is being used up very slowly, and they will begin winding it around the body and making very few knots. A hint to "hurry up, as the audience is getting restive," will also induce less careful knotting, and as they are following no regular method and several are handling the rope, they are bound to work more or less at cross purposes.

If the committee happens to be very much in earnest, and begins to make more knots than suit you, it will be well to swell the muscles, expand the chest, slightly hunch the shoulders, and hold the arms a little away from the sides. After a little practice you will find that such artifices will enable you to balk the most knowing ones. You should always wear a coat when submitting to this tie as that will be found to be an added help in obtaining slack.

It is an excellent idea to practice with a couple of assistants who know the game. Let them try their best to secure you, and you will get a great deal of needed experience. The actual escape is always possible, but practice is necessary in order to acquire speed in execution.

A sharp knife with a hook-shaped blade should be concealed somewhere on the person as it may be found useful in case some of the first, carefully tied knots, prove troublesome. A short piece cut from the end of the rope will never be missed.

When the last knot is made, you should turn to the audience and say: "Are you all satisfied that I am securely tied?" and then immediately answer your own question by saying, "Of course, you have to be satisfied, for the committee has done all that is possible, in fact, they have 'reached the end of their rope'."

After being placed in the cabinet you should call attention to the fact that it has taken six or eight minutes to bind you, and ask someone to hold a watch and see how long you require to escape.

SIMPLEX TIE

This is so easy that it can be worked by any boy with very little practice, the practice being for speed only.

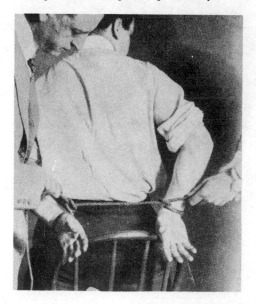

Note the way the hands are tied with a space of ten or twelve inches between them. When tied in that manner, the escape is only a matter of untying knots.

When tied to the chair, as shown, the hands can easily be brought together, and one unties the other.

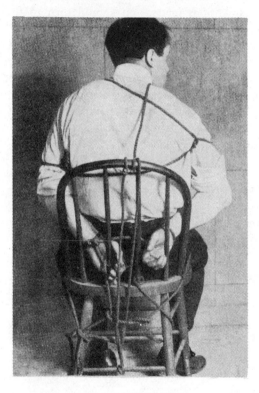

THE SIMPLEX TIE.

With both hands free, the rest of the knots can be managed without difficulty, particularly if a rather stiff rope has been used.

This belongs to the high school of escapes and should never be attempted by a beginner.

In the first place, it is absolutely necessary that the aspirant be a good swimmer, well versed in treading water, floating, and all methods of keeping afloat without the use of the hands. This is not as difficult as it at first appears, but it should be thoroughly practiced, either in a tank or in a shallow stream, and always with a friend at hand to act as a life-saver in case of accident.

It is also necessary to acquire the art of swimming with a forward and backward motion of the feet, in place of the old scissors stroke; and once having mastered the method, the body can be kept afloat as easily as by the old style. The necessity for the above is apparent when we consider that the hands must be used on the knots continuously.

Bear in mind that the release must be accomplished rapidly, not only on account of the necessity of breathing, but because the ropes shrink when they become water-soaked although this is not rapid enough to interfere seriously with your work.

UNDER WATER ESCAPE.

The hands must always be released first, and the student should practice all the methods I have explained, studying the appearance of each knot, the sort of knot he has to contend with, and the manner in which he should attack it. After the hands are free, the remainder of the knots should be fairly easy.

In the illustration, I have used short lengths of rope, but the escape is no more difficult from one length.

Deep breathing in order to strengthen the lungs and increase their capacity must also be practiced, for it will be necessary to hold the breath for a considerable time, and as the escape is bound to require rather violent struggles, this is no child's play.

Let me caution you to use extreme care and not to neglect the

UNDER WATER ESCAPE.

smallest detail. This is a dangerous business at best, and two of my imitators have been drowned when thrown overboard in manacles. If you are not an absolutely fearless swimmer, I warn you to keep away from ropes under water, and unless you are an expert of the highest order, never substitute handcuffs unless you resort to fixed cuffs which require only a pull to open, and even these might go wrong with disastrous results.

I have never used fixed manacles in any of my stunts, always allowing stage cuffs to be affixed. When I did use my own, it was only to add extra weight so that I might sink quickly to the bottom and out of sight of my audience, so that they might not inspect my method of releasing myself.

SPECTACULAR ESCAPES

Strange as it may appear, I have found that the more spectacular the fastening to the eyes of the audience, the less difficult the

THE LADDER TIE.

escape really proves to be. For example, the ladder tie here shown gives the impression of an almost unescapable restraint while in reality it is simply a slow but sure proposition.

Note carefully the manner in which the hands are tied to the sides of the ladder, and when the committee has finished the tying, start to wriggle the arms and strain at the ropes. This should give you sufficient freedom to work one of your hands to the front of the ladder, thus bringing one section of the rope within reach. This you work loose, and you will then find that knot after knot can be untied, and with one hand liberated, the rest is only a matter of time.

It is advisable to use short lengths of stiff, new sash cord, the stiffer the cord the easier it will untie. If the ladder is placed upright against a wall it should be securely fastened in place, as a fall in such a helpless condition might prove disastrous. In case the ladder is laid on the floor, the upper end should be rested on a box or something of the kind, thus leaving room to work the hands to the front side.

THE BIG WHEEL RELEASE

This belongs to the "spread-eagle" class of spectacular escapes which depend largely upon "scenery". We are always aware that many mediocre plays have attained a measure of success entirely through an artistic or realistic setting. So with the spectacular release. An audience which would go to sleep while an artist was making a really difficult escape from the wheel of a farm wagon will break into tumultuous applause over a comparatively easy one from a cannon wheel.

The first object in all these releases is to work for the liberation of one hand. After that it is only a question of untying knots, a science in which the escape artist should become expert before attempting any release. He should accustom himself to all forms of knots by having himself tied by a sailor or someone who knows how to tie real knots. I have always encouraged my assistants to devise new knots and fastenings, getting my practice in that way,

THE BIG WHEEL RELEASE.

and I'll say that they have given me some pretty hard tussles, for nearly all of them have been in the navy or before the mast in a merchantman.

Do not go before the public before you are letter perfect in the particular release that you propose to present. I have worked weeks and weeks on one escape before venturing to present it in public.

It has always been essential that my assistants be expert in the matter of tying knots, for in most of my outdoor stunts, my life depends on the manner in which my feet are lashed. For a long time, I made use of heavy padding for my ankles when hanging from high buildings in the straitjacket escape, but even that would eventually become painful.

THE NORTH AMERICAN INDIAN TIE

During one of my engagements at the Lasky studio in California, that popular leading man, Tom Meighan, who established a lasting reputation by his admirable work in the screen production of the "Miracle Man", told me of a tie that was formerly used to secure an Indian who had imbibed too freely of "fire-water". The accompanying illustration shows Meighan in the act of subjecting me to this tie. I am led to believe that he carried the process considerably farther than was the custom in the case of a bibulous aborigine, but I succeeded in freeing myself in less than four minutes.

The manner of liberating myself — or yourself — is to bend the body forward and downward as far as possible, which should enable you to get the rope off the neck, or if this is found impossible, it will allow you to reach the knots with one or the other of the hands and untie them.

This was only used when conveying the man from place to place and at a time when his wits were not at their best, which I

presume to be the reason that he did not free himself. It is not a
bad tie, however, and is shown here to give the reader an idea
when changing his program.

THE NORTH AMERICAN INDIAN TIE.

The restraint used by the Indians themselves is in a class by
itself. No ropes are used, but they find a stout sapling and place
the prisoner's legs around it, entwining his feet and resting his
body on his haunches in such a manner that he is powerless to
raise himself. By this means, they secure their man without resorting to fastenings of any kind.

Once, in Oakland, when my challengers had drawn me up
about a hundred and forty feet, I made the escape successfully,
but the ropes became twisted, and it was impossible to lower me
to the ground. There I hung suspended in mid-air where no one
could reach me. They called out the fire department, but before
they could get up their scaling-ladders, a window cleaner, who
was accustomed to doing stunts while washing high windows,
fastened himself to a window frame with a couple of towels, and
standing on the ledge, leaned far out and dragged me to safety.

This taught me a lesson. My ankles were in pretty bad shape, for I hung there a long time head downwards. My recollection is that it was about eighteen minutes, but I will not attempt to say how long it seemed to me.

After that I always had a life-line on one of my ankles, and my assistant stood ready to haul me up or in, as the case might be, to the nearest window.

During the engagement where I made this escape twice a day, at the New York Hippodrome, I adopted an ankle fastening which consisted of two strong bands of webbing. These were passed around my ankles with the ropes attached to them. After that my ankles gave me no more trouble, and I could hang upside down with ease and comfort.

THE RUSSIAN TRANSPORT TIE

This is the restraint used by Russian officials when transporting prisoners into Siberia, and it is supposed to render them helpless during the journey; but, of course, there is no reason why a prisoner should attempt a release as he is always under the eye of an officer, and such an act would probably earn him a severe beating.

In using this tie as a stunt, however, the release may be classed with the easy ones. The hands are tied in any manner in front, the ropes being carried up to and around the neck, as shown in this picture in which I am being secured by the celebrated Russian dancer, Kosloff.

For the release, you have only to bring the hands up within reach and untie the wrist knots with the teeth. With the hands free, the remainder of the knots can be readily negotiated.

Do not get the idea, however, that because easy, this escape is not effectual. Try it before an audience after you have mastered it sufficiently to acquire a measure of speed, and you will be surprised at the enthusiasm it will cause. The spectator will not stop to think that you are working at high pitch.

I can recommend this unqualifiedly to the performer who only presents one tie.

THE RUSSIAN TRANSPORT TIE.

HOUDINI'S "FULL VIEW OF AUDIENCE" RELEASE

This release, if worked with the proper dash and address, never fails to "get them", but the manner of stealing the slack is so bold that a certain amount of "nerve" is necessary in order to "put it across".

A piece of smooth rope about three feet long is held horizontally by one of the committee. The performer places his wrists fairly upon the center of it and asks that they be tied at the smallest point. As he makes this request he draws the left hand backward and points at that part of the right wrist just back of the heel of the hand. As this hand is returning to the side of the other the left little finger catches the center of the rope and draws a loop between the wrists, holding it firmly between the heels of the hands. After a little practice this steal becomes absolutely indetectable, and the grip is so secure that after the first half of the knot is made, the committee may indulge in a "tug-of-war" at the two ends of the rope without endangering the release, as shown. The committee in this case consisted of the screen favorites, Tom Meighan and Jack Pickford who, as all the world knows, is a brother of the renowned Mary.

"FULL VIEW OF AUDIENCE" RELEASE.

I have always used this as a quick release, to get a laugh, and I usually called one of the stage hands and asked him to tie my wrists as I wished to try out a new tie. After he has tied the wrists, having called another to help draw the knots tight, I ask, "Are you sure you have tied them good and tight!" To which he will probably answer, "Yes." Then I say, "Thank you; much obliged," suddenly free both hands, wad up the rope, and walk away. This is sure to get a laugh.

HOUDINI ON MAGICIANS

The field of magic in which Houdini reveled most was its history. His urge to acquire facts sometimes amounted to an obsession and once he had gathered them, he presented the details in a homely, direct way with pointed sidelights that give considerable perspective to the "history makers" as Houdini styled the old-time magicians whose lives he chronicled.

From a broad viewpoint, Houdini deserves more credit for this work than any of his other contributions to the field of magic. An art lives through the traditions established by its exponents, and Houdini, himself a performer, was the first person to delve deeply into the lives of past magicians and come up with historical facts that were more substantial than the usual press notices.

Oddly, Houdini's efforts in this direction were appreciated least by the magical fraternity itself and for a very curious reason. Houdini was highly critical of a French magician named Robert-Houdin, from whose name Houdini coined his own. Houdini's research, so he claimed, proved that Robert-Houdin had taken credit for the inventions of other magicians whose names had passed almost into oblivion. So in doing justice to those men, Houdini bitterly discredited Robert-Houdin.

The more facts Houdini presented, the more magicians stood up for Robert-Houdin, perhaps because Houdin's autobiography had long been regarded as a sort of gospel by the magical fraternity. It did not matter that Houdin himself had either ignored or belittled most of his contemporaries, or that his exaggeration of his very limited travels and comparatively brief career read like a sequel to the *Adventures of Baron Munchausen*. By unmasking Robert-Houdin, Houdini began a controversy that has raged for nearly fifty years, proving only that some minds can resent facts that disprove any fallacies, once the latter have become established.

Magicians are well able to appreciate this. For years, they have laughed at the popular belief in the Indian Rope Trick and wondered how anyone could believe such a fanciful tale. Yet any historian would become equally uproarious at the acceptance that some magicians still give Houdin 's preposterous claims in the light of the documentary evidence that Houdini produced in favor of other magicians.

Nearly all magicians bill themselves as the "World's Greatest" and as such must necessarily claim to have invented all the tricks that they perform. Houdini himself was no more immune from this egotism than other members of the trade. In fact, there is a quip that he originally wanted to call himself "Houdin" but decided to make it "Houdini" because he felt another "I" would look better. But that has no bearing on historical data other than to discount all unsubstantiated press notices pertaining to any professional magician's career.

Perhaps it was to prove this very point that Houdini persisted in biographical writings almost to the end of his career. Few of these lives of past magicians have appeared in popular books or magazines. In them, Houdini has weighed one authority against another until they fairly brim with facts, yet retain the flavor of some of their original lore.

WBG

DOCTOR KATTERFELTO

*One of the Most Interesting Characters in the
History of Magic. Magician, Quack Doctor,
Pseudo-Philosopher.*

The more one learns of the practical inventions credited to the early conjurors, the more the wonder grows that they, in common with the actors of the time, were considered vagabonds and little better than thieves.

A somewhat better standing was finally accorded to the actors; first by the uplift given to the theatre by Shakespeare, and later through the influence of Nell Gwyn at the court of Charles II, but the conjurors were obliged to work out their own salvation.

Shakespeare was fully aware of the bad reputation of the show people, but nowhere in his writings does he mention actors except to praise while his opinion of conjurors can be gathered from the following from the last act of the *Comedy of Errors.*

> . . . . . one Pinch; a hungry, lean faced villain.
> A mere anatomy, a mountebank,
> A thread-bare juggler, and a fortune teller;
> A living dead man; this pernicious slave,
> Forsooth, took on him as a conjuror;
> And, gazing in mine eyes, feeling my pulse,
> And with no face, as 'twere out-facing me,
> Cries out, I was posses'd:

And Katterfelto was a shining example of this social ostracism.

I first heard of Katterfelto through my dear old London friend, Henry Evanion, who had in his collection a number of interesting items referring to him, as well as the illustration from the *European Magazine*, a reproduction of which appears here. The more I delved into the history of this remarkable man, the more fascinated I became, and I feel certain that a brief history of his career will prove interesting to the present generation.

He was for a time one of the best known men in London. The scientific portion of his entertainment must have been, in the main, accurate and instructive; he was said to have been decidedly helpful during the influenza epidemic in London in 1782, and he made and sold sulphur matches twenty years prior to the recorded invention of the lucifer match; yet, with all these things to his credit, he never succeeded in escaping the odium of the conjuror as is shown by the fact that shortly before his death, he was committed by the mayor of Shrewsbury to the House of Correction in that city as a vagabond and impostor.

As I became more familiar with this quaint character, the more his personality impressed me. He seems to have been one of those lovable vagabonds so dear to the hearts of writers of romantic fiction, and although bombastic in the extreme, a quack and a veritable charlatan, yet he was a man of much inventive genius, of more than ordinary education, and of exceptional attainments along various lines.

All that is positively known of Katterfelto dates from the year 1782 when he opened in London with an original and attractive entertainment embodying such a subtle combination of science and humbug that it was difficult to determine where the one left off and the other began, and which, to quote the *European Magazine* of June, 1783, "repeatedly provoked risibility in all degrees, from the Archbishop of Canterbury to Dr. Johnson himself."

The following from Jones's *Biographical Dictionary*, 1822, is the only account of Katterfelto that I have ever seen in any recognized directory:

"Dr. Katterfelto, a sort of eccentric philosopher, who for several years gulled the good people of England with the exhibition of experiments in electricity, etc., which he called 'Wonderful Wonders', insinuating that his practices were magical, and performed under the supernatural agency of a Black Cat, his constant companion on those occasions. He is supposed to have been a Prussian by birth, and died at Bedale in Yorkshire, Nov. 25th, 1799."

He is described as a man near fifty years of age, about five feet ten inches tall, rather thin, and not particularly careful of his personal appearance. He wore in his performances a long black cloak and a square velvet cap. His apparatus seems to have received more attention than his person, however, as it was said to be of the best and always in excellent order. He conducted each experiment with ease and certainty, never seeming to have a failure.

He claimed to be the son of a Colonel Katterfelto, of the Death's Head Hussars belonging to the King of Prussia, and also claimed to have held a commission in that regiment at one time himself. In newspaper notices he is variously called Mr. Col. and Dr. Katterfelto

KATTERFELTO.

His entertainment quickly secured wide publicity through a series of unusual advertisements and reading notices, which were sufficiently unique to attract the attention of no less a personage than the poet Cowper, who, in a dissertation on advertising in *The Task*, says:

> The rest appears a wilderness of strange
> But gay confusion; roses for the cheeks,
> And lilies for the brows of faded age,
> Teeth for the toothless, ringlets for the bald,
> Heaven, earth and ocean plundered for their sweets,
> Nectareous essences, Olympian dews,
> Sermons and city feasts, and fav'rite airs,
> Etherial journies, submarine exploits,
> And Katterfelto, with his hair on end
> At his own wonders, wondering for his bread.

The style of Katterfelto advertising is exemplified in the advertisement reproduced here from the *London Morning Post and Daily Advertiser*.

KATTERFELTO,

As a DIVINE and MORAL PHILOSOPHER,

BEGS leave to say, that all persons on earth live in darkness, if they are able to see, but won see, that wonderful Exhibition on the Solar Microscope. He will this, and every Day This Week, and till the 22 of March next, from ten in the morning till five in the afternoon, at No. 24, Piccadilly, shew a great variety of surprizing and uncommon

NEW OCCULT SECRETS;

And such as have surprized the KING, and the Whole ROYAL FAMILY, and many of the first NOBILITY in the CITY.

And by his new-improved and greatly admired

SOLAR MICROSCOPE,

There will be seen in a drop of water, the size of a pin's head, above 5000 insects; the same in beer, milk, vinegar, blood, flour, cheese, Marechalle powder, and 200 other uncommon objects; and those insects are now to be seen to the greatest advantage. If the sun does not appear this day, he will shew them by the Compound Microscope, with his New Occult Secrets.

And this, and every Evening this week, precisely at seven o'clock, he will deliver his other various Lectures in Natural Experimental Philosophy and Mathematics, and his various Lectures and experiments are as follow, viz.

Philosophical,	Pneumatic,
Mathematical,	Hydraulic,
Optical,	Hydrostatic,
Magnetical,	Proetic,
Electrical,	Stenographic,
Physical,	Balensical, and
Chymical,	Caprimantic Art.

Mr. KATTERFELTO

Has, in his travels for these eighteen years past, had the honour to exhibit with great applause before the Empress of Russia, the Queen of Hungary, the Kings of Prussia, Denmark, Sweden, and Poland, and before many other Princes.

And after his Lecture, Mr. Katterfelto will shew and discover several new Deceptions on

Dice, Cards,	Silver and Gold,
Billiards, Tennis,	Boxes, Medals,
Letters, Money,	Pyramidical Glasses,
Watches, Caskets,	Mechanical Clocks.

Admittance, front feats, 3s second feats 2s. back feats 1s.

The whole are delivered in Twelve different nights; a different Lecture every night. And besides his Philosophical, this Evening he will deliver a Lecture on those that are

NOT BLIND BUT WON'T SEE.

N. B. His Exhibition will close in a short time, as (by command of the King of Prussia) he must be at Berlin early in the Spring.

Probably the most clever feature of these entertainments was the introduction of a wonderful Black Cat, and, while ho did not positively proclaim its supernatural endowments, he always treated It in public with a sort of reverence and seemed to invoke its aid in the performance of his wonders. This naturally caused much comment, and they came to be spoken of jokingly by the press — but quite seriously by the ignorant — as the Black Devils, and Katterfelto, taking advantage of this, made the following denial, by which it will be seen that he increased rather than diminished their Stygian reputation.

MAY THE BLACK CAT HAVE NINE TIMES NINE LIVES

KATTERFELTO is sorry to find that the writers in the newspapers have several times, and particularly within the last fortnight, asserted that he and his BLACK CAT were DEVILS. On the contrary, Katterfelto professes himself to be nothing more than a Moral and Divine Philosopher, a Teacher in Mathematics, and Natural Philosophy; and that neither he nor his BLACK CAT bear any resemblance to Devils, as they are represented in the print-shops; and assures the Nobility and the Public, that the idea of him and his Black Cat being Devils arises merely from the astonishing performances of Katterfelto and his said Cat, which, both in the day's and at the night's exhibition, are such as to induce all the spectators to believe them both Devils indeed! — the Black Cat appearing at one instant with a tail, and the next without any, and which has occasioned many thousands of pounds to be lost in wagers on this incomprehensible subject.

Another caption reads: "For the Benefit of Mr. Katterfelto's Black Cat." In this notice he says: "In the evening he will deliver a lecture solely for the benefit and emolument of the famous BLACK CAT which has of late so much excited the attention of the public," etc. Still another is headed: "Rare News!!" and continues:

Dr. Katterfelto is extremely happy to acquaint the public of an event which cannot but give universal pleasure; last Saturday his celebrated Black Cat, which has nine times more excellent qualities than any nine cats among those nine-lived animals, was safely delivered of NINE kittens; seven of which are black and two are white. So that he will be able to accommodate several of those Kings and Princes who have expressed a desire of having one of the breed of his wonderful black cat, which of all surprising animals is the most surprising, as those who have seen it can testify. And Dr. Katterfelto expects that the birth of those wonderful kittens will be mentioned in all foreign newspapers and gazettes, and that ambassadors will be sent from all the philosophers in the world to congratulate him upon so happy an occasion; therefore, Dr. Katterfelto acquaints the public, that he will remain in this kingdom for some time longer.

Then follows the usual flamboyant advertisement.

In addition to his regular advertisements, he made use of clever reading notices, which, although palpably unbelievable, could not fail to keep him in the public eye. Here is one taken from an article in the *European Magazine* of June 1783, which is characteristic:

A letter from Berlin says, the reason that the King of Prussia has taken such great notice of the Bishop of Osnaburg, since his arrival at Potsdam, more than he has done to any other Prince, is, Capt. Katterfelto, belonging to the Death's Head Hussars, having informed the King that his brother was the greatest philosopher in England, and was taken great notice of at the British Court, having discovered many useful sciences in their navy, which induced His Majesty to show the greatest respect for His Royal Highness; His Majesty has also presented Capt. Katterfelto to His Royal Highness, to give him an opportunity of conversing with the Prince about his brother now in London, and taken so much notice of by His Britannic Majesty. The King of Prussia is very proud that his army is looked upon to be the finest in Europe in the field, and Capt. Katterfelto's brother, who is a native of His Prussian Majesty's dominions, is the greatest philosopher in the world.

In another "letter from Berlin", Capt. Katterfelto is said to have obtained leave for his brother, "who travels in the character of a philosopher," to travel a few years longer as there is not any likelihood of a war in His Prussian Majesty's dominions, but he must not visit France or Spain and must return to his regiment by command of His Prussian Majesty or his General. The captain also "received power" to send his brother the fifth part of the fortune of 300,000 ducats left to him by his uncle, General Katterfelto, etc.

Still another reads:

The Queen of France is highly pleased, as is also the King and the whole Court, that Dr. Katterfelto has sent one of his celebrated black cat's kittens as a present to her majesty, by His Royal Highness the Duke of Chartres; and both the King and Queen of France have agreed to send that celebrated philosopher a handsome present, which is now making by a capital artist at Paris, and is said to be worth 8,000 livras. . . . The Queen of France is much surprised that the kitten has no tail, but if the Doctor's famous black cat kittens again, she expects that he will send her one that has got a tail, in order to propagate the breed of this wonderful cat in France.

It is said that during the influenza epidemic in London in 1782, Katterfelto was quite active as a physician and added to his nostrums the fascinations of hocus-pocus, and that, with the services of his extraordinary black cat, he was enabled to astonish and to a great extent relieve the terror of the panic-stricken lower classes. Of course this provoked the hostility of the regular practitioners, and he was bitterly attacked, but he got back at them in his own way in the following statement:

TREASONABLE CORRESPONDENCE

against the health of His Majesty's liege subjects.

Whereas, besides the many important letters Dr. Katterfelto has received, entreating his attendance in foreign Courts, he had last week divers epistles from Ireland, the Isles of Wight and Man, etc., etc., which he conceives to come from certain apothecaries, surgeons, and from others of the faculty, concerned in the destruction of the human race, as all those letters express a desire, that he will set at liberty the dangerous insects now in his possession, and which occasioned the influenza last spring, which influenza the said letter writers seem desirous of having repeated, preferring their own emolument to the health of His Majesty's liege subjects, and for which purpose they offered Dr. Katterfelto large sums of money in order to comply with their wishes.

But Dr. Katterfelto, as a moral and divine philosopher, considering the many honors and advantages he has received from the Royal Family, nobility, and people of every distinction in this kingdom, will not be guilty of such ingratitude as to lay up so many thousands of the good people of these realms for any reward or upon any consideration whatever. And he takes this public method of answering all the said letters accordingly, having reserved those noxious insects for the express purpose of exhibiting them, amongst his other curious objects, by his solar microscope, and which are to be seen at the greatest advantage this and every day this and next week, from eight in the morning till five in the afternoon; or when the sun does not shine he will show his curious occult secrets, which have surprised the King and the whole Royal Family.

The evening lecture at eight o'clock, will be continued as usual, and enriched by the presence and extraordinary performances of the black cat, by which Katterfelto doubts not of getting at least £30,000 in the course of the present year, especially if she should have kittens, as he will not dispose of any under at least 500 guineas, as several of the first nobility in different parts of Europe have already requested to have some of that most wonderful breed.

Besides the verse of Cowper, several bits of rhyme singing the praises of Katterfelto appeared in the press of the day; one is credited to a certain Dr. Hamily, and the others are anonymous;

none is particularly good, and the style of all is identical, so it seems quite evident that all were written by the same hand, whether by Katterfelto himself or a press-agent is now problematical.

It is known that it was his intention to write an autobiography entitled *Memoirs of the Greatest Philosopher that Ever Existed or Ever Will Exist*, but this work either never saw the light or has evaded my research for material.

During the height of his popularity, a burlesque of his performance was produced at the Haymarket under the title: *None are so blind as those who won't see*, in which he was characterized as Dr. Caterpillar, and even this he turned to his own advantage in his advertisements.

In 1783, Katterfelto advertised all his "Philosophical and Mathematical" apparatus for sale at £2,500, claiming that it was worth £4,000, and "would be very valuable to a school like Harrow or Winchester as many young gentlemen would reap very great advantages from them."

In the same advertisement, he says that he makes and sells phosphorus matches.

Despite his offer to sell his apparatus, he continued in London for many months after, whether long enough to wear out his welcome does not appear, but his London popularity was evidently of little advantage to him in the smaller cities of England, and after the close of his London engagement, misfortune seemed to follow him most persistently till the day of his death.

WHO WAS DR. KATTERFELTO?

In 1831, a correspondent to the *London Mirror* asked the question: "Who is Katterfelto?" and an answer which appeared in the following issue is here reproduced, so that the reader may obtain a first hand word-picture of this medical mystifier.

In reply to the question of your correspondent — "Who is Katterfelto?" I am enabled to offer the few brief paragraphs which follow. With regard to his birth, parentage and education, I am, however, not qualified to convey any information. I know not "to whom he was related, or by whom forgot." I became acquainted with him about the year 1790 or 1791, when he visited the City of Durham, accompanied by his wife and daughter. He then appeared to be about sixty years of age His travelling equipage consisted of an old rumbling coach, a pair of sorry hacks, and two black servants. They wore green liveries with red collars, but the colours were sadly faded by long use.

Having taken suitable apartments, the black servants were sent round the town, blowing trumpets and delivering bills, announcing their master's astonishing performances, which in the day time consisted in displaying the wonders of the microscope, etc., and in the evening in exhibiting electrical experiments, in the course of which he introduced his two celebrated black cats, generally denominated the Doctor's Devils — for, be it understood, that our hero went under the dignified style and title of *Doctor* Katterfelto. Tricks of legerdemain concluded the evening's entertainment.

The first night of the Doctor's performance was extremely wet, and the writer of this, who was then quite a boy, composed his whole audience. The Doctor's spouse invited me behind the curtains to the fire, on one side of which sat the great conjuror himself, his person being enveloped in an old green, greasy roquelaire, and his head decorated with a black velvet cap. On the other side of the fireplace sat Mrs. Katterfelto and daughter, in corresponding style of dress — that is to say, equally ancient and uncleanly. The family appeared, indeed, to be in distressed circumstances. The Doctor told me the following old anecdote:— Some time before he had sent up from a town in Yorkshire a fire-balloon, for the amusement of the country people, and at which they were not a little astonished; but in a few days afterward the Doctor was himself more astonished on being arrested for having set fire to a hay rick! The balloon, it appeared, had in its descent fallen upon a rick, which it consumed, and the owner, having ascertained by whom the combustile material had been dispatched, arrested the doctor for the damage. As the Doctor was unable to pay the amount, he was obliged to go to prison, thus proving that it is sometimes easier to raise the devil than it is to "raise the wind." Having been admitted behind the scenes, I had an opportunity of seeing the conjuror's apparatus, but the performance was postponed to another evening.

On the next night of the Doctor's appearance, he had a tolerably respectable auditory, and the following incidents may amuse your readers, as they occasioned much laughter at the moment. Among the company was the Rev. Mr. P., a minor canon. The conjuror, in the course of his tricks, desired a card to be drawn from the pack, by one of the company, which was done, the card examined and returned into the pack in the presence of the audience; but on the company being requested to take the card again from the pack, it could not be found. The Doctor said it must have been taken out by some one present, and civilly begged the reverend gentleman to search his pockets. Indignant at such an insinuation, the inflamed divine for some time refused to comply, but at length, being persuaded, he drew forth the identical card, much to his own surprise and the amusement of the spectators. A similar trick was also played with some money, which unaccountably found its way into the reverend gentleman's pocket, a circumstance which put him out of all patience; and he proceeded to lecture most sternly the astounded Doctor for having practised his levity on a gentleman of his cloth, upon which, and threatening the poor conjuror with vengeance, he strode out of the room. Katterfelto declared that, although he was a conjuror, he did not know the gentleman was a divine.

Katterfelto left Durham soon afterwards, and I have heard died at Bristol.

Pentonville   DUNELM.

It is the general impression today that the fact that disease germs are transferred by house flies, Jersey mosquitoes, the carniverous cootie, and like insects, is a Twentieth Century discovery, but Katterfelto's announcements of his solar microscope show that the fact must have been known to him as he often spoke of showing "these insects which caused the late influenza as large as birds."

Much remains to be said in commendation of this remarkable man and very little in censure. What his earlier life had been and where he obtained the scientific knowledge he undoubtedly possessed, I have been unable to discover.

His eccentricities may have been inborn, but I am inclined to the opinion that they were assumed for business purposes like those of Lafayette the magician, who lost his life in the Edinboro fire.

Lafayette was a modest, charming fellow in private life, and many a good laugh we have had together at his obvious eccentricities in public.

I recall one cold night in London when I saw two giant negroes standing in front of the Green Room Club as motionless as statues. There they waited, standing *à la* Napoleon, until Lafayette came out, and then with great reverence they escorted him to his motorcar as if he were a king.

Katterfelto was a natural product of his day and generation, and such of his life as I have been able to trace was helpful to his fellow man; so, surely none among us will begrudge the poor, old, forgotten conjuror-lecturer a niche in the Magician's Hall of Fame.

Photograph of Houdini soon after the authorship of his momentous volume *The Unmasking of Robert-Houdin* in which he furnished exhaustive evidence to prove that magical effects claimed by the famed French conjuror were actually the invention of Robert-Houdin's predecessors and rivals. The controversy created by this scholarly work still rages, but the *Unmasking* still stands as an important milestone in the annals of magic. Contrary to later rumor, Houdini never retracted the opinions expressed in that book.

Frontispiece from an old book on magic portraying Chabert, the famous fire-king performing his celebrated test of remaining alive in a burning oven, described by Houdini in his book on *Miracle Mongers*.

From the John J. McManus Collection.

PHILADELPHIA

A Historical Seventeenth Century Magician

Today this would hardly be considered either an appropriate or an attractive name for a magician. The famous conundrum of Shakespeare "What's in a name?" may have, in his day, merited no wiser answer than the one he gave, but in these days of high-powered press-agents, with their seven-league boots of successful endeavor by means of which they far out-distance the gold-bought publicity of past generations, there is not only a great deal in a name, but more than a little in the size of the type in which the name appears. However, the name never seems to have proved a handicap to Philadelphia himself, and he even succeeded in surrounding it with quite a distinct halo of glory.

Born in Philadelphia, Pennsylvania, on the 14th day of August, 1735, of orthodox Hebrew parents, this man, whose right name was Jacob Meyer, must have left these shores at an early age as all his successes were won in foreign lands, and I find him mentioned as a "celebrated conjuror" in 1773. It took many years to win such a title in those slow-moving days.

That he was sufficiently well known to attract the attention of a prominent writer is shown by the following:

Under the title of "Horea Subsecivae", in the *Dublin University Review*, in 1833, vol. I, p. 482, by the late Dr. West of Dublin, appeared the following amusing trifle:

Among Swift's works, we find a *jeu d'esprit*, entitled *The Wonder of all the Wonders that the World ever Wondered at*, and purporting to be an advertisement of a conjuror. There is an amusing one of the same kind by a very humorous German writer, George Christopher Lichtenberg*, which, as his works are not much known here, is perhaps worth translating. The occasion on which it was written was the

---

* Lichtenberg, George Christoph. Born at Oberramstadt, near Darmstadt, Germany, July 1, 1742; died at Göttingen, Feb. 24, 1799. A German physicist and satirist, professor at the University of Göttingen. He is best known as the discoverer of the electrical figures named after him. His works were published in 1800–05. *Century Dictionary.*

following: In the year 1777 a celebrated conjuror of those days arrived at Göttingen. Lichtenberg, for some reason or other, did not wish him to exhibit there; and accordingly, before the other even had time to announce his arrival, he wrote this advertisement in his name and had it printed and posted over the town. The whole was the work of one night.

PHILADELPHIA.

The result was that the real Simon Pure decamped the next morning without beat of drum and never appeared in Göttingen again. Lichtenberg had spent some time in England and understood the language perfectly, so that he may have seen Swift's paper. Still, granting even that he took the hint from him, it must be allowed he has improved on it not a little and displayed not only more delicacy, which, indeed, was easy enough, but more wit also.

"The admirers of supernatural Physics are hereby informed that the far famed magician, Philadelphus Philadelphia (the same that is mentioned by Cardanus in his book *De Natura Supernaturali*, where he is styled 'The envied of Heaven and Hell'), arrived here a few days ago by the mail, although it would have been just as easy for him to come through the air, seeing that he is the person who, in the year 1482, in the public market at Venice, threw a ball of cord into the clouds, and climbed upon it into the air till he got out of sight.

"On the 9th of January of the present year, he will commence at the Merchant's Hall, publico-privately, to exhibit his one-dollar tricks, and continue weekly to improve them, till he comes to his five-hundred-guinea tricks, amongst which last are some which, without boasting, excel the wonderful itself, nay are, as one may say, absolutely impossible.

"He has had the honour of performing with the greatest possible approbation before all the potentates, high and low, of the four quarters of the globe; and even in the fifth, a few weeks ago, before Her Majesty Queen Obera at Otaheite.

"He is to be seen every day, except Mondays and Thursdays, when he is employed in cleaning the heads of the honorable members of the Congress of his countrymen at Philadelphia; and at all hours, except from eleven to twelve in the forenoon, when he is engaged at Constantinople, and from twelve to one, when he is at his dinner.

"The following are some of his one-dollar tricks; and they are selected, not as being the best of them, but as they can be described in the fewest words:

"1. Without leaving the room, he takes the weathercock off St. James' Church and sets it on St. John's, and vice versa. After a few minutes he puts them back again in their proper places. N.B.—All this without a magnet, by mere sleight of hand.

"2. He takes two ladies and sets them on their heads on a table, with their legs up; he then gives them a blow and they immediately begin to spin like tops with incredible velocity, without breach either of their head-dress by the pressure, or of decorum by the falling of their petticoats, to the very great satisfaction of all present.

"3. He takes three ounces of the best arsenic, boils it in a gallon of milk, and gives it to the ladies to drink. As soon as they begin to get sick, he gives them two or three spoonfuls of melted lead, and they go away in high spirits.

"4. He takes a hatchet and knocks a gentleman on the head with it, so that he falls dead on the floor. When there, he gives a second blow, whereupon the gentleman immediately gets up as well as ever, and generally asks what music that was.

"5. He draws three or four ladies' teeth, makes the company shake them well together in a bag, and then puts them into a little cannon, which he fires at the aforesaid ladies' heads, and they find their teeth white and sound in their places again.

"6. A metaphysical trick, otherwise commonly called *Metaphysica*, whereby he shows that a thing can actually be and not be at the same

time. It requires great preparation and cost, and is shown so low as
a dollar, solely in honour of the University.

"7. He takes all the watches, rings and other ornaments of the
company, and even money if they wish, and gives every one a receipt
for his property. He then puts them all in a trunk, and brings them
off to Cassel. In a week after, each person tears his receipt, and that
moment finds whatever he gave in his hands again. He has made a
great deal of money on this trick.

"N.B. During this week he performs in the top room at the Merchants' Hall; but after that, up in the air over the pump in the market-
place; for whoever does not pay, will not see."*

Philadelphia made every effort to give the impression that he
was a real dealer in black magic or a conjuror of witches. There
was a belief among his more humble audiences that his effects
were accomplished through a power to cause a temporary blind-
ness to attack them, and he did everything he could to strengthen
this belief.

At one time he advertised to enter a certain city at both the
east and west gates at the same moment and is credited with having
made good his boast. I might be inclined to question the truth
of this statement had I not accomplished the same feat myself.
In the earlier days my face was not as well known to the public
as at present, and at that time my brother Hardeen resembled me
quite closely. It is now, I think, generally known that he is the
only legitimate imitator of some of my feats, and on this occasion
while I was appearing in New York, he impersonated me and
duplicated my stunts at Philadelphia, and as it was advertised that
I would appear at both theatres at the same time, each audience
thought that the other was disappointed.

Philadelphia was without question an excellent showman, for
while a study of his program shows that he introduced some of the
simplest tricks, still, by his clever and — for those days — extensive advertising, his making the most of his splendid personal
appearance and his natural aptitude for mathematics and physics,
he brought himself into prominence at an early age and secured a
lasting reputation.

---

* *English Eccentrics & Eccentricities*, Timbs, London, 1875.

Mit hoher Obrigkeitlicher Bewilligung

wird ein hochgeneigtes Publikum hiedurch benachrichtiget,

daß der allhier angekommene mechanische und mathematische Künstler,

Meyer Philadelphia,

Heute Mittwochen den 20ten, Donnerstag den 21ten, Freytag 22ten April die Ehre haben wird,

Funfzig neue Stücke von seiner Geschicklichkeit

zu p r o d u c i r e n

und mit sehenswehrten Künsten während seines Aufenthalts allhier zu unterhalten.

Zur beliebigen Nachricht findet er für nöthig zu erinnern, ihn nicht in die Klasse der Gaukler, Afterkünstler und Taschenspieler zu versetzen, oder ihn mit jenen zu vergleichen; denn er darf es ohne Prahlerey sagen, daß seine Künste sowohl bey dem Königl. Preußischen Kayserl. als bey dem Königl. Preußischen und Schwedischen Hofe mit allergnädigstem Beyfall angenommen worden sind, wie er denn auch in den berühmtesten Städten und Ländern allen Beyfall erhalten hat: deshalb er sich schmeichelt, auch hier in Lüneburg Zuspruch und Beyfall zu erhalten.

Er macht viele hundert Stücke, die aber wegen Mangel des Raums nicht alle benannt werden können.

Bey jedem Spiel werden Funfzig neue Stücke gewechselt.

Von den 50 Stücken, die der Künstler heute producirt, werden hier einige der vorzüglichsten angeführt, als:

1) Wird er einen Bachus mit einem Weinfasse unter dem Arm seyn auf den Tisch stellen, und ein Glas reines Wasser in dieses Faß schütten, dann können die resp. Zuschauer befehlen, was Sie haben wollen, entweder Wein aus dem Faß oder Brandtwein, und der Bachus wird es selbst aus dem Faß zapfen, ohne daß der Künstler eine Hand daran bringt.

2) Wird er mit einer Egyptischen Zauber-Uhr die Zuschauer auf eine überraschende Art belustigen, und damit viele sehenswürdige Stücke machen, die noch wenig gesehen worden sind.

3) Wird er den kleinen Talismann produciren, der schon in vielen Städten und Ländern, seiner Geschicklichkeit wegen, den größten Beyfall erhalten hat.

4) Dürfen sich 3 Personen aus der Gesellschaft am Tisch setzen zu l'Hombre, und dürfen unter sich ausmachen, wer ein Solo, oder Sond Brandre haben soll, und nach der Karten-Austheilung dürfen die andern beiden Herren noch bestimmen, in was für Couleur der 3te Solo spielen soll, in einer schwarzen oder in einer rothen Couleur; dieses geschieht mit einer ganz neuen fremden Karte.

5) Wird er 12 besondere Kartenstücke zeigen, die noch von keinem Künstler, so vor ihm hier gewesen, sind gemacht worden.

6) Wird ein Dinten-Faß auf dem Tisch gestellt, woraus ein Jeder befehlen kann, in was für eine Couleur sich die Dinte verwandeln soll. Dieses Stück ist aller Orten mit größten Beyfall aufgenommen worden.

Wenn Herrschaften sind die einige von diesen Stücken zu lernen wünschen, können nur den Künstler kund thun wohin er kommen soll.

Preise der Plätze.

Erster Platz 8 Ggr.   Zweyter Platz 4 Ggr.   Dritter Platz 2 Ggr.

NB. Wenn Herrschaften auf den Theater, wo der Künstler spielt sitzen wollen, bezahlt die Person 12 Ggr.

Alle diejenige welche auf den ersten Platz unchenirt sitzen wollen, werden gebethen ihre Billets in Voraus aus meinem Logie, bey den Hrn. Burgdorff beym Brodbänken, holen zu lassen.

Der Schauplatz ist in des Herrn Schillings Hause am Markte,

und werden die Plätze gut rangirt seyn, daß Jedermann der werthesten Zuseher unchenirt sitzen, und alles genau übersehen kann.

Die Casse wird geöfnet um 6 Uhr, der Anfang ist präcise 7 Uhr.

Shortly after leaving America, he renounced the Jewish religion and joined the Christian Church. It was then that he adopted the name of his native city.

He attracted the attention of Duke Henry of Cumberland by his mathematical proficiency, and this acquaintance helped greatly to speed him along the road to success.

He toured through Europe, appeared before the Empress Catherine, and secured the favor of Sultan Mustapha the Third at Constantinople. He won great success in Berlin and Vienna. At Potsdam he performed before Frederick the Great with marked success. After which, having amassed a considerable fortune, he retired to private life.

I have been unable to discover where or how he passed the remainder of his days, or the date of his death, but I find the imprint, Nürnberg, 1778, at the bottom of his portrait, from which I assume that he was still alive at that time.

The modern truism that "every knock is a boost" has been justified in the case of many magicians. Houdin attacked Bosco, and the result was decidedly to the advantage of Bosco; Descremps tried his best to expose and belittle Pinetti only to succeed in immortalizing him, and the same is true of Philadelphia, for the ridicule of Lichtenberg only served to brighten the luster of his name.

This reminds me that in December, 1898, at Kohl and Middleton's Museum, Clark Street, Chicago, I gave twenty-two complete acts every day, and on Saturday and Sunday, the number was increased to about thirty. After appearing on the curio platform as a conjuror, I hurried downstairs to the theatre stage where I did a turn as handcuff expert and trunk escape mystifier in the big show, and by the time this was over, I was due on the curio platform again.

Willmann, the well known manufacturer of apparatus at Hamburg, Germany, informed me that he had searched for years without success for a portrait of this man. He did succeed, however, in procuring a program, which I afterwards purchased from him, and which is, to the best of my knowledge, the only one in existence today. By this program, which is here reproduced, it will be seen that in Germany he used the name Meyer Philadelphia. I find no record of his having used the term elsewhere.

WILJALBA FRIKELL

Frikell was born in Sagan, Schlessien, Prussia, July 27, 1816. He died in Kötchenbroda, October 10, 1903. He was famed in the history of magic for having given the first simon-pure sleight-of-hand performance without cumbersome stage draperies and apparatus.

Herr Frikell, in all probability, held the record for the number of appearances as a magician. He spent 62 years in the magic circle, and next to him in years of service to his craft, stands Signor Blitz.

The material used in this article was furnished by Frau Frikell on several occasions when she received me personally. Many of the facts she gave me on the day when we first met, at the death-bed of her husband. This is the first authentic biographical sketch of Wiljalba Frikell ever published; and the information offered by Mr. Thomas Frost and his successors, concerning Frikell, is in the main incorrect and unreliable.

Wiljalba Frikell was the son of a physician and the youngest of nineteen children. When a mere boy, he traveled over the continent

WILJALBA FRIKELL IN HIS YOUTH.

as assistant to a professional magician, and at the age of sixteen he was able to give a complete performance on his own account. About this time, he returned to his native town not knowing that his family had removed from the house in which he had been born. As he neared the door of his old home, he saw issuing from it a christening procession. A baby girl was being carried to the church for baptism all swathed in white lawns and laces. Young Frikell watched the procession wend its way down the quaint street, murmuring to himself:

"Someday I will marry that girl. Then I will have my revenge on the family for moving into my old home."

And marry her he did, after watching her grow up as a charming young girl. At seventeen she became his bride, but the revenge never materialized, for they were a most happy and united couple to the day of his death.

Not that their wedded life was one long path of roses, for Frikell, like all magicians, had his ups and downs, particularly as his career as a public performer ran almost uninterruptedly from 1831 to 1896. For instance, in America he had most unpleasant experiences. In Cincinnati, Ohio, he played to packed houses for four performances, and then his manager disappeared with the receipts. At the conclusion of his engagement at Steinway Hall in New York City, another manager played him the same scurvy trick, and perhaps for this reason he held America in poor esteem.

During his numerous continental tours, he made friends with crowned heads and members of the nobility. Particularly was he honored by the King of Greece, who, after meeting him at Weisbaden, invited the unpretentious magician to visit him at his palace in Athens. The King of Denmark and the Viceroy of Egypt conferred medals upon him, and of gorgeous rings, pins, and other jeweled trinkets from the hands of the nobility, he had a remarkable collection.

His income varied as that of all old-time magicians did. Once, in a little German village, his receipts were only 1 Mark, 70 Pfennige, or about 40 cents in the coin of the United States. On the other hand, one night in St. Petersburg, Russia, after paying all expenses he cleared 2,500 rubles or $1,250 for a single performance.

It was in Russia also that he met with a very curious adventure, which was related to me personally by Frau Frikell, and which has never appeared in print, because Herr Frikell was in no wise proud of the occurrence.

When he appeared by royal command before the Czar of Russia, that monarch was so pleased with Frikell's performance that he commanded a high court official to express this appreciation by presenting to the magician a handsome diamond ring. In later years, when in less affluent circumstances, Frikell endeavored to dispose of the stone, which was a large and apparently a brilliant one, and found that he had been the victim of Russian graft. The court official had presented him not a genuine diamond as ordered by the Czar but a clever paste affair. This ring I saw framed among other souvenirs at the Villa Frikell in Kötchenbroda.

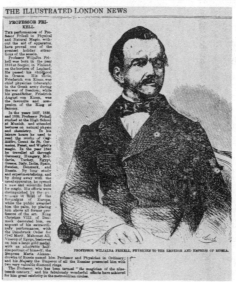

WILJALBA FRIKELL IN HIS PRIME.

Another time he was handed a counterfeit note by a clever but unscrupulous German auditor. Frikell was doing a trick which entailed borrowing a thousand mark ($250) note, burning it, and later finding it in a candle. In those days the trick was simply worked. One note was borrowed, and after the trick, another note was returned to the lender, a counterfeit note being used for the burning. The next day, on looking over his apparatus and prop-erties, Frikell discovered that the obliging man in the audience had handed him a counterfeit note and received in exchange a genuine one. Through a mere accident, he succeeded in tracing the man and under threat of arrest secured the return of his good bill. Today magicians employ sleight-of-hand, take a little more trouble, and return the same bill borrowed, not a duplicate bill.

Frikell claimed to have invented a very clever trick which he performed in public places to advertise his show. He would go to market and purchase rabbits or hares and carry under his coat a live hare. After making his purchase, he would apparently bring the dead hare to life, for a live animal would dive from his hands into the crowd, scurrying for an avenue of escape. Of course, this tale would travel throughout the town and help his attendance in the evening.

But he disclaims all personal credit for having made the greatest innovation in magical performances of his time, and that was dis-carding flowing draperies and cumbersome stage apparatus. This revolution is claimed by Robert-Houdin, but the fact remains that years before the French magician appeared before the public, Frikell had introduced the innovation, not with malice afore-thought, but because of a singular mishap. He was booked to appear in Hamburg, but his entire apparatus, most of which was in sterling silver, his costume trunks, etc., were burned, and Frikell decided to abandon his performance. Enter then the famous German poet Heinrich Heine, who insisted that Frikell should give the show with whatever properties he could scrape up. The result was a sleight-of-hand performance, pure and simple. The audience went wild over the innovation, the mere absence of draperies and flowing sleeves by which the performer could so easily deceive the eye.

From that day, Frikell was famous for the simplicity of his performance, and on this he built his large fortune.

At the age of 59 he retired, apparently in affluence. A year later the bank in which his funds were invested, failed, and Frikell, almost penniless, resumed his profession. A remarkably well-preserved man and one who believed in careful grooming and immaculate dressing, he readily deceived the public as to his years. When I saw him at 87, he could easily have passed for 50, and indeed, when he appeared before the King of Denmark in Weisbaden, that monarch could hardly believe that this was the same magician who had appeared before him in the heyday of his youth. In 1884, he celebrated his fiftieth or golden anniversary as a magician. In 1896 he gave his last performance at Weisbaden and never again appeared in public.

His farewell trick was the one which had closed his performance for years, that of the demon hat. He borrowed a hat from a man in the audience, drew from it a miscellaneous collection of articles and then handed it to his assistant to be returned. The assistant awkwardly crushed the hat, and Frikell, taking the shreds, shoved them into a cannon, and then after the shot, a perfectly restored hat soared to the ceiling and was brought back to the owner at another pistol shot.

After his second and final retirement, Frikell seldom left his home in Kötchenbroda, known as Villa Frikell. He had serious differences with relatives and determined to lead an almost hermitlike life. So completely did he isolate himself that the world of magic thought him dead, but during the course of my continental tour, in the early nineties, I learned that he was still alive, although almost inaccessible, at his Kötchenbroda home.

While playing in Cologne, I wrote to him requesting an interview. I received in reply a curt note, "Herr verreist," meaning "The master is on tour." This, I knew, from his age, could not be true, so I took a week off for personal investigation. I arrived in Kötchenbroda on the morning of April 8, 1903, at 4 o'clock, and was directed to his home, known as "Villa Frikell." Having found my bearings and studied well the exterior of the house, I returned to the depot to await daylight. At 8:30 I reappeared at his door, and was told by his wife that Herr Frikell had gone away.

I then sought the police department from which I secured the following information: "Dr." Wiljalba Frikell was indeed the retired magician whom I was so anxious to meet. Living in the same town was an adopted daughter, but she could not or would not assist me.

Armed with this information, I employed a photographer, giving him instructions to post himself opposite the house and make a snapshot of the magician, should he appear in the doorway. But I had counted without my host. All morning the photographer

HOUDINI STANDING IN FRONT OF VILLA FRIKELL AT KÖTCHEN-
BRODA, GERMANY, WHERE THE MASTER MAGICIAN, WILJALBA
FRIKELL, SPENT THE LAST YEARS OF HIS LIFE.

lounged across the street, and all morning I stood bareheaded before the door of Herr Frikell pleading with his wife, who leaned from the window overhead. With that peculiar fervency which comes only when the heart's desire is at stake, I begged that the past master of magic would lend a helping hand to one ready to sit at his feet and learn. I urged the debt which he owed to the literature of magic and which he could pay by giving me such direct information as I needed for my historical work on magic.

ANOTHER PICTURE OF FRIKELL IN HIS PRIME.

Frau Frikell heard my pleadings with tears running down her cheeks, and later I learned that Herr Frikell also listened to them, lying grimly on the other side of the shuttered window.

At length, yielding to physical exhaustion, I went away, but I was still undaunted. I continued to bombard Herr Frikell with letters, press clippings regarding my work, etc., and finally in Russia, I received a letter from him. I might send him a package containing a certain brand of Russian tea of which he was particularly fond. You may be sure that I lost no time in shipping the little gift, and shortly after, I was rewarded by the letter for which I longed. Having decided that I cared more for him than did some of his relatives, he would receive me when next I played near Kötchenbroda.

With this interview in prospect, I made the earliest engagement obtainable in Dresden, intending to give every possible moment to my hardly won acquaintance. But Fate interfered. One business problem after another arose concerning my forthcoming engagement in England, and I had to postpone my visit to Herr Frikell until the latter part of the week. In the meantime, he had agreed to visit a Dresden photographer, as I wanted an up-to-date photograph of him, and he had only pictures taken in his more youthful days. On the day when he came to Dresden for his sitting, he

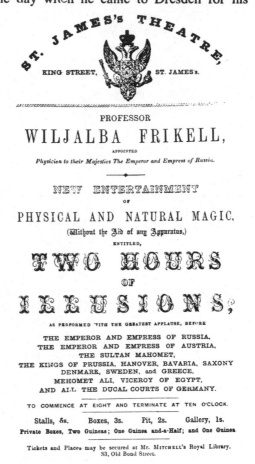

A REPRODUCTION OF ONE OF FRIKELL'S PROGRAMS ON WHICH IS MENTIONED "PHYSICAL AND NATURAL MAGIC WITHOUT THE AID OF ANY APPARATUS."

called at the theater, but the attachés, without informing me, refused to give him the name of the hotel where I was stopping.

After the performance, I dropped into the König Kaffe and was much annoyed by the staring and gesticulations of an elderly couple at a distant table. It was Frikell and his wife, but I did not recognize them and, not being certain on his side, he failed to make himself known. That was mid-week, and for Saturday, which fell on October 8, 1903, I had an engagement to call at the Villa Frikell. On Thursday, the Central Theatre being sold out to Cleo de Mérode, who was playing special engagements in Germany with her own company, I made a flying business trip to Berlin, and on my return, I passed through Kötchenbroda. As the train pulled into the station, I hesitated. Should I drop off and see Herr Frikell or wait for my appointment on the morrow? Fate turned the wheel by a mere thread, and I went on to Dresden. So does she often dash our fondest hopes.

My appointment for Saturday was at 2 p. m., and as my train landed me in Kötchenbroda a trifle too early, I walked slowly from the depot to the Villa Frikell, not wishing to disturb my aged host by arriving ahead of time.

I rang the bell. It echoed through the house with peculiar shrillness. The air seemed charged with a quality which I presumed was the intense pleasure of realizing my long cherished hope of meeting the great magician. A lady opened the door and greeted me with the words: "You are being waited for."

I entered. He was waiting for me, indeed, this man who had consented to meet me, after vowing that he would never again look into the face of a stranger. And Fate had forced him to keep that vow. Wiljalba Frikell was dead. The body, clad in the best his wardrobe afforded, all of which was donned in honor of his expected guest, was not yet cold. Heart failure had come suddenly and unannounced. The day before, he had cleaned up his souvenirs in readiness for my coming and arranged a quantity of data for me. On the wall above the silent form were all the gold medals, photographs taken at various stages of his life, orders presented to him by royalty — all the outward and visible signs of a vigorous, active, and successful life, the life of which he would have told me had I arrived ahead of Death. And when all these

LAST PHOTOGRAPH OF HERR AND FRAU FRIKELL. FRIKELL DIED
OCTOBER 8, 1903, THE DAY AFTER THIS PHOTOGRAPH WAS TAKEN.

were arranged, he had forgotten his dislike of strangers. The old instincts of hospitality tugged at his heartstrings, and his wife said he was almost young and happy once more when suddenly he grasped at his heart, crying, "My heart! What is the matter with my heart? Oh---" That was all.

There we stood together, the woman who had loved the dear old wizard for years and the young magician who had been so willing to love him had he been allowed to know him. His face was still wet from the cologne she had thrown over him in vain hope of reviving the fading soul. On the floor lay the cloths used

A POSTER USED BY FRIKELL FOR HIS ENGAGEMENT AT THE POLYGRAPH HALL.

so ineffectually to bathe the pulseless face now laughing mockingly at one who saw himself defeated after weary months of writing and pleading for the much desired meeting.

JOHANN N. HOFZINSER

"Johann N. Hofzinser. Born in Vienna, July 6, 1806. Died in his native city March 1st, 1875. A genius unheralded and unsung."

Such might well have been the epitaph written on the tombstone above all that remains of Austria's brilliant necromancer, Dr. Hofzinser. He was a genius, but only his intimates recognized this fact. Conjuring was with him an obsession, yet so long as his government commanded his services in a more practical capacity, he gave to Austria the best of his energies. He enriched magic by his clever inventions and wonderfully built tricks, but this enrichment was only temporary, for in dying he begged that his secrets should die with him, and his widow fulfilled his request.

And so it happens that while the annals of magic teem with the exploits of Pinchbeck, Fawkes, Pinetti, Phillipe, Bosco, and Anderson, and while the literature of magic uses the names of Robert-Houdin and Herrmann to conjure up images of professional success, a man from whom all these masterminds of magic might have learned much is practically unknown to professional magicians or to those interested in magic and its romances.

It remained for Ottokar Fischer, the eminent correspondent for the *Conjurors' Monthly Magazine* in Vienna, to unearth by patient, diligent, and loving research the true history and the numerous brilliant achievements of Johann Hofzinser.

The writer met Herr Fischer while playing an engagement in Vienna in 1901 and found in him one of the most enthusiastic students of magic and its history in all Europe. Though not a traveling entertainer, he knew the secrets of magic and every entertainer worth knowing who came to Vienna. In order that he might broaden his acquaintance with magicians and go to the very fountainheads of magic's history, he mastered both English and French. The latchstring of his Vienna home is always out for the magician of any nationality. He, today, is one of Vienna's most brilliant parlor entertainers. Hofzinser was one of the early Nineteenth Century magicians who particularly appealed to Herr Fischer, and the latter, in studying the history of his compatriot,

JOHANN N. HOFZINSER.

has unearthed facts invaluable to students of magic. After compiling this material for the *Conjurors' Monthly Magazine*, Herr Fischer writes:

You know how I love and worship the memory of this great magician. All dates herein given have been collected personally by myself, and it has positively taken me over twelve years to do this. I hope that you will appreciate this fact and that the article will find favor with you as well as with your readers.

Johann Hofzinser's early history is unwritten, but it is known that he came of excellent parentage, and that his education was of the best. While yet very young, he betrayed marked musical ability and often appeared as a violinist in both private and public circles. For some time he evidently enjoyed supremacy as a boy virtuoso, for one day while playing before a select circle, he met another youth, also well educated on the violin. This boy was asked to play and either equaled or eclipsed Hofzinser, for the latter's pride was so hurt by his loss of supremacy that he laid aside his violin, never touched it again, and devoted himself exclusively to his school work. Upon his graduation from the Vienna University, he was appointed to an excellent position in the Imperial and Royal Treasury Department of the Austrian Government. In that department he remained until he was pensioned, ever a faithful servant of his king.

Just when his interest in magic awoke is not known, but his letters indicate that in 1828, he had already occupied himself extensively in performing and inventing card tricks. He also used the various implements of office work as properties for sleight-of-hand work, and gradually his interest and talent absorbed all branches of magic. It was the passion of a beautiful, exquisite life. Hofzinser was a delicate man in physique, but a giant in intellectual and inventive strength. His government work for a time prevented his appearing as a public entertainer, but he gave exclusive performances in his own lodgings. After his connections with the Treasury Department were broken, he occasionally appeared in public. He was the aristocrat to his finger tips and was most acceptable to the nobility and in high social circles. For forty years he was the favorite of the Vienna social world, and no function of note was considered complete without his presence.

Occasionally, in later years, he gave performances in the Eastern Austrian provinces, but he never went beyond the confines of his native country and seldom beyond Vienna.

In 1853 he established in his home an exclusive magical parlor, called "Salon Hofzinser", and for many years gave performances patronized by the upper classes because of their exquisite delicacy; and prices were charged accordingly. He called his performance "One Hour of Deception", and in this he was assisted by his faithful wife, who was especially useful in his masterly presentation of second-sight.

Yet with all his personal charm, with all his social prestige, with all his government backing and influence, Hofzinser was not able to score financial success. He was too much the artiste, too little the charlatan. He would spend hours, days, weeks perfecting some tiny detail of a trick, and begrudge minutes needed to boom his business. After a long and painful illness, he died in his unpretentious Vienna home, March 1, 1875, leaving a widow but no children.

His wife was a most beautiful and fascinating person, and a few years after Hofzinser's death, she married a Viennese named Biela. She also survived her second husband and left her personal fortune, 250.000 florins, to the Vienna University, from which her first husband was graduated as a doctor and was later elected as professor of Experimental Physics, thus proving that even in death, her love belonged to Johann Hofzinser.

In point of inventive ability and productive faculty, Hofzinser is practically without a rival. That the world has not known this fact is due to the jealous manner in which he guarded his every magical secret and the fact, before mentioned, that at his behest, his wife burned or buried his tricks with him. So far as it lay in human power, he wiped out the record of his work. Whether this was due to disappointment or to the fact that he underestimated his own achievements is not known, but he was the typical genius, the dreamer of dreams, with all the eccentricities peculiar to such a temperament.

In creative ability, he was fully fifty years ahead of his time, and his tricks involved principles of importance and primary value, which, if understood and generally known at the time, might have revolutionized magic. Though regarded as an amateur, he came nearer the basic principles of the art than many professionals of his own time or later.

The old-time technique of magic was in vogue when Hofzinser became interested in the art. In fact, it was at a low ebb when he touched it with his wonderful revivifying hand. It stuck too closely to the "double bottom" principles. Hofzinser was not satisfied to improve tricks built upon this principle. He reached out for the new, the artistic, the brilliant effects. Often after studying an old trick, he would cast it aside and rebuild practically the same effect on entirely unique and individual lines.

Herewith is given a long list of Hofzinser's tricks. Those marked with the asterisks show his original inventions. Others were old tricks improved by his master touch.

*The Rose Mirror
*The Floating Wand
*The Wandering Coins
*The Butterflies (quite different from the Japanese method)
*The Ink of the Enamoureds (Ink-Vase)
The Box of Flowers
*The Protocol of Knots
*The Recollection of a Finger
*The Spiritist
*The Word
*The Sympathetical Influence
*The Lantern of Diogenes
*The Rose-Tree and Card
The Changement in Onlookers Hands
The Magical Bell
*The Frame for Cards
*The Card-Star with Crystal Dial-Hand
*The Crystal Ball Casket

*The Dial With Cards
*The Ducats (a coin trick)
*The Delicate Theme: egg
*The Enchanted Bankbills
*The Grandfather (fairy ninepins)
*The Corresponding Watches
*The Dial with Flowers
*A Mathematical Example
*The Library
*The Album of Poetry
The Toast
*The Bird-Sword
*The Thought of Photograph
The Coffee Trick (his own)
*The Wreath of Flowers in the Hat
*Diabolical Variations with a Ninepin
*The Exchange-Speculator
*The Billiard Balls (his own method)

In addition to this, he had his own method of presenting second-sight, and Herr Fischer found traces of incomplete tricks lost beyond repair.

Besides the completed tricks mentioned above, Hofzinser invented a number of practical contrivances for presenting tricks and worked out many subtle sleight-of-hand moves

He is credited with having invented the clock dial in which use is made of the counterweighted hand, for he found that the magnetic clock dial was limited in its scope. Still his own clock dial was a magnetic one and is now in the possession of an amateur in Vienna.

Great as this master of tricks was at magic, far more remarkable was his work as a manipulator of cards. In this line, he has absolutely no rival in the entire history of magic. No other performer has ever approached him in dexterity of hand in manipulating cards. He loved his card work passionately and called it the poetry of the magical art. To card work he devoted his very best energies, his finest inventive skill, and he had a repertoire of more than sixty card tricks of exceptional value. More than half of these tricks were buried with him, and the world of magic suffered an indescribable loss. The tricks which Herr Fischer has been able to unearth are as follows:

The Sympathetical Number
The Equal Thoughts
  (1st method)
The Four Aces
Everywhere and Nowhere
  (1st method)
The Forced Thought
Les Quatres Rois
  (The Four Kings)
La Pensée Quand Même
Think and Forget
  (2nd method)
Omnipotence of the Queens
Coeur Mariage
  (1st method)
The Wonderful Cards
Everywhere and Nowhere
  (2nd method)
Equal Thoughts
  (2nd method)
The Ace of Hearts
The Flying Thought

The Association of Thoughts
The Four Eights
The Flying and Changing Card
The Sensible Feeling
The Might of the Faith
The Forced Thought
  (2nd method)
Think and Forget
  (1st method)
Think and Forget
  (3rd method)
Do Decept Thy Neighbor!
Coeur Mariage
  (2nd method)
Think and Forget
  (4th method)
Everywhere and Nowhere
  (3rd method)
The Insolvable Impromptu
Three Like One
The Magnetical Cards
The Magical Candlestick

The Cards and the Picture

Hofzinser was opposed to endowing his tricks with bombastic titles, so we find in this list titles almost precisely alike; yet, we have evidence that they are worked on different methods and bring forth different results. The thirty-two tricks above are evidently Hofzinser's own inventions, and all are complete in Herr Fischer's possession. Besides these experiments, Herr Fischer traced to Hofzinser, but not to his entire satisfaction, the following tricks. They may or may not belong to his credit:

The Choice of Colors	Card and Cigar Box
The Changed Ace	(own method)
The Mysterious King of Spades	Exposition of Gambler Tricks
The Five Changed Cards	Carte Blanche
The Card and the Ring	The Marvellous Harmony
The Obedient Kings	The Card and the Bankbill
The Mysterious Handkerchief	The Card and the Watch
The Inexplicable Separation	Queen of Hearts and the Flowers
Successive Disappearing of Cards	The Card and the Carrot
Playing Card and Visiting Card	The Lausquents
The Diminishing Cards	Watch Your Card!

The combinations used in the above twenty-one tricks are exceedingly fine; so fine, in fact, as to indicate the hand of Hofzinser in their invention.

The beauty of all the Hofzinser tricks, and especially of his card tricks, lay in their thorough and logical combinations. To this, he added a most poetical and graceful patter. He built up his repertoire as a playwright builds up a drama, each trick gaining in interest and intricacy, step by step, scene by scene, until his performance was like a drama of magic in which each trick played a rôle, leading to a beautiful and artistic climax.

Many modern conjurers who were fortunate enough to witness a Hofzinser performance appreciated the charm of his work and copied his method. Compars Herrmann was among his most loyal admirers and painstaking copyists.

Most of his card tricks can be performed with an ordinary pack of cards. Others require prepared cards or cards in combination, which bring about results surprising even to those thoroughly versed in the secrets of magic. To handle these tricks requires great dexterity of hand, hence many dealers in magic as well as unskilled magicians have tried in vain to copy the Hofzinser tricks. Mechanical contrivances are not sufficient to gain Hofzinser results. Dexterity is all-essential. Many of these tricks Herr Fischer, himself most dexterous, has performed before the writer and such eminent manipulators as Downs, Devant, Clement de Lion, etc., and all acknowledged the beauty and difficulty of the tricks. While after years of work Herr Fischer has now ready for the press an exhaustive work on the Hofzinser Card Tricks, he admits that no mere phrases can do justice to their beauty. They must be seen to be appreciated.

The tracing of each trick represents prodigies of labor. So much of the apparatus, so many of the cards, and all writings connected therewith, Hofzinser's widow burned after his death, that Herr Fischer had to search far and near for scraps of correspondence from Hofzinser to friends, bearing on his tricks. In his research he was aided also by George Heubeck, a Vienna magician, who was Hofzinser's one and only pupil.

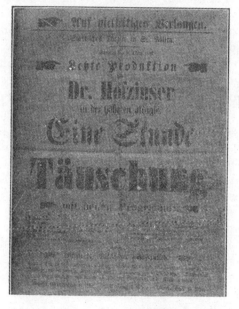

A RARE HOFZINSER PROGRAM.

GEORGE HEUBECK

In mentioning the name of this poor past grand master of magic, it must be noted that it was that staunch friend of magic, Herr Ottokar Fischer, who drafted his history. Herr Fischer obtained the minute details in person from him, for Heubeck died in poverty, forgotten, unheralded, and unsung.

It happened that one summer it was reported that Heubeck had died, and since the newspapers wished a brief account of the magician's demise, Fischer started out to get the desired information. Imagine his surprise on reaching the magician's humble hut to find the dead man alive and attending to the chores of the household. Heubeck claimed that his enemies reported him dead so that they could obtain such of his engagements as still were periodically allotted to him in the provinces of Austria.

Heubeck was for many years a picturesque figure in Austrian fields of magic, occupying the unique position of being Hofzinser's only pupil. He was born in Vienna, August 30, 1829, and died March 8, 1899, at the age of 70, in his native city.

His father, who lived at 19 Mariahilferstrasse, was a rich jeweler, but in 1841, robbers broke open his safe and not being a believer in banks, he lost all of his worldly possessions. Never afterward was he able to recoup his losses and was therefore obliged to send his son George to work for a silk dyer named Lorenz Clauser.

In 1844 George Heubeck for the first time saw the performance of a magician by the name of Hermanutz, who was engaged at the time by the elder Zobel, in Magdalenestrasse. The young dyer's apprentice evinced so profound an interest in magic that after the performance, he called upon the magician and asked to be initiated into the secrets of his tricks. Hermanutz at once took a fancy to the boy and gave him lessons in magic every Sunday, with the result that in a year's time, Heubeck surpassed his teacher. In 1846, while ordering a pack of cards to be made by a well-known mechanic, Graf, who made all mechanical cards at that time for the Viennese magicians, he became acquainted with Hofzinser, through having shown his sleight-of-hand tricks to Graf and the latter in turn having called Hofzinser's attention to the then unknown but skilled magician.

Hofzinser invited Heubeck to call on him to show him his ability in detail. After Heubeck had shown what dexterity he possessed, Hofzinser, with a quiet smile, took a pack of cards and manipulated them with such effect that Heubeck at once recognized that he had a long journey to travel ere he could reach the goal attained by the master who stood before him.

Hofzinser took a liking to the young man, who now became a

MR. AND MRS. GEORGE HEUBECK.

frequent visitor, and under his guidance, by persistent practice, became exceptionally clever, so that at Hofzinser's death (in later years), he was recognized as his only possible successor. Owing to the Austrian war, in 1848 Heubeck enlisted in the second *Steierische Schutzenbataillon*; he was wounded in the foot in one of the battles but remained until the soldiers were discharged on January 10, 1850. He returned to Vienna, where he worked at his trade as a dyer until 1852 when he gave his first public performance as a professional magician in the *Grossen Elysium bei Daum* in Johannisstrasse. There he was engaged for four months at a salary of 150 florins a month.

With the money saved from this engagement, he purchased a horse and carriage, with which he used to travel through the Austrian provinces giving performances in halls and theatres, and saved a considerable sum of money.

After an absence of three years he returned to Vienna, married, and continued his relationship with Hofzinser, who continually taught him new tricks.

Later in 1866 he was engaged in the Rappo Theatre in Berlin, where he performed for three months. Following this he was engaged for four years at the Krott Theatre, Alhambra Königsberger Theatre, then in Danzig, Hamburg, Breslau, Flensburg, Stettin, Leipzig, Dessau, Dresden, and returned to Vienna in 1870.

Here he met Compars Herrmann, who engaged him for two years at a monthly salary of 200 florins, lodgings, and all traveling expenses.

In 1873 he was engaged by Kratky-Baschik, with whom he remained until 1881, when he was engaged by Bergheer with whom he went to Hungary and Roumania, remaining with him for three years.

Heubeck during this time had shown frequently before the royal families and nobility.

In 1890 he underwent several operations which, with prolonged severe illness, exhausted his savings.

For nine years he suffered in want and penury and was assisted by Ottokar Fischer, who did all that was in his power, until the day of his death. His destitute widow had to be provided for by the city authorities.

Very few people attended the funeral of this man, who at one time numbered his friends by the thousands. His sad end was similar to that of many magicians, who, in their prime have been cheered and fawned upon by multitudes, but at their graves, forgotten!

WYMAN THE WIZARD

One of the Financially Successful Magicians of the Historic Gift Show Era

The name Wyman the Wizard means nothing to the present day public and very little even to the magician. Nevertheless, he was far more than an ordinarily successful magician and man of business. His life reflects credit on our mysterical profession.

John W. Wyman for perhaps the greater part of his career was a gift show man. He was absolutely honest personally, and the public always got a square deal at his hands. That same public, however, after getting a high opinion of the gift show through such men as Wyman was sadly disillusioned by men of the Alleyn type, whose masterpiece of magic consisted of an escape through the back windows with the gate receipts.

The exact time of Wyman's birth is not known, but it occurred at Albany, New York about the year 1816. I have been unable to learn anything of his earlier years or just when he entered the magical profession. An old friend of his, Mr. H. B. Spackman of Tuckerton, New Jersey, says that the professor never mentioned his parents.

He began in a very small way playing small town school houses and the like to the mystified delight of crowds of children between the ages of eight and eighty. These minor successes seem to have colored his entire future, for he preferred the small, but certain profits rather than the gamble of the big cities. Thus we find records of only one engagement in New York City; that was in 1850 under the management of P. T. Barnum. With this exception, I have it on the authority of Mr. Spackman, Wyman never had a manager, always conducting his own business affairs, making his own contracts; in fact, he was the whole works, chief cook and bottle washer.

His program in the earlier days included magic, ventriloquism, and marionettes, but later on he went abroad in search of novelties and returned with a very complete magical outfit. From that time on he seems to have given much greater prominence to his magic. He also purchased a large part of the apparatus of Anderson, which included a number of the very best tricks of the time.

Readers of that perennial treatise, *The Magician's Own Book*, will recall an early form of the bullet-catching trick which bears the title "Wyman's Gun Trick", but the records show that he was not entitled to this distinction as that trick was bought from Anderson. It had been performed in 1784 at Astley's Circus in London. Astley himself claims in his book, *Natural Magic, or Physical Amusements Revealed*, by Philip Astley, Riding Master, Westminster Bridge, 1785, to have invented this trick in 1762 when two of his friends fought a duel in Germany in which he acted as one of the seconds and thus had an opportunity to remove the

bullets by the same method used in the early form of the stage
trick. He was enabled by this means, as he writes, "To happily
preserve, most probably, the life of one or both of his friends."

For a long time it had been my impression that the bullet-
catching trick was the invention of Philip Astley. In fact his
modest claim to having been the inventor of it had been generally
accepted, but my old friend, R. Evanion, nephew of Henry E.
Evanion, sends me the following item copied from a book called,
Threats of God's Judgments, written by Rev. Thomas Beard and
published in 1631, which shows that this trick was known and
used over a hundred years before Astley's time.

It is not long since there was in Lorraine a certain man called
"Coulew", that was over much given to this cursed art (magic),
amongst whose tricks this was one to be wondered at: that he would
suffer harquebusses or pistols to be shot at him and catch the bullets
in his hand without receiving any hurt; but upon a certain time one
of his servants being angry at him, hit him such a knock with a pistol
(notwithstanding all his great cunning), that he killed him therewith.

Tracing the trick back to this early date will establish the fact
that neither Astley, Anderson, Eagle, nor Wyman invented it. They
may have improved the effect or presented it differently, but the
trick itself, in form and general effect, belonged to an earlier age.

That it was unnecessary to resort to crooked methods in order
to succeed in the gift show field is evidenced by the fact that Wyman
accumulated a very respectable fortune as fortunes went in his day.
This enabled him to spend the latter years of his life in comfort
in a beautiful home. There were a few others whose success stands
as a proof that there was always money in magic if honestly followed, but the majority of those whose life story is familiar to us
either died in want or very close to it. To mention a few at random:
Augoston was found dead in the streets of Berlin, practically from
starvation; Heubeck was supported by charity; Holden lost everything; John Mahr MacAllister was buried in Potter's Field; H. J.
Sargent in an infirmary at Leeds, England; the Harrington of our
own days had his trunks held up in many hotels and died in a
Chicago hospital, friendless and forgotten.

But to return to Wyman. Notwithstanding the comparatively
recent date of his death, 1881, it seems impossible to obtain anything like a complete history of his life. This is through no fault of
Wyman himself, however, as he was a most methodical man and

JOHN W. WYMAN.

kept a very complete scrapbook up to the close of his professional career.

After Wyman's death, this book came into the possession of J. H. Birch, Jr., whose father was manager of the Opera House in Burlington, New Jersey for many years. Mr. Birch sent the book to George M. Cohan and, not having heard of its arrival, concluded that it had best be given to my collection. Upon investigation, however, it was discovered that the book had vanished, and Mr. Cohan tells me that he never even heard of it. So that most valuable book is lost, the express company cannot trace it, but perhaps some day it will be discovered for sale in some book shop.

A complete description of Wyman's stage-setting will be found in Kit Clarke's *The Story of the Gift Show*, in *M. U. M.*, No. 58, Vol. 7, January 1918. In the later years of his professional career, he caught the fever of the day for high-sounding titles, and billed himself as:

BILLS FROM THE HOUDINI COLLECTION.

PROF. WYMAN!

Monarch of Magicians, in a Grand Coup d'Etat in Necromancy and the Magical Art of Scientific Diablerie.

In the same bill, to a long list of gifts valued at from 50 cents to 50 dollars, he adds the testimonials of many persons who had received building lots in New Jersey. These lots may not have had a great money value, but you may depend on it that the titles were clear, if Honest John said so.

After his retirement, he resided in Philadelphia for a number of years and then removed to Burlington, New Jersey, where he invested quite heavily in real estate, and there died on July 31, 1881. Only his wife and Mr. Spackman were with him in his last moments, and together they took the body to Fall River, Massachusetts, for burial among his wife's relatives.

Wyman is almost unknown to the present generation, but there are still among those whose hair is silvered by the snows of many winters, a few whose pulses quicken at the mention of his name.

HOUDINI ON CHALLENGES

In many of his performances, Houdini specialized in challenges, escaping from devices provided by a committee or effecting his release under what amounted to challenge conditions. This was an outgrowth of his handcuff act, in which he invited people to bring their own regulation cuffs. In these larger challenges, anything might be supplied from a straitjacket to a steel vault.

There were stand-bys among these, such as the mail bag, which is included in this section. How these descriptions and explanations came to be preserved, largely in Houdini's own language, is an interesting story in itself.

At the time of his death, Houdini's published material on escapes was comparatively small. Since he had featured the escape act, he kept many of its more important secrets to himself, even destroying the original notes from which certain of his larger escape devices had been built.

However, Houdini intended some day to produce a book on escape secrets and this could have been of an encyclopedic nature, had he decided to include everything available in rough notes as well as devices actually constructed. Much of his planned material was in the hands of his attorney, Bernard M. L. Ernst, who, pursuant to Houdini's own wishes, arranged to have it published.

I was given this work because of my literary connection with Houdini, particularly where technical material was concerned. In my book, *Houdini's Escapes*, a preface appears by Mr. Ernst stating: "Had Houdini lived, he would have written this book." This carries a special point, as my association with Houdini was such that I would have worked with him in its final preparation.

Much of the Houdini material consisted of rough notes and diagrams that required considerable research to reconstruct into final form. But in one department, "Houdini's Challenges", most of the descriptions were given in full detail in Houdini's own style. Some in fact carried more of the Houdini flavor than a great many of his published writings as they were spontaneous and not subject to the exacting revisions so common in technical explanations.

In *Houdini's Escapes*, I quoted liberally from his statements but interspersed them with my own descriptions and comments of the effects involved. This was somewhat necessary to conform to the nature of the work itself. Now, in revising "Houdini's Challenges" for the present volume, I have gone back to the original notes, keeping only Houdini's actual wordage, subject to whatever editorial revision and rearrangement seemed necessary for greater clarity.

Having made a thorough study of Houdini's writings both in manuscript and printed form, I feel that the material in this section adheres much more closely to his original style than do many of the published works that appeared under his name. This may be due in part to the fact that Houdini was covering the subject closest to him: escapes.

As to the challenges themselves, a few preliminary facts will be important. Challenges came under two categories: those where Houdini invited people to bring some standard article, such as a mail bag; and those in which the challengers dared Houdini to attempt an escape from a device of their own construction, such as a brewery barrel.

As is evidenced in Houdini's own frank statements, he could not risk a "strange" escape unless its conditions allowed some opportunity of introducing his familiar methods. As a result, most challenges were planned beforehand. For example, Houdini might agree to escape from a barrel or basket of a certain pattern, even supplying blueprints for the construction of same. This was fair enough from the challenger's standpoint, especially as Houdini frequently called for an object more formidable than the one they would normally supply.

Where the challenger himself came up with an idea, there was always some discussion of the device to be used. Not until the terms were finally agreed upon would the challenge be made public. Usually, the challenge was worded as though the challenger had made it, but comparisons of "challenges" received by Houdini in various cities show a surprising similarity of ideas. People in one town, however, were unaware of what happened in the next, hence the general conviction was that Houdini was meeting each test for the first time, and this frequently enhanced the performance and enriched the box office as well.

Houdini added to the popular misconception by referring in his publicity to "freak" escapes, such as his release from a tangle of automobile chains or his escape from the interior of a giant football. These were simply adaptations of his more common escapes, but gave the impression that he could free himself from anything on call.

Copies of printed challenges issued to Houdini make a sizeable collection in themselves. These are also reflected in Houdini's theatre programs, giving them an individual touch, because often such programs gave a day by day listing of the challenges scheduled during Houdini's entire engagement.

When people talked about the escapes that they had witnessed early in the week, public interest was naturally roused for those that appeared later, giving Houdini's stay a cumulative effect, again translatable in the universal language of the theatre: box office.

Few of Houdini's escapes — challenges or otherwise — were effected in full view. The straitjacket, some rope releases, and others of this type were done openly because they did not reveal the secrets of mechanical devices but did give Houdini an opportunity to display his strength and skill at wresting free of bonds that would have held most of his less wiry rivals.

The rest were done within the confines of a cabinet curtained from the audience's view. This must be taken for granted when reading the descriptions and explanations. The articles used were examined by a committee, usually both before and after the escape. With most challenges, it was necessary for Houdini to smuggle certain tools or implements in with him in order to effect a release. The music of the orchestra covered the sounds that came from the cabinet.

WBG

THE SAILOR CHALLENGE

In presenting the Challenge Escape Act, I have time and again received challenges from sailors, both in America and abroad, specifying that I escape from ropes with which they were to bind me. Since sailors are known to be skilled at the art of tying knots, such challenges always rouse popular interest in the places where they are issued.

From the performer's standpoint, such a test often becomes a usual rope escape though on a more elaborate scale than ordinary. It can prove tedious to the audience, however, as well as tiring to the performer, when sailors insist on tying a superfluous number of knots to no special purpose. To render such challenges more spectacular, I have had sailors bind me to a wooden plank, every step of the procedure being thus impressed upon the audience and adding materially to the general effect.

The articles used are an eight-foot plank, a strong broomstick, and three ropes; one for the hands and knees, one for the feet, and one for the body. As the audience witnesses it, I am lashed to said plank with the broomstick behind my knees and my hands secured at each side of same.

The knees and wrists are bound first. A long, soft cord or rope is used for fastening the stick to the knees. I start in a sitting position; the stick is placed under my knees; that is, behind them. The rope is put around the center of the stick and is fastened to my knees. Both my hands are then placed under the stick and tied firmly to it.

I am now laid on the plank, which ought to be at least an inch and a quarter thick and nearly eleven inches wide so that I can rest easily on my back. I am lashed to the plank with heavy rope, starting under my arms, crossing over my body, and coming back to my neck. This rope should be sufficiently long as well as heavy, and when the neck has been fastened with the same rope, it is tied off at the end of the board.

My feet are now tied together with the last rope, which should also be heavy, though shorter than that used for the body tie. This rope is also tied off at its end of the board.

All is now ready for the escape to begin. There are two methods of release, as follows:

One is to be able to pull the feet out. This can be done with a great deal of effort, but it depends very much upon how my ankles have been bound. If, for instance, the rope is tied around both ankles together, it is almost impossible to secure my feet closely.

Should I gain the benefit of this or other slack, I first maneuver to release my feet. When they are loose, I can twist more freely upon the board and get my mouth to the rope that holds my hands and untie it with my teeth.

The other method: In this case, the hands are released first. After working a while, I manage to push the broomstick out from my hands. This will make me virtually loose, and from then on, the escape is comparatively easy.

THE WET SHEET TEST

This test, I class as one of the best of all challenges, its being a regular method sometimes used to subdue and restrain dangerous maniacs. I first learned of it when I was featuring the straitjacket escape with the Circus Busch in Germany when an asylum attendant related the details of the wet sheet restraint. It is one of the most difficult tests that I have ever undertaken as will be appreciated by reading the following description:

For the test, I am dressed in a bathing suit, and I am first secured with a piece of cloth tied around my body binding my hands to my sides. In the center of the stage is a sheet; I am placed in this and rolled up tightly by the committee. Thus wrapped in the sheet, I am placed on another sheet which is also rolled about me. The committee then rolls me in a third sheet to serve as an outer wrapping.

Thus bound, I am placed upon a bed with a strong frame, and heavy cloth bandages of the type used in hospitals are wound about my ankles, knees, waist, and neck. The lower pair of bandages measures about four yards in length; the upper pair, about five yards. The ends of these bandages are secured individually to irons fitted permanently in the sides of the bed frame. Four additional bandages, each three yards in length, are run lengthwise from my head to my feet to make the binding firmer. These are also secured to irons fitted in the bed frame.

Now comes the part that renders the escape still more difficult. I am thoroughly drenched with buckets of hot water — about 110 degrees Fahrenheit — which soaks the sheets so that they stick together. The same applies to the cloth with which I was first bound, as well as to the bandages that hold me strapped to the bed.

From this restraint, escape would seem impossible. In fact, the test is so hard that several times I have had barely enough strength to walk off the stage after it was over. Endurance is what counts as it is necessary to worm your way out of the sheets toward the head of the bed. I have had committees refuse to allow my wearing a silk bathing suit, insisting on cotton which will not slip as readily as silk — their purpose being to prevent me from wriggling free.

The factor that the committee overlooks is the length of the two upper bandages, particularly the one at the neck. The irons on the sides of the bed are placed at intervals, almost the full length of my body. By having my feet fastened first, my body is drawn down toward the bottom of the bed. Thus my neck is below the line of the upper irons when the top bandage is fastened there. That bandage slants upward in both directions.

This gives some slack as I wriggle upward, and finally, I come clear of the sheets and can roll to the floor. There, I am able to slip the long cloth down over my feet and get at the knots with my teeth. The cloth may be handled in that fashion as it was wound around my body to begin with.

In case the sheets will not allow you to wriggle out, you can as a last resort sometimes untie your hands, slip them out of the sheets, and undo the knots outside. One time I failed to release my hands in such an emergency and was forced to resume the wriggling process, which succeeded when I was on the point of utter exhaustion. So this is a test in which I must actually struggle for freedom with all my strength.

THE BLANKET RESTRAINT

Ever since I first undertook the Wet Sheet Test, the idea was in my mind of attempting an escape from a heavy blanket which

Scene on August 5, 1926, at the swimming pool of the Hotel Shelton, New York, with preparations under way for Houdini to outmatch the "under water burial" of the self-styled Egyptian fakir, Rahman Bey. Houdini disputed the fakir's contention that this required a cataleptic trance condition and declared he could do better by normal means.

Actual lowering of the box containing Houdini. By conserving his breathing, Houdini stayed under water 1 hour and 31 minutes as opposed to Rahman Bey's then existing record of only 19 minutes at a river bottom. Houdini repeated this in other cities during his final tour. After his untimely death in Detroit, his body was shipped to New York in this "under water" casket, the only box from which Houdini never attempted an escape even when alive. *From the John J. McManus Collection.*

Bill-poster used by Houdini during his first season with his big show (1925-26) heralding the exposé of fake mediums which featured his performance. *From the John J. McManus Collection.*

Photograph of Houdini in his prime, showing him in one of his characteristic moods.

would be strapped tightly around by body in such a manner that the head alone is uncovered. As a great finishing or opening trick, this was the best thing I ever thought of to take the place of the straitjacket.

First, my hands are strapped to my sides with straps and buckles. This is done in such a way that I can always get at least one hand free, as in various other escapes. My body is then rolled in the blanket and straps are fitted around me: One about the neck, one over the shoulders, one over the hips, one over the knees, and one at the ankles.

When the blanket is placed around the body, it fits way over the head, but after the neck strap is fastened, the top portion of the blanket is folded down and makes a sort of collar for the blanket. When I get my hand free, I can release the neck strap through the blanket and struggle out.

With the "collar" hiding the neck strap, I can do the ecsape in full view, working up to a great finish for the escape. By turning over I can kick the restraint way off, so I can make a quick get-up for a bow. This means first loosening the lower straps through the blanket and slipping my feet free.

By having the lower portion of a blanket made of leather, the freeing of the feet and kicking the blanket clear can be done together. But once a special type of restraint is used, it is better to add a novel arrangement that makes a very spectacular escape. In this form, the whole contrivance is made of leather and it is swung between two jacks, so that I am swinging while working.

One jack is at each side of the stage, like those the wire-walkers use, so that all that has to be done is to hook me up first by my head, then by my feet and I can start in working. Since the material used is leather, it is impossible to strap me too tightly. But to speed an escape of this nature, I must be sure of an immediate release from the wrist straps.

This is done by having a secret pocket in my clothes, containing a small, sharp knife and a duplicate strap for my wrists. The pocket, of course, is located in a reachable position. If the straps prove too tight to slip one hand, I obtain the knife and use it to cut one strap. Later, I put the cut strap into the secret pocket along with the knife and remove the duplicate strap so that the committee will suppose it is the one that was used to bind me.

THE PASTEBOARD BOX ESCAPE

Since the object of an escape is to leave the audience and committee mystified as to the how and wherefore, some very effective releases may be introduced with flimsy containers instead of formidable ones. A huge pasteboard box, thoroughly examined before and after the escape, leaves the audience utterly baffled. This, too, is an excellent challenge as the box may be manufactured by some well-known company whose word that it is unfaked will be accepted by all present.

In fact, the box is quite ordinary, as long as it fulfills required specifications. When examined, the very simplicity of its cardboard construction convinces people that it is free of trickery. In this escape, you are placed in the box, the lid is put on, and the box is roped like a huge package. Yet soon after it has been covered by the escape cabinet, you emerge free, and both box and rope may be examined. the box still tied as at the start.

First, the box must be made to your order. Mine is generally about 30 inches high, 24 inches wide, and 37 inches long. The inside is strengthened by a light wooden frame. If possible, I use a dark paper covering, not figured but all black or brown glazed.

The top or lid must be about 12 inches high, fitting like a telescope and fitting easily. The bottom of the box has two holes or spaces cut away below its upper edge, each going to the depth of 9 inches and being cut curved, looking as though they were there simply for the hands to take hold of in lifting.

In order for you to escape, the ropes must be cut. For this you must carry a very sharp and extra long knife. The cutting of the ropes would be difficult but for the "handle" spaces at the sides of the box. By pushing the long blade out through these, it is fairly easy to cut the ropes from inside the box.

You may cut all the ropes on the sides, and it still may happen (and has happened) that the longest rope was unreachable and could not be cut from the side. The only way to beat that is to carry with you a sheet of paper exactly like the kind with which the box is covered and some photo paste. Feel along the bottom of the box for the rope and deliberately cut a slot on the bottom edge. Keep cutting until you have cut the rope.

In challenges where I cut this rope, I try to use a cheap cord that resembles sash cord. This cuts easily and can be carried wrapped around the body. But it is best to use as heavy a rope or cord as possible, as it makes the trick appear more difficult. The object of having a solid color on the box is that in case you tear it or have to cut it, you can repair same and this will be almost impossible to detect.

Once I had to do a new job on the side-holes as the pasteboard was weak and was badly torn. But I had scissors, paste, brush and a sheet of the paper used on the box, and thus I repaired the damage well enough for the box to stand later inspection. It must be remembered that the box can not move after you once enter because your weight would break it. So the best plan is to allow it to remain on the same spot and move the cabinet over the box.

The sash cord that you carry wrapped around your body is used to replace any lengths of ropes that you have cut. The knots must be duplicated so that ropes as well as the box will look exactly the same. The cut rope is wrapped about the body or hidden in the cabinet.

As a challenge, this is not as strong as those requiring heavier contrivances such as packing boxes. Always go into these weak challenges as heavily manacled as possible as this strengthens the trick.

THE PAPER BAG ESCAPE

An escape from a paper bag, as from the pasteboard box, is convincing because the item used is too simple and easily examined to be faked in any way. It has the same element of mystery in its presentation and has taken its place among the most puzzling escapes.

The bag must be made of stiff, strong paper and must be large enough to hold you comfortably so that after you are inside it, you can raise your hands above your head with ease, this being very important to the success of the escape as will be seen later. The bag I use is generally 7 feet and 6 inches long and about 40 inches in circumference. You can easily find your required measurement by trying one beforehand.

In presenting this escape, call attention to the fact that you are not going to destroy the bag but will escape from same leaving it intact. You also emphasize that only one bag is used, this bag being on display in the theatre lobby or at present in the possession of the committee. To prove that only one bag is used, you take the bag immediately after the committee has brought it on the stage and allow members of the audience to write their names on it or to make secret marks that they will be able to identify later.

Be careful not to have any of these too near the top of the bag, for a reason that will be later evident. This point is easily handled by telling people that the upper part of the bag is reserved for seals which the committee will place upon the bag for final identification.

You come back on the stage, allow yourself to be handcuffed, and then enter the bag feet first. The bag is tied with cord which is wound about the neck of the bag a given number of times. Sealing wax is then placed upon the knots and marked with seals by the committee. These seals may also be affixed upon the bag itself.

As you can not move after you are in the bag, the cabinet must be pulled over the bag. In from five to ten minutes, you escape, and coming from the cabinet, you bring out the bag, uninjured and still sealed.

The paper bag, as stated previously, is entirely unprepared, but you must have a duplicate of the seals to be used by the committee. This can be done by supplying them with a stock seal of some ordinary type. If the escape is done as a challenge, you must obtain a duplicate of the seal that the challengers intend to use.

Another point which is helpful, though not an absolute necessity, is to show the committee men how to wind the cord around the neck of the bag. This will enable you to gauge the number of turns that will be made, and the rope will be tied the way you want it, something that is also to your advantage.

As you have furnished the cord for the bag, you have a duplicate cord of the same length. This, plus a sharp-bladed knife, you have concealed upon your person when entering the paper bag. The duplicate cord, as in the Pasteboard Box Escape and others of this category, is wrapped around your body to begin with.

You make your escape by cutting the cord around the neck of the bag with the sharp knife. You must cut through the paper to do this. After you are out, look at the cord and see how many knots have been tied. Retie the bag and reseal it with the duplicate seals, using wax that you have taken along.

The more sealing the committee does, the better, hence you encourage them in this. The reason for this is that when the bag is retied, though the duplicate cord itself covers the hole in the paper, any wax that may be added will hide the cut all the better.

In sealing, the committee usually seals the cord to the bag, so this of course is the best place to make your cut, close to a sealed spot. After you repair the bag, the new seal is placed over the old one. In all this sealing you must use wax matches or tapers that will light without making a noise. These you must have on your person with the knife.

Also see that your cabinet will not show light from the inside. If it does, line it with black cloth before attempting this escape. As further precaution when you are resealing the bag, place your body so that it will shield the light from the committee; that is, toward the front curtain of the cabinet.

THE BASKET ESCAPE

The Basket Escape is an excellent challenge as it is worked with an unprepared basket, supplied by your challengers. It is not as good as being nailed up in a box but will do for a change. Of course, a lot depends upon the type and appearance of the basket, both from its effect upon the audience and from the standpoint of your own escape. The basket should look formidable and at the same time be free of too many complications.

The easiest basket to escape from is the so-called "Laundry Basket" made from split elm. This basket has a wooden top and can only be tied with ropes. To get out of this, you have two ropes; one you hand to your challengers, the other you have wound about your body. The ropes, of course, are identical.

The committee can tie you in, any old way; but the best way

is to rehearse them, getting them to tie the basket with three ropes one way and one the other. This will enable you to retie the basket more quickly than will be possible if you have to study how to retie it.

You carry a sharp knife with which you can cut the original ropes from the interior of the basket. Here, the construction of the basket is a factor; with some, you can work the knife out through the weaving and thus cut the rope. Where this is impossible, you must depend on the flexibility of the basket. By gripping the rim inside the cover, a space is obtained by bending the basket inward. By pushing the knife down through this space you are able to cut the rope without great difficulty.

In getting out of a basket that has a lock, accept only a basket which has holes at the side through which you can reach out and get at the lock, which may be picked or unlocked with a duplicate key.

Always be sure to try the basket before having it announced as a challenge. Make conditions to suit yourself. When you have the basket in your dressing-room, you can change the locks or cut off the hinges if you wish. But make it dead certain of not holding you. Of course, it is possible to fix hinges or put on those of a type that can easily be removed from the inside and replaced later as with hinges found on certain trunks.

LADDERS AND ROPE CHALLENGE

This escape is based upon a challenge made by a building material dealer in England while I was playing a theatre there. The challenger's letter ran as follows:

Dear Sir: Will you submit yourself to a test I have to propose as follows: I will furnish three of my strongest building wrecking ladders about 12 to 18 feet in height and laced together in the form of a tripod; rope your feet or rather your ankles to an iron staple-ring secured to the floor; encircle your neck with rope, knotted, and tie the long ends securely to the top rungs of the ladders.

Even with your hands free, you could not untie your feet or neck, but to make assurance doubly sure, I will secure an iron bar or steel tube three feet in length behind your back, your elbows encircling same, bringing your hands in front where I will tie your wrists in such a position as to render them absolutely useless to you; and will lash different parts of your body to the ladder rungs so that you will be utterly unable to move in any direction whatsoever.

If you accept, name your night, and I will come upon the stage with a number of my employees and test your abilities to the limit. You must make the attempt to escape in full view of the audience.

I performed the escape as described with success in 1910 and also made similar escapes in subsequent years. As described, three ladders are used. They are secured together and fastened to the stage so that they will not slip. Next my feet are tied with thick rope; this prevents the knots from holding fast and I can slip from them if required.

The two ends of the rope are tied into a ring or staple in the stage. I can eventually untie these with my toes after sliding off my shoes. This will dispose of any knots that give me special trouble.

A gas piping forty inches in length is placed behind my back; my elbows encircle it. Sash cord is tied about one hand, then to the other; the pipe is secured to my elbows. Care must be taken to make all the ropes encircle the bar or they will deaden my arms and make me helpless.

I must have my wrists tied as low as possible, so they will not pain, whereas if they are tied as high as possible, it will not only make the escape harder, but will cause unbearable pain. The sash cord is so long that one end is tied to the end of the bar and then to the ladder; another rope is taken and eventually two ropes are tying me from the bar to the ladders, back and front. My legs are tied around the knees and lashed to the ladders, back and front. The long rope for the neck is encircled about my neck, tied, encircled twice or thrice and tied; then it is taken up and tied off away from my hands.

Once my feet are free, I can raise my body and work my hands upward, to get at the ropes around my neck. By pulling one loop of rope, I can tighten the others, thus working one loop over my head, which must be done rapidly because the others are meanwhile choking me. Sometimes to do this, knots must be loosened first. I release my hands by working the bar out, as with the broomstick in the Sailor Challenge.

One time when I tried this escape, I managed to get my head

out first. Then, by taking off my shoes, I untied the knots that
held me to the floor, which allowed me to pull my feet free and
after that it was easy sailing. As with all rope releases, much
depends on the way you are tied.

For cabinet work, this is an excellent escape and you do not
have to worry about more difficult knots as you have more time
to operate. Also, in a test like this, if done behind a curtain, it
is best to have a knife to cut ropes if necessary. Such a knife can
be concealed under the belt, where reachable with one hand. Ropes
hidden in the cabinet can be used to replace any you cut.

THE GREAT CELL MYSTERY

As a spectacular stage escape, this is a great advertising scheme.
It can be billed as a new system of mystery with no faked hinges,
no faked screws. It requires a large cell lined with aluminum or
any non-ferrous metal, and you can offer a reward to anyone who
can work his way out or can find that the cell is not properly made.

The escape artist is locked in the cell and from the inside, it
is absolutely impossible for him to help himself. The locks are
on the outside and there is no trap, no faked rivets or faked hinges.
Yet after a few minutes, during which the cell is curtained off from
sight, the performer is free.

The secret depends upon locks of a special pattern. Each lock
looks exactly like a very fine Chubb; in fact, it is a complicated
lever lock, the same as used on a safe. But it is made to open
from the inside of the cell, with a strong magnet, which you have
concealed.

After I make my escape, the key to the cell is used to lock it
again. But the key given to the committee locks twice. When
the lock is locked twice, no one can get out as the magnet will
not work. This is so that the reward can be offered to anyone
who can get out of the cell.

The door should be held inside by a rather long sheet of metal
which prevents it from coming in. When this sheet is removed
from the inside, it allows the door to come in just far enough to

allow me to squeeze out. Or the door may be made so that after the lock is open, you can lift it up from the inside and thus allow it to be easily pulled inward. Then the closing is easy enough. This must be made to work very quickly.

By having the door open inward, the cell can be chained or roped all about, as with the trunk escape. These will not impede the opening of the door and it is easy to work your body out between them. It is a good idea to use a good straitjacket and be strapped inside the cell and then get out of both. While they are securing the cell outside, there is ample time to release yourself from the jacket. I worked the straitjacket this way with the Circus Carré.

An added feature is to have a bolt on the cell. This is arranged so that by removing a strong screw, a stiffened wire may be inserted; pushing the wire will release a powerful spring that will pull back the bolt. This can easily be fixed so that it can never come back by accident but will require pressure. When pressure is released, it will relock.

THE BARREL CHALLENGE

One of the most effective challenges is the escape from a large unprepared barrel or cask. This challenge is usually accepted by a brewery, so when delivered, the bottom of the barrel is already in place. As soon as you are inside, the top is put on the barrel and the upper band driven firmly in place.

Before entering the barrel, make a speech stating that you are not certain of escaping and that you will try for at least an hour before giving up. Actually, you should be able to do the job in thirty minutes. There are various time-taking details as will be described.

Naturally, you must have air to breathe while endeavoring to make an escape, so it is understood that the barrel must be provided with air-holes. The logical place for most of these is in the top, where your body will not impede the air. My original method took advantage of this. I would specify that the top of the barrel be made in three or more sections with plenty of air-holes. The middle board should have at least five or six — the more the better — in a cross-row.

I would first obtain some duplicate boards from the brewery and have these concealed in the cabinet. I took a dozen fine keyhole saws and a strong handle with me into the barrel, also two stage screws, all hidden on my person. Inside the barrel, I would fasten the stage screws in the top and then start cutting with the saws along the air-holes, to cut the board in half. After cutting the board I would give a few hard pulls on the stage screws and thus draw the sections of the board inside the barrel. (Stage screws are wood screws with large heads that may be grasped and turned by hand.)

You can use two rows of holes so that in case the board is in too tight, you can cut both lines of holes. This enables you to take out a piece of the board, making the rest short enough to draw out, no matter how tightly it may have been placed in.

Be sure and try this escape before you go after it. Also take along a couple of electric pocket lamps; they will come in handy as this gag takes a lot of work. After starting the cutting with the keyhole saw, it is a good plan to have a small fine hardwood saw also. This will cut more quickly.

When the center board is out, you can generally pull away the others intact, but if damaged, you have others to replace them, like the middle board. After your escape, take a muffled hammer — any hammer that you have padded beforehand — and knock the hoops up from the barrel. This is easy after you have taken the top out. Replace the boards and drive down the hoops. Hide the hammer in the cabinet with the cut board.

If the barrel top has cross cleats, these must also be sawed and replaced, which takes additional time. With some barrels it is better to escape by cutting through the bottom, which is also made in sections. If air-holes are needed, you must conceal a small brace and bit to make them. In fixing the bottom of the barrel, use a duplicate middle board of pliable wood, slightly shortened so it can be forced into place.

An ingenious escape can be effected if the middle board of the top can be made pliable. In this case, the air-holes should be bored in the other sections of the top, but none in the center board. You use a special wrench consisting of a screw device with two projecting arms or clamps. These latter are adjustable, and you hook them in the air-holes of the side boards, thus applying the screw device to the middle board. As you increase pressure with this wrench, the board bends upward until it finally comes free.

This same board can be forced back into place again once you are out of the barrel. It works especially well with a large cask, but there must be no air-holes in the board, or it may break under pressure.

THE MAIL BAG ESCAPE

The escape from a United States government mail bag is the most genuine challenge that I have ever been forced to accept. Absolutely nothing is done in the way of faking the bag itself, and the article itself is the regulation type available in any city. No special tools or implements are required, so there is no chance of damaging the bag. This means it can stand thorough examination both before and after the escape. Because of the availability of these mail bags or pouches, I consider this to be the greatest test possible in the United States of America.

Here is a copy of the challenge as given in Los Angeles, when I was touring the Orpheum Circuit:

Houdini will be locked into a leather mail pouch by post office officials. This pouch will be secured with the patent Rotary Government Mail Locks used on registered mail pouches. These locks are made by the government for the sole use of the post office department. They are never allowed to leave the post office and should Houdini fail to release himself, he must be taken to the central post office to have the lock opened.

Such mail bags are sealed by means of a leather strap running through a row of metal staples fixed in the leather collar of the bag. The strap goes over a final staple and is held there with the lock described. The only way of getting out of the mail bag is by unlocking said lock with a duplicate key. Such keys are obtainable, but the big problem is how to use the key while you are locked inside the bag.

The secret is to have the key securely tied to the end of a long string which in turn is attached to your belt or some part of your clothing where it is concealed. There is sufficient space at the top of the bag to push out the key. You then grope through the canvas of the bag, obtain the key, and working through the folds of the canvas, get it to lock which you proceed to open. Due to the string, there is no danger of losing the key if it falls outside the bag. The string can always be drawn in to start operations anew.

Escapes from non-regulation bags are made by means of a steel bar which is pushed through holes in the top of such a bag, with padlocks locked in holes at the end of the bar itself. This is done with a special bar that unscrews in the center. The joint is so smooth and perfect that it can not be noticed by persons who examine it, nor can they unscrew it.

Only when the padlocks are in place can you get the grip and leverage that will unscrew the bar. You do this by taking hold of the padlocks through the canvas of the bag. When the sections of the bar are drawn apart, the bag opens and you can step out, then replace the bar through the holes in the bag. Thus, any locks may be supplied and sealed by the committee.

A duplicate bar of solid steel is kept on hand for exhibit with the bag. This is switched for the faked bar before and after the escape. Fraud mediums have used this bag escape to produce manifestations in their cabinet, then getting back into the bag and replacing the bar, they will be found in the bag at the finish.

THE SPANISH MAIDEN

The Spanish Maiden used in this escape resembles the famous instrument of torture. It is shaped like a human body, and the front is painted to resemble a maiden. The device hinges open at the side and both sections of the interior are lined with iron spikes.

When you enter the device, you take a position between the spikes. The front is then closed, so that the spikes completely trap you within. Padlocks are attached to staples on the outside of the Maiden to prevent you from opening the device. Nevertheless, soon after the cabinet is placed over the Spanish Maiden, you make your escape.

The secret depends upon specially constructed hinges that are practically indetectable. They are pin hinges, but each is cut like a ratchet on one side, and two springs inside the tube hold the pin in position. When the box is open, the lower spring swings around and engages a groove in the opposite side of the pin holding it in place.

When the front is closed, both springs engage the ratchet, and by gripping one of the spikes at the hinge side, you can work the front upward by degrees, gradually forcing the pins out of the springs. The looseness of the padlocks permits this; when the operation is complete, the padlocks serve as hinges while you open the other side of the box. The pins are replaced by pushing them up through the hinges from the bottom, and the Spanish Maiden may be examined by the committee after the escape.

THE DOUBLE BOX ESCAPE

In this spectacular escape, the performer is locked in a large box which is also strapped and encased in a canvas cover. The box is then placed in a still larger box which is also locked, strapped, and laced in canvas. Nevertheless, an escape is made and the boxes may be examined before and after the exhibition.

There are three horizontal boards in the back of each box. The middle board is attached to the lower by two long, thin metal rods. The top board prevents the middle from being lifted off these rods. Spring catches in the upper edge of the middle board engage openings in the top board. These are actuated by a single rod set horizontally in the middle board.

Into an air hole just below this rod, you insert a special U-shaped implement which can be pushed upward to release the hidden catches. This enables you to pull in the center board and lift it, allowing space for your body to pass through. First, however, you must loosen the lacing on the canvas cover.

This is done while the outer box is being locked and laced inside its cover. You find the air hole of the outer box and operate its secret mechanism as you did the inner. The outer canvas is also unlaced, and the escape made. Then you must slide the boards back into place, tightening each canvas cover in due turn.

You need sufficient space between the boxes to allow for the raising of the special board in the outer box. The boxes must be well constructed to stand thorough examination, and the release is rapid as well as spectacular.

HOUDINI ON SPOOKS

No phase of Houdini's career created more controversy and furore than his attacks on fraudulent spirit mediums and psychic swindles during the last few years of his life. It has been charged that this crusade brought him publicity in due proportion. That is quite true, and what is more, the publicity tied in with the magic show and lecture that Houdini was presenting at the time he died.

But it is also a fact that Houdini was inspired by an overwhelming sincerity in this campaign and went beyond all normal limits to carry through his purposes. During his appearance in Philadelphia, for example, he was challenged to a debate by a spiritualistic group. The time for the meeting was set on the day after Houdini's show closed. Naturally, Houdini belonged in the next city on his route where press conferences had been arranged prior to the opening of his show.

Instead, Houdini returned to Philadelphia and met the challenge. The headlines he received came one season too soon to serve as local publicity. But his action was in keeping with his claim that he was serving the public well through his attacks on what he believed to be outright fraud.

It is difficult today to picture the stir that Houdini's activities fomented. The wave of spiritualism that followed World War I had been fanned to the proportions of a tempest by Sir Arthur Conan Doyle when he toured America affirming his belief in spirit communication. Every parlor medium was basking in the implied endorsement of that deductive genius, Sherlock Holmes, whose fictional prowess was supposed to belong, in fact, to his literary creator.

In taking the opposite side of the question, Houdini automatically plunged himself into something more than a controversy; namely, a full-fledged career. He was rugged enough to meet the imprecations heaped upon him by the fanatical opposition. Doyle's adherents would have been outraged had anyone suggested that their champion was out to hoodwink the public. Yet, they lacked the good taste or fair play to grant Houdini the same consideration. Through it all, Doyle and Houdini themselves maintained a cordial regard for each other, but that had little bearing on the local situations that Houdini encountered on tour.

Today, the question still exists, in fact was given a fresh impetus during World War II. If Houdini were alive today, he would be training his guns on masqueraders who style themselves mind-readers, spiritualistic mediums, fortune tellers, and others of that ilk. His challenges to such would readily be adaptable to television programs. Indeed, he might well have roused Congressional interest in the investigation of a field that looms as a growing menace to the mental health of the nation.

Therefore, Houdini's own opinions on the spook question, the account of his effort to have Congress outlaw psychic fakers, plus some of the methods used in spirit trickery, are perhaps as timely today as they were in Houdini's own lifetime.

WBG

SPIRITUALISM SWEEPING THE WORLD

The great wave of Spiritualism which is sweeping the world at the present time has caused many deep thinkers to go into the subject, if possible to discover for themselves just what there is in it.

When in 1848, the Fox Sisters started the mythical snowball of Spiritualism rolling down the snowclad mountain of Time, there was no thought that it would survive seventy-five years of criticism, exposure, and consequent opposition, and would have developed

A faked "spirit photograph" of Houdini, with an "extra" of Lincoln. The spirit photography racket began soon after the Civil War, and Lincoln's portrait became popular as a "spirit extra" partly because his widow was an avid believer. Usually the "extra" is superimposed upon a prepared plate, so the "spirit" will be looking over the sitter's shoulder. By turning the plate upside down before it goes in the camera, an investigator can upset the spirit photographer as well as the "extra".

Marquee of theatre during Houdini's last stand in Chicago, showing the challenge to local mediums which he featured in every city he played.

to the stupendous proportions made manifest by careful observation in this year 1923.

When I started to investigate Spiritualism more than twenty-five years ago, I did so with an open mind and a sincere desire to learn if truth was involved in Spiritualism. During all those years, more than a quarter of a century, and up to the present moment, I have not received any convincing evidence, and of all the mediums I have encountered, not one of them has satisfied me with the genuineness of psychical phenomena. To the contrary, I have never failed to detect a fraud, or at least a possible solution on a perfectly rational basis.

In June, 1922 while visiting with the family at their hotel at Atlantic City, Lady Doyle, at the suggestion of Sir Arthur, favored me with a séance, and in their combined desire to establish the truth by circumstantial evidence, Lady Doyle in a "trance state" produced a letter "automatically" which purported to having been dictated by my sainted mother, and while I respectfully accepted the proffer and reverently considered the epistle, analytically, I was not in any manner convinced that the hand of Lady Doyle had been guided by the spirit of my mother. In fact, I am quite positive it was not dictated or inspired by the spirit of my mother.

I fully appreciate the courtesy bestowed by Lady Doyle in giving me a private séance, but my conscience rebels against accepting or endorsing that epistle as being genuinely communicated by my mother. I would be wrong, if for the mere purpose of politeness, I should assent to what I do not believe.

I have given this episode very careful, thoughtful consideration, for I would have given my right hand for any evidence that may have proved to be true and put me in actual touch with my sainted mother. I regret exceedingly that I must put myself on record as not having been convinced that my angel mother guided that pencil over the message which was delivered to me through the instrumentality of Lady Doyle.

Magicians are trained for magical work, therefore, they detect false moves more quickly than ordinary observers who might chance to witness a séance without knowledge of the subtleness of misdirection.

Misdirection and malobservation are oftimes explanatory of what might, and perhaps is, put down as subconscious action of

the mind. Many times I have retired at night with a problem unsolved and awoke in the morning with a consciousness of that
problem solved. The explanation is plain. On retirement, my
brain was fatigued and incapable whereas at the dawn, it was re-
freshed, and the thoughts which had been harbored, *subconsciously*,
through the night hours, became acute and *responsive*, and a solution seemed, apparently, automatic.

It has been stated in print by a staunch believer in Spiritualism
that I possess psychic power, but were I to accept that statement
as being true, I should be pluming myself with false feathers.

The belief in Spiritualism is getting to be a very serious thing,
and it is high time that the truth should be established beyond
peradventure of doubt by undeniable evidence, which result, if
my judgment is not in error, the pending challenges are sure to
bring about.

I am not an irretrievable sceptic. I am not hopelessly prejudiced. I am perfectly willing to believe, and my mind is wide
open; but I have, as yet, to be convinced. I am perfectly willing,
but the evidence must be sane and conclusive.

HOUDINI BEFORE CONGRESS

1.

The *New York Times* of February 27, 1926, featured this
story:

WASHINGTON SPIRITUALISTS FIGHT BILL
TO FORBID FORTUNE TELLING FOR FEES.
HOUDINI TAKES THE OTHER SIDE.

The clashes of magician Houdini with astrologers whom he challenges amuse hearers. Members of Congress are numbered among the
callers for advice on spiritualistic mediums in Washington, but who
they are is a dark secret.

This was one of the revelations this afternoon before the Senate
Committee on the District of Columbia when Harry Houdini, magician,
appeared in support of the Copeland-Bloom bill to prohibit fortune
telling for fees in the District of Columbia.

One medium declared she had told Mrs. Harding her husband
would become President, and later warned her of his death.

Mr. Houdini engaged in repartee with various fortune tellers. Once he issued a general challenge to them to tell just what his mother called him when he was a boy, but no Spiritualist ventured to furnish the information, and Houdini did not offer it.

According to Houdini, it was possible for anyone to become a spiritualistic minister, in proof of which he displayed a parchment to show that he himself had obtained such a charter.

Mme. Marchia said: "There are men in the Senate and Congress who consult us constantly."

2.

Two days later, on March 1, 1926, the *New York Times* editorialized:

Of the many mediums who gathered at the public hearing in Washington to protest against the passage of a law making most of their pretended activities a misdemeanor, one indignantly declared, in defense of her art, that she was frequently consulted by both Senators and Representatives, and that they considered her advice good and followed it.

The statement is far from incredible, but surely it should lead in both branches of Congress to demands for a further questioning of the seeress and insistance on her disclosure of the names of her legislative clients, for subsequent publication in the justly celebrated *Congressional Record*.

There is where they belong, and nobody who is under the guidance of spirits can be reluctant to have the fact known.

3.

Extracts from the CONGRESSIONAL REPORT OF THE SIXTY-NINTH CONGRESS, FIRST SESSION, HEARINGS OF COMMITTEE — 69th Congress, H. R. 8989, Feb. 26, May 18, 20 and 21, 1926.

Examination of Harry Houdini before the Congressional Committee:

Mr. McLEOD:—Do you care to make a general statement? I understand you are a proponent of this bill 8989.

Mr. HOUDINI:—Yes, sir.

Mr. McLEOD:—You may proceed to make a general statement.

Mr. HOUDINI:—In thirty-five years I have never seen one genuine medium. Millions of dollars are stolen every year in America, and the Government has never paid any attention to it, because they look upon it as a religion.

Mr. RATHBONE:—Is there anything in this bill that deals with Spiritualism?

Mr. HOUDINI:—Yes.

Mr. RATHBONE:—If so, will you be good enough to point it out to me?

Mr. HOUDINI:—Well, under the guise of mediums they tell fortunes. They claim to be clairvoyants, but there is no distinction. That is their way of telling things; they may not charge you any fixed price, but they beat it by taking donations. They pretend that they are looking into the past and the future by mediumship, and when a medium is arrested and brought before a magistrate, she will say: "I am the Reverend Josie Sharman; I am an ordained minister"; and the magistrate does not know that you can be an illiterate and yet be an ordained minister. You need not study; you don't have to go to school to be a reverend. One of my investigators has been ordained six times, and as a pastor twice. And I would like to tell you in front of everyone that in many towns the men are degenerates. When they have women in the room — I have this under oath — they get the women alone, and they have put their hands all over their bodies. I have examined 300 mediums, and this town is the worst I ever struck.

Mr. REID:—Washington, you mean?

Mr. HOUDINI:—Washington, absolutely. If you want sworn affidavits about some of the men degenerates here, I will be glad to let you have them. They act under the cloak of religion. There is nothing in the Bible that says the dead can come back and commune, but Spiritualists interpret it so. Every medium, with few exceptions, would sell my investigators lucky charms. They spent at least $2,000 in buying lucky charms.

Mr. RATHBONE:—Mr. Houdini, you are attacking Spiritualism.

Mr. HOUDINI:—No, I am attacking fraudulent mediums. If there are any genuine mediums, I have never met one.

Mr. HAMMER:—I understand you to say that all spiritualistic mediums are frauds.

Mr. HOUDINI:—I do think so.

Mr. GILBERT:—I concede all that. But what is the use of us legislating?

Mr. HOUDINI:—You will stop people being robbed under the guise of mediumship. It is time to do something in this regard. If you were to die and your wife went to a medium, they would rob her of every penny by claiming to bring your spirit back.

Mr. McLEOD:—It is possible to have a genuine clairvoyant, is it not?

Mr. HOUDINI:—It is impossible. I will give $10,000 to any clairvoyant in the world that will do one test. I would not believe a clairvoyant under oath, so help me God.

Mr. McLEOD:—Would you by proof?

Mr. HOUDINI:—By proof, yes; certainly by proof.

Mr. HAMMER:—You don't claim to be able to do anything by divine power?

Mr. HOUDINI:—No, sir, I am human. But mediums are trying to say I am psychic. That is not true.

Mr. BLOOM:—Everything you do is just as a magician?

Mr. HOUDINI:—Yes, sir; I call it mystification. But I do tricks nobody can explain.

Mr. HOUSTON:—You have never tried to catch a clairvoyant on a test, have you?

MR. HOUDINI:—On a test? [Turning to the audience.] Tell me the name my mother called me when I was born. [No response.] Tell me the pet name my father used to call me. [No response from the mediums.]

Mr. BLOOM:—Mr. Houdini, tell us about Washington.

Mr. HOUDINI:—Washington is the only place where you can buy a license for $25 as a clairvoyant with which to blackmail and rob the public. You are protecting those fortune tellers who, under guises and titles, pretend to see the future. They have not got one genuine medium in Washington.

HOUDINI SUBMITTED THE FOLLOWING STATEMENT
TO THE CHAIRMAN

May 20, 1926

Hon. Clarence J. McLeod,
Chairman of Subcommittee of Judiciary,
Committee on the District of Columbia,
House of Representatives, Washington, D. C.
My dear Sir:

I hereby wish to change the conditions of the $10,000 challenge, especially for today, if any medium present will read and properly answer five sealed questions that I will write; if they will put the sign of the cross on a slate or if they will make any inanimate object move three times in my presence; in fact, if they will do any physical manifestation which they claim to do by spirit agency — should I fail to detect, expose and duplicate what they have done, they may immediately take possession of the $10,000. The Congressmen present are to act as judges.

HOUDINI

A MARVELOUS COINCIDENCE

Occasionally coincidences occur in the performance of magical feats that are so startling as to cause even the artist surprise, and such might easily be mistaken for actual manifestations of something occult by those who are believers in such things.

In Gilbert K. Chesterton's play *Magic*, the performer astonishes himself by actually producing magical effects that he had not supposed possible and which he himself realized that he actually had no hand in, materially speaking.

Something very like this occurred at a banquet given in my honor by the Los Angeles Society of Magicians at the City Club, the night of April 12th. All the members presented brief experiments and among them a druggist of Glendale, California, named Robinson, essayed the feat of changing a rolled cigarette paper into a live moth. Unfortunately, the moth when produced was dead. But just as the metamorphosis was to occur, a living moth appeared from somewhere and circled about his head! It vanished as it came, and a believer might well have decided that it was the astral body of the dead insect which appeared, or that in some way the powers of darkness had conspired to assist the magician.

Of course it was a coincidence, but a miraculous one. I was myself startled, and so was everyone else, the performer possibly most of all. I have never seen anything like it in my experience with the art of conjuring.

THE SPIRIT KNOTS

As a rule a spiritualistic phenomenon is produced in total darkness or a dimly lighted room — and when your audience is made aware of that as being a fact, you are ready to present the following under like conditions:

A twenty-five foot length of clothesline is necessary. The performer holds this line coiled in his hands and calls attention to the fact that there are no knots in the rope — that it is a continuous piece from end to end without knots. When that has been done, one end of he rope is tied around both wrists of a volunteer assistant, and the other end is tied around both wrists of another assistant in similar manner. These knots may be sealed.

The assistants thus secured are stationed about five or six feet apart. The light is now turned out, and the medium, or performer, gives the looped rope in his hand a twist or half turn and approaching one of the assistants, deftly slips the coils over the head of the assistant and guides them to the floor. This can be done quite unobserved by passing the hands over the shoulders as if guiding the assistant to a slightly changed position, the real object being to force him to step out from the loose coils you have just dropped to the floor. This change in position effectuates the tieing of as many knots in the slack rope as there were coils, each coil being converted into a knot. When the change of position has been effected, the performer lifts the knotted coils from floor and simultaneously calls for light. On stretching the rope out it will be found that the spirits have tied the knots.

To perfect the illusion, the performer should draw the rope through his hands just before calling for light, which will have the effect of tightening the knots.

THE VANISHING KNOT

Another interesting knot trick with a rope is the reverse of the move just described.

A bit of clothesline or stout cord about three feet in length is used. A single knot is deliberately tied in the center, after which the two ends are tied together into a double knot or three or four.

The light is turned down, and the spirits cause the knots in the center to dematerialize. This little effect, though very effective, is extremely simple.

Under cover of darkness, the performer loosens up the knot and slips it along to one end of the rope, close up against the knots joining them, draws it tight. The addition of a knot at the joining will never be noticed.

THE SPIRIT RELEASE

Requirements: A volunteer assistant, a large handkerchief, and a five foot length of stout cord.

The wrists of the assistant are securely tied together with the handkerchief, the hands being clasped, or palm to palm. Two or three knots are made to render all secure.

One end of the cord is now passed around the handkerchief, and between the wrists, the ends brought together and tied, or held firmly by a third person. The conditions are now such that the joined hands and arms act as a large link, and the cord forms a second link. The problem is to separate them.

It may be accomplished under cover of darkness or a large scarf or foulard.

The Secret: The "bight" of the cord is between the wrists. Pass it under the handkerchief close to one of the wrists, then over the hand, draw down on opposite side, and in this downward course pass it again between wrists and handkerchief, whereupon the cord will be released and may be drawn away freely.

If this release is deftly done unobserved the effect is very mysterious.

TABLE LIFTING

Cut a slot in a ring which you can place on one of your fingers as is depicted in the accompanying illustration. Then drive a common pin into a small lightweight table (as per illustration), which you intend to lift. By slipping the slot of the ring behind the head of the pin, you are able to get quite a firm hold on the table and so can lift it from the floor.

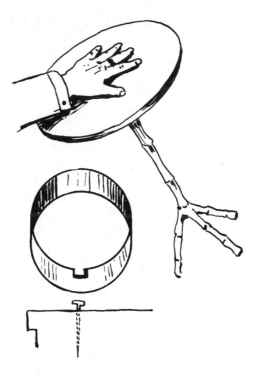

TABLE LIFTING USING RING AND COMMON PIN.

Place your hand on the table and casually slip the slot of the ring behind the head of the pin and slowly and carefully raise the table, which will make it appear to the audience as if you lifted it with your finger tips.

To add effect to this, you can now spread a silk handkerchief over the top of the table to show there is no preparation, for it will not prevent you from slipping the slot of the ring over the head of the pin. You can now lift the table and move it about to the accompaniment of music, and with the last movement, remove the pin and hand the table around for examination.

SPIRITUALISTIC SECRET: LIBRARY DIRECTORY SERVICE

There is one trick that we have never explained, and that is to go to a public library and look up the old directories to trace old addresses, and then give the oldest inhabitants information that seems wonderful. We know of a Spiritualist that had access to the Public Library in St. Joseph, Missouri, and he would hold his séances near this place; whenever necessary he would sneak out the back entrance of the building, rush to the library, and search the old directories for the names and addresses asked of him, and always made a hit by correctly giving the desired information to the "Seekers after truth."

THE ZAN ZIC SLATE

This trick seems to have been the one with which the lately deceased Zan Zic made his money. In fact, he fooled the best of them, and I do not know of any better trick that can be worked in a parlor for private sittings than the one in this number.

In a room in which you give your "sitter" a private reading, have a table, two chairs, and an innocent looking chiffonier. This chiffonier has all the drawers cut away, in fact, it is only the shell of the real article. In this you have concealed your confederate,

METHOD OF READING SEALED LETTERS AND OF OBTAINING SPIRIT
SLATE WRITING ATTRIBUTED TO THE LATE ZAN ZIC WHO WAS ONCE
UNDER THE MANAGEMENT OF JACK CURREY.

who has a good supply of slates, envelopes, strings, wires, seals,
knife, scissors, in fact everything with which he can reseal any
envelope or slate that he has handed to him. The "sitter" is seated
with his face toward the window and his back towards the
chiffonier.

Zan Zic would walk up and down, whilst his "sitter" would be
writing the questions and placing them in envelopes. After all the
questions had been written, Zan Zic would stand behind the "subject", and taking up an envelope with his right hand, would place
it on the head of the unsuspecting "sitter", and with his left, he
would reach for an envelope that the concealed confederate passed
to him from the chiffonier. With a shaky movement he would
exchange the envelopes, and ask the "sitter" to hold the envelope
so as to get more "magnetism." The confederate would tear open
the envelope, and hold the message out of the drawer, enabling
Zan Zic to read it. After the message was known, the confederate
would reseal the letter or question, and it would be handed back

and "switched" for the "dummy" envelope that was being held on the head of the "sitter." To obtain writings on sealed slates, the slates would be exchanged the same way, the confederate would open the slates, write the message, and reseal or rivet them and put them back in the original position. This test, worked properly, is the strongest that has ever been known.

The above "test" has been described to me by several people, foremost amongst whom were Prof. S. Baldwin, Harry Stork, and Llywellian.

Note: The Zan Zic mentioned in this article is not to be confused with the more famous Julius Zancig who performed an amazing mental act with his wife, under the title "Two Minds With But a Single Thought". *WBG*

THE TALKING SKULL

The skull trick is worked with the aid of a long thread which is stretched across the stage; after the skull has been examined, two assistants, one on each side of the stage, take hold of each end of the thread and lift it up to the level of the skull's jaw and here insert the thread. By holding the thread taut, they can at will cause the skull to answer, either by moving the jaws or causing the skull to rock.

As the magician asks the questions in a loud tone of voice, the concealed assistants hear everything and move the skull's jaws or rock the skull accordingly. Prof. S. S. Baldwin made use of a common piece of board. Delprade used a borrowed high hat. And both entertainers obtained satisfactory results.

SPIRIT PHOTOS

The *New York Sunday World* (1907) has a two-page article most interestingly illustrated as only a gigantic paper like the *World* can illustrate, informing us about the great scientists who believe in the dead being able to revisit us after the soul has left the body. While it makes interesting reading, we cannot agree with any of it as those spirit photos are so simple of production, and the various effects reported so easily duplicated, that the only thing we can say is that Flamorien, Stead, and several of the other great minds mentioned, have lately been compelled to keep in close confinement so as to evade questions that they could not answer.

THE VEST TURNING MYSTERY

This effect has been attributed to "Spirit Mediums", but there is no authentic record of such having been the case. It is simply a mystery effect that classifies with curious puzzles.

The trick, or puzzle, is to turn the vest wrong side out and button it on backwards after the hands have been secured by a bit of rope about three feet long. Each end of the rope is securely tied to a wrist, and the knots sealed with wax or sewn with a needle and thread.

The way it can be done:

After the rope is tied around wrists, the manipulator steps behind a screen so that his action is unobserved, and unbuttons his vest. Both hands then grip vest at back of neck and bring the entire vest over his head to a position directly in front of his body. He then turns vest inside out by passing the entire thing through one sleeve hole, with the result that the vest is now wrong side out. In this condition it is easily slipped back over the body with buttons to the back. It is only necessary now for the hands to be lowered; straight down the hips, and the "bight" of the rope passed under both feet by stepping through which allows free play of hands at back for purpose of buttoning the vest. When this is accomplished, the rope is brought to its original position in front by stepping over the "bight" from back to front.

"MARGERY" THE MEDIUM EXPOSED

In 1922 I was asked to write a series of articles on Spiritualism for the *Scientific American* but had to refuse owing to pressure of work.

I explained that the research work involved was such that I could not entrust it to anyone else and that it was impossible for me to spare the time which this and the writing of the articles would require, but I advised them to form an investigating committee and said if the other members were honest, reliable, and qualified, I would serve as one without pay with the stipulation that I was to have the right to reject any person proposed as a member of the committee with me. My reason for this was, as I explained to them, that while an ordinary investigator, whether layman, professor, or scientist, could make a mistake and later correct himself without damage to his standing, I was in a different position, for due to the peculiar nature of my work my reputation was at stake and I could not run the risk of having it injured. This was agreed to before they left my office, but sometime afterwards hearing that they had selected a committee without consulting me I wrote the following letter to protect myself.

November 13, 1922.

Mr. J. Malcolm Bird,
Scientific American,
233 Broadway,
New York City.
Dear Mr. Bird,

I have just been informed by Mr. Hopkins that you have already selected a committee to serve as investigators for the $5,000.00 offered to the mediums.

So, that there is no mistake in this, I would like to have it understood emphatically, that when I consented to be one of your committee, it was under the condition that,

1. I am to know each and every man so selected.
2. That all conditions placed before the mediums should be thoroughly gone over with me, so that there could be no loop-hole for anyone to misconstrue the conditions of the manifestations required.
3. Another condition is that the selected committee will go to a number of séances for investigation purposes, so that we could get a line on each other regarding the capability of actually recording in writing what was seen, as mal-observation is the curse of all description.

It was also stipulated in my conditions that we are to hold conferences to see whether all the committee are agreeable to each other, because we must work in harmony.

I have more at stake than the money you are offering, and that is, my reputation as a psychic investigator, and I, therefore, ask you to give me your full confidence, as I am giving you mine. I intend to serve you faithfully, and with all the knowledge I possess, but I ask to be fully protected in this.

May I suggest that it might be advisable for us to get together again before publicity is given, so as to prevent any mistakes on all our parts. I am keenly and intensely interested in the subject and will deem it a compliment to be on the committee, but if any of the above conditions do not meet with your approval, please count me out.

Yours sincerely,

HOUDINI.

HH.JLD

————————

The Committee as finally formed consisted of Dr. William McDougall, of Harvard University; Dr. Daniel F. Comstock, formerly of the Massachusetts Institute of Technology; Dr. Walter Franklin Prince, of the Society of Psychical Research; Hereward Carrington; and Houdini. Mr. Bird has acted as Secretary for the Committee and Dr. Austin C. Lescaboura, another editor on the *Scientific American* Staff, has assisted in arranging the tests and been present at most of the séances.

Following the *Scientific American's* offer of a sum of money as a prize to any medium who could successfully pass its tests, several presented themselves and gave sittings before the Committee. Among them were the Tomsons, Mrs. Josie Stewart, Valentine, and Pecararo. Bird did not invite me to the major part of the séances, whereas, as Secretary, it was his duty to do so, therefore, on learning of the Pecararo tests, I traveled from Little Rock, Arkansas, to New York, to be present at one of the Pecararo séances.

In all these investigations it would seem that Mr. Bird allowed the mediums to believe that they had practically won the prize and this is mirrored in the press reports given out by him. Dr. Prince and I strenuously objected to this course.

So far as I knew there was no other investigation under way when, on picking up a copy of the *Scientific American* early in 1924, I was surprised to find an announcement of a series of séances being held by the Committee with a certain "Margery" and judged from the reading of it that the Committee was on the verge of awarding her the prize. In the next issue of the magazine I again found mention of the mysterious medium whose identity was being hidden behind the name of "Margery," *but as most all American papers carried stories giving her correct name and address before I was called into the séances, and as later she gave interviews to newspaper men, and one in particular in my presence, without denying her name, it would be ridiculous for me now to do other than call her by her right name also, Mina Crandon, wife of L. R. G. Crandon, a well-known Boston surgeon.*

The *Scientific American* reports, written by Editor Bird, were such as to lead an ordinary layman to believe that the magazine had found a medium who had successfully passed all its crucial tests and to all intents and purposes was "genuine." In addition the lay reader, and the uninitiated reporter as well, were left with the impression that the Committee had approved this medium, whereas the articles only represented the opinion of Mr. Bird, who, garbing himself in a mantle of authority, had written whatever he desired, always, however, being careful to so phrase his material that later, in case the necessity arose, he could claim a certain alibi. A careful reading of the articles makes these subtleties obvious.

Shortly after the appearance of the articles, I received the following letter from Mr. Bird:

SCIENTIFIC AMERICAN,
233 BROADWAY, NEW YORK.
June 18, 1924.

MR. HARRY HOUDINI,
278 WEST 113TH ST.,
NEW YORK CITY.
MY DEAR MR. HOUDINI:

As you will observe when you get your July *Scientific American,* we are engaged in the investigation of another case of mediumship. Our original idea was not to bother you with it unless, and until, it got to a stage where there seemed serious prospects that it was either genuine, or a type of fraud which our other Committeemen could not deal with. Regardless of whether it turns out good or bad, there will be several extremely interesting stories in it for the *Scientific American;* and these will run in the August and following issues.

Mr. Munn feels that the case has taken a turn which makes it desirable for us to discuss it with you. Won't you run in, at your convenience, to take lunch with one or both of us, and have a talk with Mr. Munn? Better call me in advance, and make sure that he and I will be in at the time you select.

Faithfully yours,
(Signed)   J. MALCOLM BIRD,
Associate Editor.

P.S. Mr. Munn left the office today, to be gone until Monday morning.

I made the appointment requested in the letter and on meeting Mr. O. D. Munn he explained that he had been anxious to get in touch with me, and in fact had been trying to for a week, but Bird had been side-stepping the matter, and that he thought we should go to Boston together and sit in at the "Margery" séances. After we had talked the matter over he called Bird into his office and turning to him I asked point blank:

"Do you believe that this medium is genuine?"

I asked him this because, although a raw amateur at investigating, which amounts to a profession in itself, and with no experience with or knowledge of "the production of mysteries" he had nevertheless, given his approval to several mediums and failed to detect their conjuring trick methods. His reply, as near as I can remember, was:

"Why, yes, she is genuine. She does resort to trickery at times, but I believe she is fifty or sixty per cent genuine."

"Then you mean that this medium will be entitled to get the *Scientific American* prize?" I asked.

"Most decidedly," he answered.

"Mr. Bird," I replied, "you have nothing to lose but your position and very likely you can readily get another if you are wrong, but if I am wrong it will mean the loss of reputation and as I have been selected to be one of the Committee I do not think it will be fair for you to give this medium the award unless I am permitted to go up to Boston and investigate her claims, and from what you tell me I am certain that this medium is either the most wonderful in the world or else a very clever deceptionist. If she is a fraudulent medium I will guarantee to expose her and if she is genuine I will come back and be one of her most strenuous supporters."

Then turning to Mr. O. D. Munn, I said:

"If you give this award to a medium without the strictest examination every fraudulent medium in the world will take advantage of it. I will forfeit a thousand dollars if I do not detect her if she resorts to trickery. Of course if she is genuine there is nothing to expose, but if the *Scientific American* by any accident should declare her genuine and she was eventually detected in fraud *we would be the laughing stock of the world*, and in the meantime hundreds of fraudulent mediums would have taken advantage of the error."

"Well, then you and I will go up together and see," he replied.

"All right, I am at your service," I told him.

We were given to understand that this first séance which I attended on the evening of Wednesday, July 23rd, 1924, was the forty-eighth in which Mrs. Crandon had been tested, but I learned later from a letter written by her husband that it was nearer the eightieth, and by the time Mr. O. D. Munn and I had finished our fifth séance Dr. Crandon claimed that the total was ninety. All séances were *dark*.

At this séance Dr. Crandon sat on the medium's right and held her right hand and I, Malcolm Bird, as had been customary in their previous séances, circled with one of his hands the fingers of both the medium and her husband. This left one of Bird's hands free for "exploring purposes" as he said.

I sat on the left of Mrs. Crandon and held her left hand with my right. My right foot was placed against her left foot, pressing against her ankle.

FIGURE 1

Anticipating the sort of work I would have to do in detecting the movements of her foot I had rolled my right trouser leg up above my knee. All that day I had worn a silk rubber bandage around that leg just below the knee. By night the part of the leg below the bandage had become swollen and painfully tender, thus giving me a much keener sense of feeling and making it easier to notice the slightest sliding of Mrs. Crandon's ankle or flexing of her muscles. She wore silk stockings and during the séance had her skirts pulled well up above her knees.

One of the successful (?) demonstrations which she had been giving, and which none of the Committee had been able to expose, involved the use of an electric bell enclosed in a box fourteen inches long by six wide and five deep.

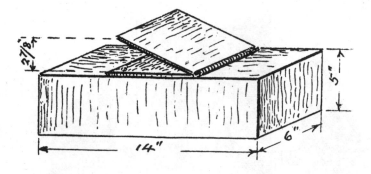

BOX WITH SPRING HINGE FLAP

This box (Fig. 1) was stoutly fastened on all sides except the top, which was covered with boards. Inside the box with the bell were dry batteries which rang it whenever a certain pressure at the top of the box completed the circuit. In previous séances when this box had been placed in front of Mrs. Crandon and the sitters supposed they had her perfectly controlled (held by hands and feet so they could detect any motion) the bell had been rung repeatedly and the explanation given was that "Walter," the medium's dead brother, had closed the circuit. Not only had the bell been rung but it had been used with a code and answered questions.

On the evening in question the bell-box was placed between my feet with my right foot between it and Mrs. Crandon's left foot. As the séance progressed I could distinctly feel her ankle slowly and spasmodically sliding as it pressed against mine while she gained space to raise her foot off the floor and touch the top of the box. To the ordinary sense of touch the contact would seem the same while this was being done. At times she would say:

"Just press hard against my ankle so you can see that my ankle is there," and as she pressed I could feel her gain another half inch.

FIGURE 2

When she had finally maneuvered her foot around to a point where she could get at the top of the box the bell ringing began and *I positively felt* the muscles of her leg flex and tighten as she repeatedly touched the ringing apparatus. There is no question in my mind about it. *She did this.* Then, when the ringing was over, I plainly *felt her leg slide back* into its original position with her foot on the floor beside mine.

During the second intermission "Walter" asked for an illuminated plaque to be placed on the lid of the box which held the bell and Bird went to get it. This left the right hand and foot of the medium free. Bird had difficulty in finding the plaque and while he was searching "Walter" suddenly called for "control." (See Fig. 2.)

Mrs. Crandon placed her right hand in mine and gave me to understand that I had both her hands. Bird was requested to stand in the doorway, but without any warning, before he could obey, the cabinet was thrown over backwards violently. *The medium then gave me her right foot also, saying:*

"You have now both hands and both feet."

Then "Walter" called out:

"The megaphone is in the air. Have Houdini tell me where to throw it."

"Toward me," I replied, and in an instant it fell at my feet.

The way she did these two tricks is as follows: when Bird left the room it freed her right foot and hand. With her right hand she tilted the corner of the cabinet enough to get her free foot under it, then picking up the megaphone she placed it on her head, dunce-cap fashion (Fig. 3). Then she threw the cabinet over with her right foot. As she did so I distinctly felt her body give and sway as though she had made a vigorous lunge. As soon as this was done "Walter" called for "better control" and she gave me her right foot. Then she simply jerked her head, causing the megaphone to fall at my feet. Of course with the megaphone on her head it was easy and simple for her to ask me or anyone else to hold both of her feet and also her hands, and still she could snap the megaphone off her head in any direction requested. This is the *"slickest"* ruse I have ever detected, and it has converted all skeptics.

FIGURE 3

The next day Mrs. Crandon told us it would be impossible to either kick or push the cabinet as it was hinged on the inside and would double up in the middle, but that afternoon Mr. O. D. Munn and I went upstairs alone and while sitting in the medium's chair I put my right foot under the right-hand corner of the cabinet and easily tilted it so that the slightest movement caused it to fall over.

The second séance of Mrs. Crandon's which I attended was on the evening of July 24th, at Professor Comstock's hotel. At this time I discovered without question that she used her head and shoulders to push back the table. Her great asset in disguising the muscular movements which she uses in doing this is the arm chair in which she sits. As she is unusually strong and has an athletic body she can press her wrists so firmly on the arms of the chair that she can move her body and sway it at will without the sitters, who have hold of her hands, detecting the movement (Fig. 4).

FIGURE 4

That evening I was in charge of her left hand which rested lightly on the palm of my right. With my index finger I could feel her pulse. In fact I used the secret system of the "touch and tac-

FIGURE 5

tics "of the mind or muscle performer, (I had given performances or tests in this field of mystery) who is guided by the slightest muscular indication in finding a hidden article. *I was able to detect almost every time she made a move. Frequently she stretched out her arms to rest them and once I caught her using this motion as a subterfuge, leaving only her elbow on the chair while she pushed the table with her head* (Fig. 5).

"Walter," her guide and aide, is very autocratic, seldom asking anything but usually directing, and this evening he ordered everyone to move back from the table around which we were sitting so that he might gather force. This was simply another ruse on the medium's part, for when all the rest moved back she moved back also and this gave her room enough to bend her head and push the table up on over. *I caught her doing this twice.*

Before going to the séance Mr. O. D. Munn and I had determined to explore things to our satisfaction and had arranged a code of signals. At the séance he sat at my left in the circle, I holding his right hand. At the first movement of the table I pushed his hand under it and let go and began groping around with my left hand. As I did so I felt Mrs. Crandon's head at the edge of the table pushing it up and forward until the box with the bell had slipped off to the floor. I reached over and whispered to Mr. O. D. Munn what I had detected. Then to check up and assure myself of the deception I reached out again into the dark and *she ran her head directly against my outstretched fingers.* I do not think she was more surprised than I. She then said something about losing hairpins and after the séance her hair was loosened. This was done for effect and to offset my discovery.

While I knew she was still using her head, I pulled Mr. O. D. Munn's ear to my lips again and whispered:

"Will I denounce and expose her now?"

"You had better wait a while," he replied.

"Now is the time," I urged.

"No, better not for a while," he answered.

After this demonstration the bell-ringing test was gone through again. The box was placed between my feet with her ankle against my right foot like the night before. I had rolled my trousers up as on the previous evening. She began with exactly the same tactics, but nothing happened. Finally she said to me:

"You have garters on, haven't you?"

"Yes," I replied.

"Well, the buckle hurts me," she said.

I reached down to undo the garter and found that the buckle had caught her stocking so fast that it prevented her from sliding her ankle enought to get room to tap the bell. After I took the garter off she was able to reach the bell as she had the previous night. When the spirit asked Mr. O. D. Munn how many times he wanted the bell rung and Mr. Munn said "five," she made so bold a sliding movement with her ankle to reach the box that I think she was under the impression that I was badly fooled or was going to help her like others. After the five taps on the bell she slid her foot back into position on the floor beside mine.

When the séance was over Mrs. Crandon left the room to dress for the street. I had Mr. O. D. Munn call the Committee into a room by themselves and I explained the trickery which I had discovered and there was a discussion as to whether I should expose the medium then or after our return to New York. The Committee finally decided that we should return to New York first; that Mrs. Crandon was not to be informed that I had detected her, and I was to make an affidavit for the Committee covering the details of my discoveries. *Bird opposed my demands to have her exposed as quickly as possible, but I called his attention to the rapid exposure he had given the others* and he replied:

"We will do it differently this time."

I strongly suspected his motives and told Mr. O. D. Munn so after we had left.

Directly after this séance Mr. Munn and I started for New York, although Bird stayed on for three days as the guest of Dr. and Mrs. Crandon and later when called to task before Mr. O. D. Munn admitted that he gave them information concerning my discoveries and the talk of the Committee. Before I left my hotel that night I wrote the following letter which I handed to Mr. O. D. Munn at the same time telling him that I did not want Bird to write an account of my findings.

July 24, 1924.

THE COPLEY-PLAZA,
BOSTON.
DEAR MR. MUNN:

Please if I may, allow me to see the exposed article before it is published, as all of the other articles were not written so as to properly place the real thing before the public.

Mr. Bird in your presence, said he believed the medium was fifty per cent genuine, when this evening there was no chance of anything she pretended to have been accomplished by "Walter," but was so done by herself. In fact she is *one hundred per cent trickster or fraud* judging by the first séance I attended, after forty or more were given.

I ask you in all *fairness* that in the future, Mr. Bird be not permitted to send any report speaking for the Committee, unless the Committee has read the account and agreed that it should be published.

I have been unfairly treated in this case being only called in when according to Mr. Bird's personal statement and in print made, to the effect that the medium, Mrs. Crandon, was fifty per cent genuine, and publishing in two articles of your publication, facts such that could not have been written by a competent investigator, and I would like a personally written statement from all those who were present on the Committee, to check up their findings.

Most important of all, in the future, the entire Committee should be called to the séances in a systematic manner and not in a haphazard way as has been done.

Believe that whenever material is published in reference to the Committee or work probably to be done by it, that the names should be mentioned and they are not to be treated in a slighting manner.

If any of those conditions do not meet with your approval, will you kindly accept this letter as my resignation.

    (Signed)   HOUDINI.

At this time the September number of the *Scientific American* was on the press and in it was another article by Bird in which he spoke of the "wonderful mediumship of Margery." The first thing Mr. O. D. Munn did when we got to New York was to stop the presses and have this article of Bird's thrown out.

"Houdini, stopping presses and throwing out that thing of Bird's is a pretty costly proposition," he said.

"Yes," I replied, "but it will save the reputation of the *Scientific American,* and that is cheap at any price. Bird has not a penny invested in your magazine, but nevertheless is using it to suit his own purposes."

He evidently agreed with me and as a result when the September number came out it had no reference to the investigation. Bird's articles in the *Scientific American* were so uncalled for, so unreal and so misleading that Dr. Prince and I agreed that they must stop, for Bird was- making statements as though Dr. Prince were in accord with him, which was not the case, and it was jeopardizing Dr. Prince's reputation and position. So concerned was Dr. Prince about it he told me he was going to resign and I replied if he did I should also terminate my dealings with the Committee.

I then made a special trip to see Mr. O. D. Munn, explained the situation to him and told him that if we were going to Boston again I wanted Dr. Prince retained on the Committee and taken along with us, for I trusted implicitly in his integrity. I got Dr. Prince on the telephone and asked him to come to the *Scientific American* office immediately, which he did, and before leaving he agreed not to resign if the following conditions were adhered to:

1. No reports of experiments with which the judges have to do at any stage, and no opinions, positive or tentative, regarding their results or quality, shall be made public, either in the *Scientific American,* or any other publication, prior to the conclusion of the series of which they are a part. Not only the management of the *Scientific American,* but all the judges shall agree to this.

2. No representative of the *Scientific American* shall ascribe to the Committee of Judges, in that periodical or elsewhere, conclusions or opinions which are not strictly authorized by the official statement of that Committee, which, or so many members of which as participate in the experiments, shall draw up its own report of conclusions. If the individual members of the Committee are quoted or opinions or acts ascribed to them, the names of such members shall be stated in connection.

He also made this suggestion:

It has come to my knowledge that many persons are not clear in their minds that the Judges have no interest in the financial factor involved in the offer of prizes, and that they are quite independent of the *Scientific American.* This has probably come about from the facts that one

THE CABINET BOX AS IT WAS THE FIRST NIGHT. THE FRONT WAS
PUSHED OUT BY THE MEDIUM, SINCE IT WAS HELD IN PLACE BY
ONLY TWO BRASS STRIPS.

of the editors of that periodical is termed Secretary of the Judges, and that the Judges' decisions have invariably and solely appeared incorporated in his articles. I suggest that the title "Secretary to the Committee of Judges" shall no longer be borne by any member of the *Scientific American* staff and that the official decision of the Committee of Judges shall, whether or not incorporated with the article describing the sittings, appear under a separate title, with the names of the participating members appended.

But although Mr. O. D. Munn assured Dr. Prince that he believed his position was perfectly correct and that his conditions and suggestions would be adhered to and gave Bird written instructions to follow them it was not long before Dr. Prince and I were forced to object to newspaper articles with such headings as: "BOSTON MEDIUM BAFFLES EXPERTS," "SCIENTISTS PLAN MORE TESTS," "HOUDINI THE MAGICIAN STUMPED," "BAFFLES SCIENTISTS WITH REVELATIONS, PSYCHIC POWER OF MARGERY ESTABLISHED BEYOND QUESTION," "EXPERTS VAINLY SEEK TRICKERY IN SPIRITUALIST DEMONSTRATION" — and statements which, as Dr. Prince said, showed that if Bird was being correctly quoted he was telling the reporters one thing and us another. In fact we seemed unable to curb Bird until after my strenuous objection to his being in the séance room and Dr. Prince had again insisted that his resignation must be accepted unless we could have a more dependable guarantee that nothing would be said until after the the series of séances was over.

Following the séances of July 23rd and 24th, 1924, Dr. Prince, Dr. Comstock, and Mr. O. D. Munn asked me to construct some sort of a comfortable restraint for the medium which would prevent her from using any of the tactics which I had detected, such as moving her hands and feet. This was agreed to by the whole Committee and I set to making a cabinet-box which was entirely closed except openings for the medium's neck and arms.

It had been arranged that the Committee should meet in Boston on August 25th. I went up from New York taking the cabinet-box along and also my assistant in case there were any changes to be made. The first séance, which took place that same evening, was in a room at the Charlesgate Hotel. Previous to the séance at which the Committee was present Mrs. Crandon gave a private one at which it is said there were wonderful phenomena.

At the official séance the box with the bell was placed on a table in front of the cabinet. As the lid of the cabinet was only fastened with two thin brass strips Mrs. Crandon, by lifting her shoulders, was able to force the lid and ring the bell with her head. They tried to make it appear that "Walter" had forced open the cabinet-box, which of course was simply an effort to hide the fact.

FRONT VIEW OF THE CABINET

BACK VIEW OF THE CABINET

While we were in another room, after the séance, I suddenly missed Dr. and Mrs. Crandon and walking into the room where the séance had been held I discovered them by the cabinet-box talking in subdued tones. Their backs being toward me, they did not see me enter and I watched them measure the gap in which the neck was secured. Before that they had insisted on cutting this aperture larger, but when I spoke to them again about it, they said they were perfectly satisfied with it and to let it remain as it was.

That night at the hotel after the séance while Mr. O. D. Munn and I were talking it over, he said he wanted the next séance a total blank as the fooling must be stopped. In order to do this the next afternoon I fixed up the cabinet-box so that we could lock the front portion with four hasps, staples and padlocks in such a way there would be no possible chance of the lids being forced open again.

Mr. O. D. Munn told me that he had arranged not to have Bird at the séances of August 25th, 26th and 27th. Bird though in Boston was absent on the evening of the 25th but on the 26th he came and demanded to know why it was that with no apologies he had been literally and unceremoniously put out and the door of the séance room slammed in his face and what were our objections to his being present. Dr. Prince and I, in view of the disclosures which Bird had made, considered it best that he stay out. Dr. Prince is a better diplomat than I, but I openly said:

"I object to Mr. Bird being in the séance room because he has betrayed the Committee and hindered their work. He has not kept to himself things told him in strictest confidence as he should as Secretary to the Committee."

He denied this but I called his attention to the fact that Mrs. Crandon had told me a number of things which he only knew and that he had admitted to Mr. O. D. Munn that she had wormed things out of him.

"Well, then I will resign as Secretary to the Committee!" he exclaimed.

"That is not necessary," I replied, "as according to the letter written by Dr. Prince, the conditions of which were accepted by Mr. O. D. Munn, you can only speak for yourself and not for the Committee."

But the Committee decided to accept his resignation, as a matter of form, and Dr. Prince was elected Secretary. Bird then left the room.

THE SECOND NIGHT. FOUR MORE HASPS AND STAPLES WERE PLACED ON THE CABINET BOX, SO THE MEDIUM COULD NOT FORCE OPEN THE FRONT OF THE BOX AS SHE HAD DONE ON THE FIRST NIGHT.

This brush with Bird, and the usual preliminary examinations over, the séance proceeded. I had been asked by the Committee to construct a humane, fraud-proof restraint to held the medium and in thinking what would be necessary to make me helpless I

HOW THE TWO-FOOT RULE MANIPULATED BY THE CHIN CAN PRESS THE BELL AND CAUSE IT TO RING. NOTICE THAT BOTH HANDS ARE BOARDED UP INSIDE THE CABINET BOX.

had figured out the cabinet-box. Then in thinking of possible ways to beat the Committee it occurred to me that were I the medium, and the cabinet was closed I could get ready, some concealed instrument, with which to reach the bell while the Committee was fastening the locks.

Having this in mind I allowed her the greatest freedom while she entered and was being locked into the cabinet-box, but standing at one side I carefully watched her face and could tell by the way she pulled down on her neck that she was "reaching" for something, so I asked Dr. Prince to hold her right hand and I took control of her left which she put out through the opening at my request. She was now locked in the cabinet-box with her head and arms protruding. Believing that she had something concealed, *I repeatedly told Dr. Prince not to let go of her right hand until after the séance was over and the cabinet-box unlocked.* I repeated this so often that Dr. Prince not knowing what I had in mind, good-naturedly resented it, thinking I thought he did not understand. Finally Mrs. Crandon asked me sharply what I meant by saying it so often.

"Do you really want to know?" I asked.

"Yes," she replied.

"Well, I will tell you. In case you have smuggled anything in to the cabinet-box you can not now conceal it as both your hands are secured and as far as they are concerned you are helpless."

"Do you want to search me?" she asked.

"No, never mind, let it go. I am not a physician," I told her.

Soon after "Walter" appeared in the circle saying:

"Houdini, you are very clever indeed but it won't work. I suppose it was an accident those things were left in the cabinet?"

"What was left in the cabinet?" I asked.

"Pure accident was it? You were not here but your assistant was," "Walter" went on and then stated that a ruler would be found in the cabinet-box under a pillow at the medium's feet and virtually accused me of putting it there to throw suspicion on his sister winding up with a violent outburst in which he exclaimed:

"Houdini, *you* G— d— — — — —, get the hell out of here and never come back. If you don't, I will!"

This just expressed Mrs. Crandon's feelings toward me for she knew I had her trapped, and despite all objections I insisted that this abusive remark be made part of the record. Dr. Comstock then suggested that in working around the cabinet-box, it was quite possible for someone to drop a ruler into it accidentally. Thinking that my assistant might have forgotten or dropped the ruler I said that if it was not his I would make a statement, but I laid particular stress on a request that someone should speak to him so Mr. O. D. Munn left the room and brought him in. The assistant assured Munn that he knew nothing about it and told us the same, saying that it could not be his for he had that in his pocket. He then took it out and showed it to us. I made him swear to his statements with a solemn oath and he left the room.

The séance then proceeded for some time with no results and at my suggestion the cabinet-box was opened, Dr. Prince and I meanwhile keeping tight hold of the medium's hands. After it was open I made a search and sure enough on the bottom of the cabinet was a new, cheap, two-foot rule which folded up into a *six-inch length.*

Regarding this ruler found in the box; *I accuse Mrs. Crandon of having smuggled it in with her.* When folded up it was only six inches long and she could have done it. The stenographer, Miss McManama, who examined her was incompetent for the purpose and the reader will find, by looking up the records, that other mediums have concealed implements in, or on, their persons which those who examined them failed to find but which were discovered later when the mediums were seized by investigators.

At her suggestion, it had been arranged that in the second part of the séance the arm holes in the cabinet-box were to be boarded up with her hands inside free and uncontrolled. However, she could easily have stuck the rule out past her neck and rung the bell which was directly before her on the table eight and one-half inches away.* *Mrs. Crandon, knowing that she had been caught,* made the accusation to clear herself.

The foregoing description of the occurrences at the séance of August 26th, 1924, are corroborated in all respects by the official minutes of the séance signed by the Committee.

On the afternoon of August 27th, Mr. O. D. Munn, Dr. Prince, Mrs. Crandon and myself went to a dinner some distance out of Boston. At that time she told me of having heard that I was going

---

* The space permitted this for the hole was eighteen inches in circumference and the night before she had demonstrated that she could push three-quarters of her hand up past her neck. It was then she was trying the space to see if she could reach with anything to press down the board which controlled the bell.

to denounce her and say that she was a fraud, and that I had called her a liar. I asked her to tell me who it was that had told her these things but she told me that she was bound by her word not to tell

EXPLANATION OF THE PSYCHIC POWERS

The medium is controlled. The bell box placed on the floor either to her left or right. In a short time the bell rings and the investigators are convinced of the authenticity of the medium's psychic powers.

but would ask permission so I could face my accuser. I told her repeatedly that Bird had openly confessed that as he was living at the house he was compelled to tell her something and that she had gradually wormed it out of him, but she insisted that Bird had told her nothing.

Being afraid that I was going to denounce her from the stage at Keith's Theatre she said to me:

"If you misrepresent me from the stage at Keith's some of my friends will come up and give you a good beating."

"I am not going to misrepresent you," I replied, "they are not coming on the stage and I am not going to get a beating."

"Then it is your wits against mine," she said slowly as she gave me a furtive look.

"Yes, certainly, that is just what it is," I told her.

PROVING (?) THAT A SPIRIT RINGS THE BELL

Under cover of darkness she stealthily moves the chair during the course of conversation until the bottom rung of chair forces down the hinged flap which causes contact and the bell rings.

At the séance of August 27th, Dr. Comstock insisted that the medium place her feet in a wooden box control which he had provided. This was an arrangement in which the medium and an observer, sitting opposite, put both their feet into a box which reached half way to their knees. It was so built that a board could be locked over the knees of both absolutely preventing withdrawal of the feet. The box with the bell was placed just outside this control-box at her left. No table or anything was placed in front of her. While we sat there waiting for something to happen, Mrs. Crandon remarked that she wished I would be seized with a trance for it would be a wonderful thing and her husband turning to me said:

"Some day, Houdini, you will see the light and if it were to occur this evening, I would gladly give ten thousand dollars to charity."

"It may happen," I replied, "but I doubt it."

"Yes, sir," Dr. Crandon repeated, "if you were converted this evening I would willingly give $10,000 to some charity."

As the cabinet-box prevented the medium from using feet, head or shoulders and her hands being securely held by Dr. Prince and myself, there were no manifestations and the séances were blanks. Turning to me Mrs. Crandon said:

"I do not believe any medium could manifest under these conditions."

"Well," I replied, "I am not so sure about that. I am not a medium, but still I could allow myself to be stripped nude, searched by your husband who is a surgeon, you control one of my hands and Dr. Crandon the other, and still I could ring the bell or tie knots in handkerchiefs that are on the outside of cabinet box."

"You must possess psychic power then," she answered.

"No," I replied, "I am just a mystifier. Do you care to put me to the test? *I'll do it right now!*"

"That would not prove anything," Dr. Comstock remarked.

"Oh, yes it would," I replied, "it would prove that these things could be accomplished by trickery."

I charge Mrs. Crandon with practicing her feats daily like a professional conjuror. Also that because of her training as a secretary, her long experience as a professional musician, and her

Houdini giving a demonstration for ministers of the New York Federation of Churches at the Palace Theatre. By drawing his foot from a shoe equipped with a rigid metal frame, Houdini shows how a fake medium can ring bells and produce other "manifestations" while his hands are held by a client whose feet also press upon the medium's.

Houdini showing how fraud mediums produce molds of "spirit" hands. The medium dips his hand in paraffin, then in water, which hardens the paraffin into a coating which is carefully removed. These are found in the medium's cabinet as proof that a spirit was there. Clenched and folded hands are obtained by using rubber gloves which are filled with water, bent as required, then dipped in paraffin. After the wax hardens, the water is poured from the wrists of the gloves which can then be drawn out, empty, without injuring the mold.

athletic build she is not simple and guileless but a shrewd, cunning woman, resourceful in the extreme, and taking advantage of every opportunity to produce a "manifestation."

In closing I want to add that Dr. Prince in his original report strongly suspected the medium of resorting to conjuring and I will go on record that it has required my thirty years of experience to actually detect her in her subtle moves. They may not seem so slick as one reads of them in the open daylight but in the dark room there was no wonder that such a clever manipulator completely fooled her investigators.

The foregoing is a brief account of what I readily and immediately discerned and in absolute darkness at the five séances which I attended and if the medium has other or improved methods or claims to possess any so-called psychic power, whatsoever, I will be glad to attend further sittings with her as an investigator.

Duly appreciating that Dame Nature will eventually demand her toll and realizing that I will then no longer be here to give a personal account of my connection with these séances, I deem it a duty I owe the public to set forth the above facts for future reference.

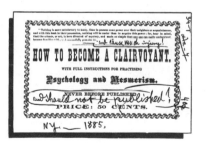

Cover of pro-Spiritualistic booklet published in 1885 with notations in Houdini's handwriting expressing his opinion of the pamphlet. Houdini's collection numbered thousands of such rare brochures.

The Museum of the American Circus at Sarasota, Florida, has included a magic section featuring many of Houdini's playbills, handcuffs, escape devices and anti-Spiritualistic equipment including rare Houdiniana and special motion picture films.

HOUDINI ON TRICKS

At the time of Houdini's death, I was engaged in the preparation of a large amount of magical material which was to appear
under his authorship. This was mentioned several years later
by Bernard M. L. Ernst in his preface to my book *Houdini's
Escapes* where he stated:

"During Houdini's life, Mr. Gibson had practically completed
two volumes of a proposed series of books on 'small magic' pro-
jected by Houdini; but because of the latter's untimely death the
publication of these works was abandoned."

In addition to the two books mentioned, a third was well under
way, its material still being in the course of selection from a greater
quantity already approved by Houdini, which was to form the
subject matter for further volumes in the series.

Much of the material was drawn from sources available to
both Houdini and myself. We checked lists of suitable tricks, and
I shaped those into an accepted pattern which conformed to
Houdini's own descriptive style. Having first approved the original
data, Houdini later okayed the final copy. This was done in
batches, so to speak, so that all that remained was for Houdini
to pass upon the actual contents of each individual volume, which
at most would have necessitated only minor changes, not only
because he was already familiar with the material, but because
the arrangement of such was chiefly the result of his own
suggestions.

Much of the preliminary work was done during my frequent

visits to Houdini's home in New York where we went over material in his study. Sometimes he dictated notes to his secretary while riding in taxicabs to appointments. I remember once discussing tricks between the overhead rumbles of trains on the Sixth Avenue El while Houdini and I were walking to the Hippodrome where he had business with the manager.

Even more vivid are my recollections of meetings with Houdini in magic shops, particularly Brema's in Philadelphia, where he was having some special equipment built. In that comparative seclusion, with every variety of apparatus and appliance available, Houdini and I were able to speed through the details of many tricks and routines that might otherwise have escaped us.

Equally productive were my backstage meetings with Houdini which began when he was appearing in vaudeville and ended during his final tour with his full evening show. Except when publicity appointments interfered, Houdini was able to give full attention to the various phases of magic that we had under discussion.

In fact, it was on such an occasion that Houdini gave his final approval to the great bulk of the material chosen for the contemplated volumes. Houdini was appearing in Worcester, Massachusetts. Rather than wait to contact him farther along his route, I arranged with my brother, Professor Theodore W. Gibson, who was then living in Worcester, to go over all the existing copy with Houdini.

This made it possible to proceed with the books themselves rather than to delve for more material. I was anxious to see the first volume in print because upon its reception would depend the frequency at which the others would appear. On the chance that this would be rapid, I planned to deliver the second book immediately after the first.

By that time, Houdini had died in Detroit and the books were no longer needed by him. It was because of my work on those volumes, however, that I was assigned the task of completing and arranging Houdini's unpublished notes on escapes and magic that he had set aside as a future project. Meanwhile, the material on smaller magic was forgotten.

In the preparation of this section, "Houdini on Tricks," I have therefore drawn from the material which Houdini authorized and also from some of his actual notes, as they appeared in my book *Houdini's Magic*.

Also included are some tricks that appeared under his by-line much earlier in Houdini's career. To these have been added a few Oriental magical effects described by Houdini plus some excerpts that he once published from an early work on magic and which he doubtless would have inserted in one of the many prospective volumes that he contemplated but was never able to complete.

WBG

COIN AND GLASS

A half dollar is borrowed, placed beneath a handkerchief, and dropped into a small goblet. Everybody hears the coin land in the glass, but when the handkerchief is whisked away, the coin has completely vanished.

In one version, this trick is accomplished with the aid of a small glass disk, cut to the size of a half dollar. This disk is hidden in your hand where it is very easily concealed. When you place the coin beneath the handkerchief, you exchange it for the glass disk which is held beneath the cloth so that spectators can see its shape.

The disk is dropped into the goblet which contains a small amount of water. Its clink causes it to be mistaken for the coin. When the handkerchief is removed the coin is gone because the glass disk can not be seen. The water may even be emptied from the goblet because the disk will adhere to the bottom.

There is an improved version of the trick which requires a trifling amount of skill but enables you to dispense with the glass disk, using nothing but the coin itself. The procedure is the same; the coin is dropped from within the folds of a handkerchief into a goblet, only to vanish immediately afterward.

The goblet has a foot, and in this method, you must have it standing on your left hand when you drop the coin with the right. You actually do drop the coin in this case, but unknown to your audience, you tilt the glass at an angle beneath the handkerchief or napkin before you drop the coin. Therefore, the cloth must be thick enough to be opaque.

The coin, when dropped, hits the *outside* of the glass and falls to the base of the goblet. The sound is a perfect deception; anyone hearing it will think that the coin actually landed in the goblet. Actually, it is lying on your hand. It is possible at this point to shake the goblet up and down letting the coin bounce from base to goblet, sounding as though it were being shaken within the glass itself.

Finally, you simply lay aside the goblet with your free hand retaining the coin in the other. Thus the coin is vanished from the goblet when someone lifts the cloth.

A neat subterfuge is to reach into your pocket for a rubber band, taking the coin along, while the other hand holds the goblet through the cloth. You drop the coin into the pocket, bring out the rubber band, and put it around the mouth of the goblet, cloth and all.

This makes it impossible for the coin to leave the glass, but it is gone when the spectators remove the handkerchief and have a look. Such touches add greatly to the effect of a trick.

FOUR COIN ASSEMBLY

This is an excellent impromptu trick. It requires a certain amount of skill, but is less difficult than a pure sleight-of-hand demonstration, as the misdirection is well arranged, and every movement is completely covered.

To the audience, the trick appears as follows: The magician borrows four coins, all alike. He lays a handkerchief upon the table. He weights down the corners of the handkerchief by placing a coin upon each corner. He takes two pieces of paper, each about four inches square, and covers two of the coins, one with each sheet.

He picks up a loose coin and places it beneath the handkerchief with his right hand. A snap of the fingers — the coin is gone. The empty right hand lifts the sheet of paper at one corner. Two coins are revealed. The coin has apparently joined its mate. The sheet of paper is replaced above the two coins. Another loose coin is magically passed beneath it. Now there are three coins beneath one sheet of paper; one coin beneath the other. At the magician's command, the single coin passes to join the three The papers are lifted. The four coins have assembled!

The first deception occurs when the performer is explaining what he intends to do. Having put the four coins at the corners of the handkerchief, he exhibits the two sheets of paper, holding one in each hand, fingers beneath, thumb above.

"When I cover the coins nearest me," says the magician, suiting the words with the action, "you see the coins that are farthest away." He lifts the papers and holds them over the other two coins. "When I cover the coins farthest away from me, you see those that are nearest to me."

It is at this point that the performer makes his first movement. The right hand is holding the paper above the coin at the outer right corner. The second finger presses against the lower part of the coin. The right forefinger raises the edge of the coin. Thus the coin is clipped between the fingers, at the back of the hand. Only the fingers are out of sight beneath the paper. The open palm is clearly seen. There appears to be no chance for deception.

The magician raises the left-hand paper from the coin that it is covering. He brings the left hand over to the right. As the left paper covers the right paper, a few inches above it, the right hand drops its paper and takes the paper that the left hand is holding. During this movement, the right fingers are constantly concealed from view. The right hand places the paper that it has taken upon

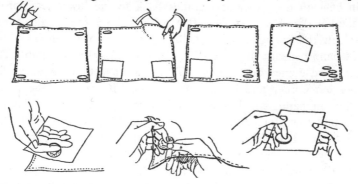

TOP: HOW THE TRICK APPEARS. BOTTOM: CLIPPING FIRST COIN; TRANSFER OF EACH "PASSING" COIN; COIN CONCEALED WHEN PAPER IS TRANSFERRED.

the coin at the lower left corner. It holds the paper there and still retains the coin. The left hand points at both sheets of paper, while the magician remarks: "When I cover the coins diagonally, the other two coins are visible."

The right hand, still carrying its hidden coin, moves to the upper left corner and covers the coin there. It drops the paper and leaves the coin beneath it. Then both hands point to the coins at the lower corner and the magician says: "I shall use the coins that are nearest to me."

He picks up the coin at the lower left corner, lifting it with the right hand. The left hand raises the corner of the handkerchief. The left fingers are beneath the corner. The right hand slowly slides its coin under the handkerchief. In so doing, it transfers the coin to the left hand which clips it between the first and second fingers, at the back; just as the right hand previously clipped a coin.

The right hand continues a bit beneath the handkerchief. Then the fingers are snapped. The right hand comes back. It is shown entirely empty. The right hand picks up the paper at the upper left corner of the handkerchief. Two coins are seen there. The left hand is still holding the corner of the handkerchief. The right hand brings the paper over to the left hand. The left moves away from the handkerchief and takes the sheet of paper. This transfer completely covers the coin that is held behind the left hand.

The right hand, being free, moves to the right to take the coin at the lower right corner. The left hand quietly lays the paper upon the two coins at the upper left corner. It leaves its clipped coin beneath the paper and comes back to the lower left corner of the handkerchief. As the left hand lifts the corner of the handkerchief, the magician repeats his previous move. He puts the right hand beneath the cloth. The left fingers clip the coin. The right hand comes out empty. It lifts the sheet of paper at the upper left corner and shows three coins. It transfers the paper to the left hand, which drops the corner of the cloth. The left hand puts the paper upon the three coins, leaving the fourth coin with them. The right hand points to the sheet of paper at the upper right corner of the handkerchief.

The last transfer should be done as mysteriously as possible. The spectators think that there are three coins beneath one sheet of paper and one coin beneath the other. As a matter of fact, all.

four coins are under one sheet of paper. The magician makes the most of this situation. He commands the last coin to pass and makes a motion with his fingers. He lifts the paper at the upper left corner with the left hand. This reveals the four coins. The right hand lifts the paper at the upper right corner and shows that the coin has gone. Coins, papers, and handkerchief may be thoroughly examined by the spectators.

If this trick is done properly, the keenest observer will be mystified. The entire routine is natural; the magician is always one step ahead of the onlookers. There should be no great speed. The trick is most effective when done deliberately, as the sleights may be accomplished without fumbling. With a reasonable amount of practice, this becomes a fine mystery, suitable for close-up presentation.

HYPNOTIC MATCH BOX

An ordinary wooden match box, emptied of its matches and laid upon your hand, rises to an upright position and then gradually lies down again at your command.

This trick depends upon the simple expedient of pinching a bit of flesh between the cover and the drawer of the match box. However, to get real results, this must be done properly.

After dumping the matches from the box, the drawer should be replaced upside down — something that no one will notice but which aids materially in the trick. When the box is set on the hand with the label up, the inverted drawer gains a better pinch with its edge than would the bottom of the drawer, which sometimes fails to gain a grip at all.

Simply push the drawer open slightly and set the box on the back of your hand, the open end toward the wrist. Press the box shut, catching the flesh. Now, by tightening or relaxing the fist, the box will rise or fall forward on the hand.

Another system is to place the box in the palm of one hand, pressing the drawer shut so that it grips the flesh at the base of the fingers, when the hand is slightly cupped. By straightening the fingers imperceptibly, the box will rise forward toward them. When you relax the fingers, the box will settle back on the palm.

After either version, take the box with the other hand and remove the drawer rapidly, so you can give it for examination before anyone realizes it was inverted in the box.

THE UNCANNY GLASS

This is one of the most baffling of impromptu table tricks as it requires just enough practice or experiment to give it a genuine touch.

You use an ordinary drinking glass partly filled with water. Calling attention to what you class as a most difficult trick, you set the glass on the table at an angle of about forty-five degrees, steadying it there as it wavers back and forth.

At last you find the balance point. You move your hands away, and the uncanny glass retains its precarious tilt, balancing at its surprising angle.

During your preliminary experiment, the observers are satisfied that you are attempting something impossible, but once you have succeeded, they suppose that they can duplicate the stunt. The more they try, the more they fail, even though they attempt it with the very glass that you used.

The secret is not in the glass at all. Beforehand, place a wooden matchstick under the tablecloth at a convenient spot for your balancing experiment. Set the bottom edge of the glass against the hidden match, using it as a base to facilitate the otherwise impossible balance.

By having a thread tied around the match and running off at your side of the table, you can secretly draw away the match from beneath the tablecloth immediately after you have demonstrated the trick.

A SPOOKY BALL

While this trick has been described in print and is known to many persons interested in magic, it is included here because Houdini's notes add an effect that gives the trick a most surprising finish.

The trick is best performed on a dinner table. The magician exhibits a steel ball-bearing that measures about one inch in diameter. He places the ball on the table and makes mysterious passes toward it. Slowly the ball begins to roll away across the table. It stops and advances at the magician's command.

The magician lays a lady's handkerchief in front of the ball. The ball rolls along the tablecloth and on to the handkerchief. The magician seizes the four corners of the handkerchief and raises it while the ball is still rolling. He gives the handkerchief and the ball for immediate examination.

A simple apparatus is utilized — a small thin ring attached to a thread. The ring is under the tablecloth. The thread goes to an assistant at the opposite side of the table. The magician lays the ball on the hidden ring. When the assistant pulls the thread, the ball moves across the table, away from the magician. The assistant is apparently an interested onlooker. Every one is intent upon watching the ball in its course.

The added effect is the rolling of the ball into the handkerchief. This is simplicity itself; the weight of the ball enables it to do the trick automatically. The lifting of the handkerchief is the assistant's cue to pull the ring completely away from beneath the tablecloth.

THE ASTONISHING EGG

The trick of balancing an egg is always popular and is particularly adapted to presentation at the dinner table. You simply take an ordinary egg, set it on its larger end, and it balances at your command.

All you need to accomplish this is a small quantity of a substance already available; namely, salt. Secretly spill some salt on the table and press it into the form of a little mound. To balance the egg, set it on this mound, and you easily make it stay upright.

Afterward, as you hand the egg for examination with one hand, you can brush away the salt with the other as though smoothing the tablecloth. This is hardly necessary with a sheer white tablecloth as the salt remains unnoticed.

There is another procedure that will work with a cloth of any color. It also makes a good alternative method, should you be doing the trick before people who have seen it previously. In this case, secretly put some salt into the palm of your left hand or have some ready on the table, away from the spot where you plan to do the balance.

Moisten the right thumb, and in getting the egg, apply your thumb to the large end of the egg. Set the egg momentarily in your left hand or on the spot where you have the salt. It will pick up a quantity of salt sufficient for the balancing stunt.

The salt still adheres to the egg after the trick, but you can easily brush it off with your fingers as you lay the egg aside. Anyone who looks at the tablecloth expecting to find evidence will be totally disappointed.

A NEW DYEING TUBE

This device will be of special interest to magicians as it is an improvement over the old tubes used for changing the colors of silk handkerchiefs. In order to make the idea plain to the reader, we must first briefly consider the effect of the usual "dye tube." The magician rolls a sheet of paper and pushes white silk handkerchiefs through it. One silk comes out red, another white, the third blue. These three are then pushed through the tube. They are transformed into a large American flag.

The tube seen by the audience is simply made of paper or cardboard, but there is also an inner tube, which may be termed the "fake tube." The fake holds the other handkerchiefs and the flag. When the different silks are pushed into the bottom, the others emerge from the top.

The whole problem of the dye tube — from the magician's view — is the secret insertion of the fake and its subsequent removal. These are necessary to make the trick convincing since the paper tube must be shown empty before and after the deception. In the dye tube about to be described, two devices play an important part: one is a nickeled tube with small holes in it, the other is a special fake to which a hook is attached. This hook is in a groove, so that while it cannot come free of the fake, it can be drawn upward or dropped downward.

At the beginning of the trick, the fake rests in the nickeled tube. The metal tube is standing on an undraped table. The hook of the fake projects over the upper edge of the nickeled tube, which is slightly longer than the fake. The fake is painted black. The interior of the nickeled tube is black. Hence the nickeled tube appears to be empty.

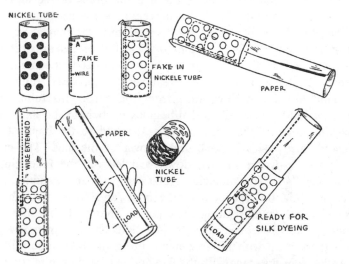

DETAILS OF THE NICKEL TUBE SHOWING PHASES OF THE TRICK.

The magician exhibits an empty tube of cardboard. It is slightly less in diameter than the nickeled tube, but its diameter is greater than that of the fake tube. It is twice as long as the nickeled tube. The magician picks up the nickeled tube. His finger and thumb enter holes in the side of the tube and thus keep the fake from dropping. The left hand holds the nickeled tube. The right hand pushes the cardboard tube up into the nickeled tube. At this point, the left finger and thumb release their hold. The fake drops to the full length of its loose wire. It hangs in the cardboard tube. The magician may pause to turn the nickeled tube in front of a light. The spectators glimpse the light through the holes and know that the nickeled tube is empty. The cardboard tube is now pushed up through the nickeled tube. The white cardboard shows plainly through the holes. The cardboard tube disengages the hook, so that it alone holds the fake. The cardboard tube is very long, so the hanging fake does not emerge at the bottom.

Now comes the dyeing. Handkerchiefs are pushed into the bottom of the cardboard tube. The nickeled tube is centered on the surface of the cardboard tube. As the fake is pushed upward, the left thumb and finger press through the holes of the nickeled tube and hold the fake firmly in the center of the cardboard tube.

When the flag is produced, an assistant aids the magician. The flag is quite large. The assistant drapes it over his outstretched arm. As soon as the flag is completely produced, the magician, standing at the assistant's side, removes the nickeled tube with one hand drawing it downward from the cardboard tube. The hand that holds the cardboard tube goes up behind the flag. The projecting hook of the fake is deftly attached to the back of the assistant's arm. This is done under cover of the flag. The cardboard tube is drawn straight downward leaving the fake hidden behind the flag. The magician walks forward and exhibits both tubes, pushing the cardboard tube back and forth through the nickeled tube, demonstrating quite plainly that both are empty.

During this procedure, the assistant folds the flag over his arm and gathers it up with his free hand lifting the fake tube with it. He walks from the stage with the flag and carries with him the only clue to the mystery — the fake tube with its load of silk handkerchiefs which were supposed to have been blended together in the formation of the flag.

SPIRITS OF AQUA

Though actually an after dinner trick, this must be done with all lights out as it involves "spirits" as the principal factor even though water is the liquid used!

To give your audience this introduction to spookdom, you first take some strips of gummed paper or Scotch tape and use these to criss-cross the top of a drinking glass that is on the table and partly filled with water.

The object of such preparation is to prove that no one can get at the water other than the spirits which you expect to summon. The more careful this preparation, the more impressed the audience will be, both now and later, so make a good job of it. The space between the strips that cross the mouth of the glass should be so slight that it would be utterly impossible for anyone to lift the glass and pour water from it without damaging the papers. You may use half a dozen or more, as you desire. Also the strips may be marked by spectators.

Lights are turned out and on again when you call for them. In the brief interval of darkness, the spirits have done their work. Nearly all the water has vanished from the glass, yet the papers that run across it are intact and dry!

The secret is simple but clever; the rest is up to you. In your pocket you have a drinking straw. As soon as the lights are out, slide it down into the glass and drink all the water you want, afterward pocketing the straw, without leaving a trace of where the water went!

MAGNETIC MATCHES

Though of brief duration, this clever trick with a box of safety matches is one of the best impromptu mysteries available and an excellent introduction to other tricks that will require either an empty match box or some loose matches.

You show a match box well filled with matches and turn it over as you pull out the drawer. Holding the inverted drawer with one hand, you drop the cover with the other hand, which promptly makes hypnotic passes.

As a result, the matches remain in the drawer although it is upside down. Apparently, they are held by some mysterious magnetic force, or at least you so allege.

Before the baffled witnesses can prove otherwise, you command the matches to drop. They fall from the drawer, landing in a pile on the table, while you pass the drawer for examination and proceed with some other trick.

The secret to this trick is a broken match. You break it beforehand and wedge it across the drawer near the center, above the other matches. In opening the drawer part way, this wedged match is not seen before you turn the entire box over. It holds the matches in place when you remove the drawer.

To make the matches fall, simply squeeze the ends of the drawer, releasing the wedge which falls with the matches and is buried beneath them. In picking up the matches to replace them in the drawer, or to show some other trick, you can easily find the half-match and remove it unnoticed.

THE TRAVELING DIE

This trick requires a plate, a hat, a red silk handkerchief, and a large die. These are the principal properties seen by the audience. The die is shown to be solid. Attention is called to its large size — it almost fills the interior of the borrowed hat. The die is placed upon the plate. It is covered with a sheet of paper, which is pressed around it and twisted at the top.

The magician exhibits the silk handkerchief and rolls it between his hands. The handkerchief disappears. The paper is lifted from the plate. The handkerchief is found there; it has replaced the die. The hat is turned over and the solid cube of wood falls to the floor.

A reference to the accompanying illustrations will show the effect of this trick and also the principal points that form the explanation. The construction of the die has a great deal to do with the trick. The die is covered with a thin shell which is open at the bottom. The shell is white on the inside, to resemble the paper

THE SILK REPLACES THE DIE BENEATH THE PAPER, AND THE SOLID BLOCK IS DISCOVERED IN THE HAT. EXPLANATORY DIAGRAMS SHOW HOW DUPLICATE SILK IS KEPT BETWEEN DIE AND SHELL, AND HOW DIE IS LEFT IN HAT AND SHELL REMOVED.

that will later cover it. A duplicate silk handkerchief is pressed between the top of the real die and the inside of the shell. It is held in place by a rubber band which can instantly be released by removing a blackened bit of match stick that holds one end of the loop.

It is a simple matter to demonstrate that the die is solid, by tapping the bottom of the genuine die. In showing that the die almost fills the interior of the hat, the magician dips his hand and releases pressure on the thin shell. The genuine die drops into the hat. Only the shell is retained by the performer.

The shell is placed upon the plate and the paper is molded about it. This action gives the magician the opportunity to release the rubber band so that the silk handkerchief fills the interior of the shell die. Now the magician vanishes the handkerchief. This may be done in various ways. The most suitable is with the aid of a "pull" — a cup-shaped metal container which is beneath the coat, fastened to the end of a length of cord elastic. The magician obtains the pull, works the handkerchief into it, and releases the cup. The silk and its container fly beneath his coat. The hands are shown empty.

When the paper cover is lifted, there is no trace of the die. The shell is picked up with the paper and the space formerly occupied by the die is now taken by the silk handkerchief. The solid die is in the hat and the magician concludes the trick by tilting the hat and letting the cube drop to the floor.

If desired, the shell die may be made of light cardboard; this will permit the magician to crumple the paper after lifting it from the plate. This adds to the effectiveness of the trick; it also means the destruction of the shell each time the trick is performed. The cost of the shell die is a trifling matter, however, if the magician finds that the apparent destruction of the paper makes the deception more convincing.

RESTORING A MATCH

In this artful bit of trickery, a wooden match is wrapped in a handkerchief and someone is allowed to break the match through the folded cloth. In due course, you unfold the handkerchief, and the match falls out whole. You may spread the handkerchief to show it entirely empty, thus completing the mystery.

Of course there is an answer, and anyone who suspects that you use a second match is on the right track. What throws such people off is the fact that the duplicate — or extra — match is the one you break; not the original.

The second match is concealed in the hem of your handkerchief, near the corner. Use a handkerchief with a fairly wide hem, open a few stitches, and insert the match so it will be ready for the trick.

In wrapping up the original match, bring the corner of the handkerchief up beneath into the very center of the cloth. You may then extend the handkerchief to some person who can break the match, or you may break it yourself after people have felt the match. Of course the one that is broken is the match in the hem. That accounts for the original remaining intact.

Have another handkerchief in your pocket so that when you put away the handkerchief with the broken match bits in its hem, you can bring out the other in its place. Do not even mention that it is "unprepared", but simply use it in other tricks as occasion demands. By the time some people get around to suspect the handkerchief, they will forget that it was gone briefly from their sight.

But suppose you should be called upon to repeat the trick, or worse, what if someone who has seen you perform it on another occasion should offer you a handkerchief and say: "Show us the match trick!" What then?

Then you must do it the hard way, by breaking a match inside the handkerchief and actually restoring it, Yes, this can actually be done, but you must break the match yourself and to make it really effective, you should use a large blue-tipped match of the common kitchen variety.

You wrap the match in the center of the handkerchief, hold it close to people so that they can both see and hear you break the match, not just once but twice. Yet when you unfold the handkerchief, the match drops out restored.

The reason: Though you actually break the match in one direction, its segments do not come apart, as you will find by trying it. The cloth conceals this from your audience. As you start to unroll the handkerchief, straighten the match through the folds, and it will appear to be restored when it falls on the table.

Even the sharpest observer will not notice that the match is actually broken but simply put back into temporary shape. You can pick up the match and show it, but do not let anyone else handle it. In this case, you must switch the match instead of the handkerchief for another match that you have ready in your pocket.

TRI-COLOR CARDS

Three colored cards, about the size of playing cards, are used in this mystery. The cards are colored respectively: red, white, and blue. A borrowed hat is also required.

You show the three cards separately then drop them in the hat. From the hat you take the red card, then the white, placing these two in your pocket. You then ask the color of the card remaining in the hat and the reply is, "Blue."

To prove that seeing is not believing, you slide the card from the hat and let it fall upon the table. Instead of blue, the card is white. From your pocket, you take the missing blue card along with the red one that you placed there.

Someone always suspects chicanery where the white card is concerned, but when such a person turns the card over, expecting to find it blue on the other side, he is disappointed as well as baffled further. The card proves to be white on the other side as well.

Oddly, the trick is actually accomplished by the subterfuge of a double-sided card, its sides respectively white and blue, but the ruse is employed early in the routine, and the card is dispensed with before anyone suspects its use.

At the start you show a red card, a white, and the special card, blue on one side, white on the other, which passes as a blue card. You show the red both sides before dropping it in the hat; the white the same way. Hence when you come to the blue, suspicions are lulled, and no one gives a passing thought to the fact that you show only one side of the blue card when tossing it casually into the hat.

You bring out the red showing both sides. But when you remove the "white card" from the hat, actually take out the trick card with its white side showing. You place these two cards into your pocket where the "white" card is promptly exchanged for a valid blue card — blue on both sides — that is in your pocket already.

The white card found in the hat naturally turns out to be quite ordinary, white on both sides, unless, as a special "gag", you resort to the following: Have the word "Stung" printed or written on one side of the white card. In showing the white card originally, let the audience see only the blank side. At the finish, the "wise" person who snatches the white card expecting to find it blue on the other side will find himself neatly "Stung" by the result.

There is a neat twist that can be added to this trick: Hold a card by its sides between the tips of your fingers and your thumb, but curl the forefinger in back of the card. Now, a forward flip of the forefinger will turn the card over, catching it between the tips of forefinger and second finger.

Use this method of showing both sides of an ordinary red card or white card before dropping same into the hat. But with the "blue" card, turn your hand over, bringing it back up, just as you make the flip. This shows the *same side* twice with never a glimpse of the other. It can be used when removing the "white" card from the hat and putting it into the pocket thus making the mystery perfect.

THE IMPRISONED CARD

A card is chosen from a pack. It is placed in a prison; namely, a thin oblong box fitted with crossbars just large enough to receive the card. The magician also exhibits an envelope. He shows that the envelope is large enough to hold the entire box. He seals the envelope and throws a handkerchief over the box. When he removes the cloth, the card is gone from the prison. Everyone can see through the spaces between the slats. The card is found in the envelope.

The box that is used has special slides behind the slats. These fall into place when the box is inverted, so that they fill the spaces between the slats. The slides are portions of a playing-card; they duplicate the card that is used in the trick.

The box is first held upright; the opening into which the card is inserted points upward. The real card is put in. It goes behind the slides. The back of the box is shown, and the back of the real card is seen there. At this moment, the box is inverted; the slides come down, but their movement is not seen because of the card.

Turning the box to show the front, the magician picks up the envelope and shows it empty. He starts to put the box in the envelope but does not do so. At this point, he releases the genuine card. It falls into the envelope. Its progress is invisible because of the presence of the front slides, which cover it. The envelope is sealed. The box is covered with a handkerchief. It is inverted beneath the cloth. The slides go back out of view. The box will now appear empty.

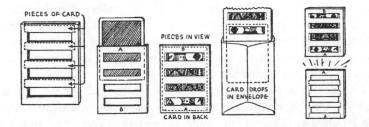

CONSTRUCTION OF SPECIAL BOX FOR VANISHING THE CARD. NOTE HOW SECTIONS OF CARD SLIDE FROM SLATS; ALSO HOW GENUINE CARD IS SECRETLY DROPPED IN ENVELOPE.

The magician removes the handkerchief in a suspicious manner. He shows the box empty from both sides and lays it on the table. Everyone suspects that the card is in the handkerchief. The magician appears annoyed for a time; finally he shows that the handkerchief is empty. In fact, he passes it out for examination.

This puzzles the spectators, as they no longer have any suspicion of the box. A member of the audience is allowed to open the sealed envelope, and when the chosen card is found therein, the trick arrives at its surprising conclusion.

THE HOUDINI CARD

Here is a playing card which makes an escape, Houdini style, from a cell — represented by an envelope — in which it has been bound under conditions that would make release seemingly impossible. All in all, it is a very surprising and unusual trick.

The card used can be a regulation playing card, such as the King of Spades, or for that matter any other. As it is used only in this trick, however, it is effective to have a card bearing a portrait or simply the name HOUDINI in large letters. Otherwise, the card is quite ordinary except for one special factor emphasized to the audience.

This card has a hole punched near its center — a trifle above the center, to be exact. This is simply a round hole made with an ordinary punch about a half inch in diameter.

Other articles used are: an envelope a trifle larger than the card, the type of envelope used by jewelers, which opens at the top; and a ribbon threaded on a large needle.

To begin, you introduce the Houdini card, allow it to be examined. You then insert it into the envelope and seal the latter. Now, taking the needle, you run it through the envelope at a spot which will strike the hole in the card. The envelope can have a bull's eye marked on it to indicate the precise spot.

The needle is removed, spectators hold the ends of the ribbon, and you clip off one end of the envelope. Now, you demonstrate the Houdini card's amazing ability to escape. You reach into the envelope and bring out the card intact leaving the envelope threaded on the ribbon! All articles are left in the hands of spectators for immediate inspection.

The only preparation is a slit along the bottom end of the envelope. This is not noticed as you do not give the envelope for examination until later.

When you have placed the card in the envelope and sealed the latter, hold the envelope upright extending upward from your left hand. Thus, the envelope is retained in the bend of the palm and fingers with the thumb in back supporting it. A slight squeeze of the sides of the envelope, and the Houdini card will slide down into your hand where it is stopped by the little finger, which should be bent a trifle more than the others.

This brings the card just below the bull's eye marked on the envelope, the indicator which presumably tells you where the hole in the card is located. Gripping the envelope tightly at its lower end, you thrust the needle through the mark and draw the ribbon through after it. This is from the back of the envelope to the front.

You remove the needle and let the ribbon dangle. The next move is very important but equally easy. You bring your right hand toward your left and extend the right thumb so that it encounters the lower side of the hand. Thus, you can push the card up into the envelope with your right thumb and bring your right fingers to the top edge of the envelope, taking the envelope away between right thumb and finger tips all in one action.

This pushes the center of the ribbon up to the top of the envelope so that the ribbon actually runs around the end of the card. The motion of the hands prevents people from observing the way the ribbon suddenly loses length; if the ribbon is reasonably long, there is no chance whatever of detecting this.

Note the subtle move that follows: To show both sides of the envelope, you turn it over, bringing the right thumb upward. This inverts the envelope so that the bottom is now the top. When you announce that you will open the envelope again, you pick up a pair of scissors and clip a narrow margin along what was originally the bottom edge. This disposes of the secret slit that served so usefully a few moments earlier.

While spectators hold the ends of the ribbon, you dip your thumb and forefinger into the envelope and whisk out the Houdini card as though actually pulling it from the ribbon. Your other hand grips the envelope and at the same time thrusts it forward, thus taking up the ribbon's slack. All items may then be examined to the mystification of the persons concerned.

For a dramatic climax, you can make the card perform a mysterious rise from the envelope in connection with its escape. In this case, use an envelope that is a trifle long, so that the spot marked for the ribbon is below the center of the envelope.

Proceed as previously described, but let the envelope dangle on the ribbon, where it will hang upright, bottom up, because it is off center. Take the ends of the ribbon from the spectators; at the same time, draw slowly, imperceptibly, on these ends. The straightening ribbon will eject the Houdini card up and out of the envelope.

MULTIPLE CARD PREDICTION

As a vest pocket mystery, this trick definitely qualifies. Though it is a prediction involving the names of playing cards, miniature cards are used, the toy variety that can be purchased at many novelty stores.

The reason for such small cards is that you also utilize a penny match box which is emptied of its matches so that the pack can be placed therein. However, the pack is first shuffled by a member of the audience. Then it is placed in the box, face down, and the drawer is pushed shut.

Now you begin to name cards one by one. They are taken from the top of the pack by a spectator, who opens the match box to remove each card. You call off the names of half a dozen cards, and you are correct at every try.

There is a simple secret to this matchless mystery. You previously remove the cards that you intend to name, remembering both their names and their order. These cards are wedged between the drawer of the match box and the top of the cover, the drawer being pushed half way open or more. The wedged cards, set face down, are thus completely hidden.

The match box is first shown in this half-opened condition. It is inverted and the matches are dumped out. You give a spectator the pack of toy cards — less the several already hidden in the box — and the spectator shuffles them thinking the pack is complete.

When the pack is dropped in the drawer, and it is closed, the extra cards fall on top of the pack. You may then name them one by one as though you have some mystic vision.

THE PHOTOGENIC CARD

In these days of so-called "thought impressions" and other marvels of the mind, the trick to be described will have a marked effect upon its witnesses. Apart from its "psychic" aspects, it makes one of the best impromptu tricks available.

You show the spectators a small pay envelope, the type that has a short flap at the top. When they are satisfied that the envelope is quite empty, you let them examine a blank bit of sensitized photographic paper which some spectator can drop into the envelope. The paper is about the size of a thumb nail or a little larger. The envelope is sealed with the paper inside.

Now a pack of playing cards is introduced. It is placed upon the table and anyone is allowed to cut it anywhere he desires. As

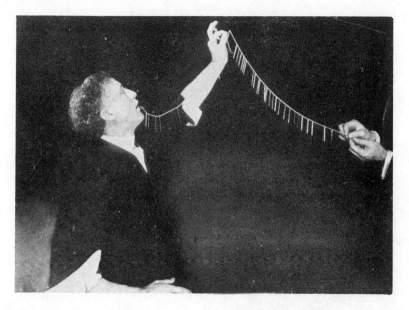

Houdini performing the "East Indian Needle Trick". Needles placed visibly in the mouth were "switched" for a threaded set concealed between the upper gum and cheeks. After these were drawn out threaded, Houdini disposed of the original set along with a glass from which he took a drink of water. Adroit manipulations with the tongue were required in the "switch" and at one stage, the extra needles were kept hidden beneath the tongue itself, so the space between gums and cheeks could be proved empty. Houdini's skill with the needle trick is a clue to where and how he concealed small keys in some of his escapes.

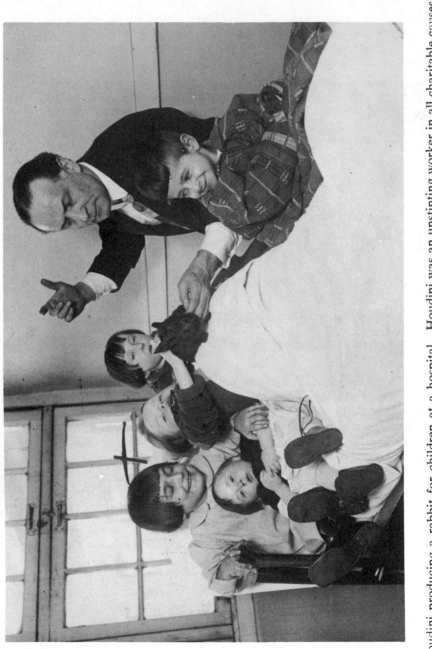

Houdini producing a rabbit for children at a hospital. Houdini was an unstinting worker in all charitable causes as well as War Bond Drives and other patriotic campaigns.

soon as the pack is cut into two heaps, you drop the envelope upon one portion and tell the spectator to complete the cut by adding the rest of the pack on top. That is, without touching the pack that the spectator himself has cut, you place the envelope between, so that it projects from what is now the center of the pack.

After giving the sensitized paper time to pick up an impression, you ask someone to lift the upper portion of the pack. This is done, and you cut open the flap of the envelope letting the paper slide out to the table and then showing the envelope to be empty as before. One person is told to turn over the paper; he does so and to his surprise finds a miniature card printed upon it, the Eight of Hearts. When the upper half of the pack is turned face up, the visible card proves to be identical, namely, the Eight of Hearts.

This is the only card whose face actually contacted the envelope containing the sensitized slip of paper, thus it seems to have registered its impression in some uncanny fashion.

For this trick you require a "double envelope" which is made as follows: Cut out the face or front of an envelope, trimming its edges very slightly. Put a slip of photo paper bearing the imprint of the Eight of Hearts into another envelope. Then insert the face that you cut out and gum its flap to that of the actual envelope. This is done by moistening the gum on the envelope proper.

Done neatly, this leaves no change in the appearance of the envelope. It can be shown as an ordinary empty envelope as your printed photo card is between the two faces.

The pack of cards, which is in its case, has the Eight of Hearts all set as its bottom card. Thus prepared, you are ready to begin.

Show a blank slip of sensitized paper, drop it into what appears to be an empty envelope, and seal the flap. When someone cuts the pack of cards, lay great stress on the fact that the cut is made at any spot he chooses. Then place the sealed envelope on the *upper* portion of the pack and tell the person to complete the cut, which he does by laying the *lower* on the envelope.

Thus no matter where the cut was made, the result is the same. The bottom card, the Eight of Hearts, comes directly upon the sealed envelope. This is a very subtle procedure as the audience, not knowing what is to follow, will remember later that the pack was cut at random and will assume that the envelope was inserted at that precise spot.

In opening the envelope, cut between the two flaps with a knife blade. Thus you actually open the secret section of the envelope allowing the imprinted slip to slide out. Then show the envelope apparently empty, which is easy enough as the blank slip is now concealed in the other section of the trick envelope.

In your pocket, you should have an ordinary envelope, empty, but sealed and with its flap cut open at the top exactly as you have cut open the double envelope. While people are turning up the slip of sensitized paper and are turning over the top half of the pack, you pick up the envelope, put it into your pocket, and take out the empty envelope planted there.

No one will notice this as they are all amazed by finding the imprint of the eight of hearts, the very card that faces them on the top half of the pack. If your action should be noticed, it will seem that you are simply bringing out the original envelope as an afterthought, for you showed it empty as soon as you let the slip of paper slide out.

Drop the duplicate envelope on the table and just forget about it. If some suspicious party suddenly decides to examine the envelope, he can — to his further mystification.

Instead of a slip of sensitized paper, you can use a miniature playing card in the envelope, beginning the trick with a blank card of the same size. On different occasions, use a different card — not always the Eight of Hearts.

CUT AND RESTORED STRING

New versions of the cut and restored string trick are constantly appearing. Like so many others, this one has points of novelty that will be of interest to magicians. It possesses that degree of difference which makes it deceptive.

The string used is about two feet in length. The magician measures off three or four inches and holds the string at that point. between his left thumb and forefinger. The right hand takes the long end of the string and weaves it between the left fingers: over the first, under the second, over the third, under the little finger. He winds the string around the little finger a few times, brings it over the little finger, under the third, then over the second and under the forefinger, letting the long end extend.

He picks the spot where the string passes over the second finger (on its return journey) as the approximate center of the string. He clips the string at that place. Then, drawing the string from his fingers, he shows it to be fully restored!

This trick depends upon a very subtle manipulation. It should be noted that the string, on its return journey, apparently crosses the knuckles of the little finger and the center finger, the back of the hand being upward. But the string does not go over the second finger. When his right hand draws the string under the third finger

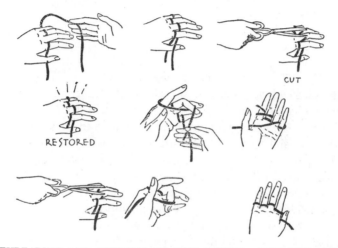

THE THREADING AND CUTTING OF THE STRING. HOW THE SHORT END IS DOUBLED BACK.

of the left hand, it is hidden from view. It picks up the short end of the string (which is still downward between the left thumb and forefinger) and brings the short end over the second finger of the left hand. The long string passes clear under the second finger of the left hand and also under the first finger. It extends between the left thumb and forefinger. Thus there is just a tiny end over the second finger, and that end is clipped between the second finger and the forefinger. Yet it appears to be the center of the entire string.

The magician uses a pair of scissors to clip the string at the point designated. When he draws the string from the left hand, the short end is retained between the fingers and is later dropped on the floor.

This is a good version of the cut and restored string as it is almost impossible for anyone to note the switch. It should be practiced carefully until the performer can weave the string in a natural, easy fashion. Once the idea is fully understood, the trick presents very little difficulty. It is advisable to start slowly with the weaving to show that everything is fair. The left fingers should be spread after the cutting to let the string pull free; at the same time, care should be taken to retain the bit of string that was cut from the short end.

CONE AND EGG

Houdini enjoyed performing old tricks that were classics in magic and which had been almost forgotten in the modern era of conjuring. His notes contain many references to tricks of this sort. In the material was the following routine with the old cone and orange. It is probably intended for a small-sized cone as an egg is used instead of an orange.

The cone is a wooden article. It is actually a truncated cone with a special rounded top. The magician borrows a hat and places it on a side table. He exhibits the wooden cone and wraps a piece of paper about it, fastening the paper with pins. He sets a large plate on the hat and puts an egg on the plate. He lifts the paper cover from the cone and sets the paper cover on the egg.

He raps the solid cone with his wand and covers it with a handkerchief. He walks forward and tosses the cloth in the air. The cone has vanished. The magician lifts the paper cover and reveals the cone upon the plate. A moment later he produces the egg from his elbow.

He replaces the cover over the cone. He makes several passes with the egg and finally squeezes it between his hands. The egg disappears completely. The cover is lifted to reveal the egg upon the plate. The magician sets the plate aside and places the cover with it. He tilts the hat and shows the cone inside it. He concludes by breaking the egg, crumpling the paper, and returning the hat to its owner, at the same time bringing the wooden cone for examination.

There are actually two solid cones used in this trick; also a thin metal shell that fits over a cone and is painted to resemble it. At the outset, one cone is on a servante (hidden shelf) behind the side table. The magician borrows the hat and uses it for some byplay, finally taking it to the table where he secretly "loads" the cone into the hat. It remains there awaiting the finish of the trick.

A "BACK-STAGE" VIEW OF THE IMPORTANT MANOEUVRES.

Next the magician exhibits the second cone — the first seen by the audience — which is already covered with the thin metal shell. He forms a paper cover, using the cone as a mold and when he raises the cover, he carries the metal shell along inside it. He sets a plate upon the hat and puts an egg on the plate. He covers the egg with a supposedly empty paper cover.

He vanishes the solid cone by covering it with a handkerchief of double thickness. Between its layers, the cloth has a pasteboard disk. The magician inverts the cone as he places the cloth over it. He is standing behind his center table at the time and he lets the cone drop to a servante at the rear of that table. The cardboard disk retains the shape of the bottom of the cone. The spectators believe that the cone is still in the large handkerchief. The cone seems to vanish when the magician tosses the handkerchief in the air.

While the cloth is still falling, the magician turns toward the side table. As he steps in that direction, he obtains a duplicate egg from beneath his vest. He lifts the paper cover leaving the metal shell cone. The vanished cone has apparently replaced the egg. The magician produces the duplicate egg at this elbow. He puts the paper cover back over the shell cone.

Now comes the byplay — false passes with the egg. In one maneuver, the magician pretends to carry the egg beneath his coat with his left hand. He suddenly shows the egg in the right hand and smiles at the suspicious glances of the spectators. This false movement to the coat enables the magician to obtain a special "pull" — a spring-wire holder attached to a length of cord elastic that passes beneath the coat. The egg is wedged into the pull. It flies beneath the coat under the cover of the arm. The hands are shown empty.

The magician approaches the side table and lifts the paper cover. He carries the shell cone with it. The egg has returned. Lowering the cover behind the hat, the magician releases the metal shell. It falls into the servante behind the table. The cover is laid on the center table with the egg and the plate. The solid cone is produced from the hat.

Having disposed of the shell, the magician can now crush or otherwise destroy the paper cover. He breaks the egg to show that it is genuine and when he returns the hat to the audience,· he carries with him the only remaining article — one solid wooden cone.

CARD IN EGG

You show a pack of playing cards, shuffle them, and allow one to be selected. Allow this card to be torn up and while it is being destroyed, walk to your table and pick up a black box into which you allow the torn card to be placed.

After the torn card is in this box, take one torn-off corner of the card and hand it to someone to hold. The black box is now also given to someone to hold and while it is being held up in full view, you again turn to your table and bring down a plate full of fresh eggs.

You allow an egg to be selected by someone at the opposite side of the card selector. After the egg has been selected, you ask the person to hold the egg in the air on a small plate that you have for the purpose. At command, the torn card will leave the black box and on breaking open the egg, the card is found in it restored, but with one corner missing. On matching the other corner which has been held by the spectator, it will be found to fit exactly the card that has just been taken from the egg.

The card selected must be forced; that is, you compel the party selecting a card virtually to select the card that you almost push into his hand. If you do not wish to take any chance on the trick, the best way is to use a "forcing pack" in which all the cards are alike.

Advance Preparation: Let us suppose that you are going to force the Jack of Diamonds. Before the performance, take a Jack of Diamonds, tear off one corner, fold the card into three parts, make a roll of it, and place it into the end of a hollow wand which contains a rod that can be pushed up and down inside of it. This wand is painted black so as to look like any ordinary wand.

Place the torn-off end of the card into the bottom compartment of a mechanical black card box. (Its mechanism will be described later on).

To perform: Take a pack of cards and ask someone to take a card, either forcing the card or if using a "forcing pack", allow any card to be taken from the pack. Ask the selector of the card to tear up the card completely and to place it into the mechanical black card box. Now this has a flap on the side which is held down by a small hook that releases the flap when you close the cover of the box and so takes up the torn-up card and makes it appear that the card disappeared and brings to view the torn-off corner of the card you have prepared in advance. Now hand this torn-off corner to the person that selected the card, and say that he had better retain it in his possession. Next take an egg which you have previously allowed someone to choose from the plate full of eggs, and break it with the tip of your wand that contains the rolled up card, and as you break the shell gently, push the card into the egg by forcing it out of the wand by means of the rod. Suddenly you spy the card and show the audience that you really extract the card from the egg. Next, unroll the card and hand it to the card selector, proving to him that it is the card he selected and that the corner he has in his hand exactly fits the missing corner of the card taken from the egg.

Note: Any amateur can perform this trick, and the mechanical card box, wand, and forcing pack of cards can be purchased from all reliable magical dealers.

FINDING A CHOSEN CARD

In many cases, you may be unable to get hold of a card that has been selected and often when doing a card trick, some "wise one" will almost spoil the trick about to be shown simply because he knows how to shift the pass or slip the cut or whatever name you wish to call the movement in which you exchange the top half of the cards for the bottom. However, with this simple subterfuge, you may be able to deceive even a knowing conjurer as you can even allow the selector of the card to take the pack from your hands and replace his card into the pack himself thus proving that you do not shift the selected card and bring it to the top or bottom of the pack.

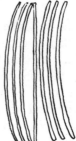

Suppose you have had a card selected and must gain possession of it, and you cannot do so with the aid of sleight-of-hand. First of all, allow a card to be selected. While attention is being drawn to the selected card, you take the pack of cards in your hand and bend them into an oval shape as in the illustration.

You now have the card returned and as that card alone has not been bent or "ovaled" or shaped, by simply straightening up the cards, you can easily select the chosen card, as it is the only straight card among all the bent ones.

THE BALANCING MAGIC WAND

The effect of this is to cause your wand to adhere to your fingers in many positions. The secret of this is to procure for yourself a blonde lady's long hair, knot it, and make an endless loop. This you can have lying on your table on top of a sheet of paper or in some position where you know how to reach it and

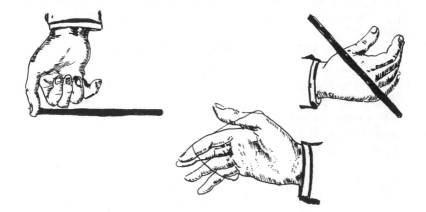

when ready for the trick, you push your right hand into this loop as per illustration and by careful pressure, you will be able to balance all light objects. Properly used, this light hair is positively undetectable, and many good results can be obtained from same.

CIGAR ON HAT

A peculiar little trick that we once saw the Berliner Herrmann perform was the balancing of a borrowed cigar on a borrowed hat. It was quite puzzling, and for the benefit of our readers we will illustrate the apparatus he used.

Have concealed in your hand before borrowing the hat or cigar, a common cork, in the center of which you have forced a sharp needle.

Borrow a hat, take it with your right hand, and place it over your left hand in which you hold concealed the "needle-cork". Now ask for a cigar. When it is handed to you, go through all kinds of motions trying to balance it until eventually, you insert

the needle into the tip of the cigar. Then you are ready to go through your various gags in balancing the cigar and making it do the hootchy-koochy dance.

Hand back the cigar with your right hand and after it is returned, take the hat from your left hand and return it with your right. This allows you to repeat the trick, if called upon to do so, and also allows you to return the needle to your pocket. Do not forget that a needle is sharp, so it is best to rid yourself of the cork and needle by placing it into your side coat pocket where you run no danger of being stung.

EXCHANGING A MARKED COIN

In case you have to exchange a genuinely marked coin in the course of your performance, you can try the following method once and will find that it is most effective. No false movements are required.

First of all, take two ordinary playing cards and place them face to face. Now place them in this position on a table or chair with the coin that you are going to exchange for the borrowed one underneath in such a position that you can easily pick it up. Advance to the audience, and ask for a half dollar as that is the magician's favorite size.

When you have been offered the coin, say, "I have no wish to touch the coin as I wish it marked before it leaves the loaner's hands." You look about for a plate, and not seeing one (for the simple reason that you have no wish for one), accidentally on purpose spy the playing card. Walk deliberately up to it, pick it up, and say that you will ask the gentleman to place the coin on the card. Ask them to watch it very carefully. When the marked coin is placed on the card, simply hold it on its place by using only your thumb. You are now holding the concealed coin with only your index finger as you show the audience the

coin on top. With a slight movement, turn the card around and show the coin under your index finger. You can now go ahead with your trick as it is hardly possible that anyone would suspect you are deliberately and boldly deceiving them right in front of their eyes.

THE RIBBON ESCAPE

Here is an impromptu "release" or "escape" trick that you can turn into a most puzzling and entertaining mystery. It involves a length of colored ribbon, but instead of your escaping from that ribbon, it actually escapes from you!

First, your wrists are tied with a handkerchief. The handkerchief is simply wound around both wrists together and tied with a double knot. State that you do not want it tied too tightly because that is not necessary. Everything will be done in full view so that people will see that your wrists are bound at all times.

Now the ribbon is placed within the circle formed by your bound wrists. Since your hands are tied, a spectator must put the ribbon in that position, holding it by both ends, so that the ribbon is stretched vertically.

In brief, you have trapped the ribbon and there is no way that it can be removed without untying your hands or releasing one end of the ribbon.

No other way?

After all, there is a magical way and if you didn't have one, you wouldn't be a magician. To prove your point, you tell the person holding the ribbon to relax the ends and then draw them tight. Meanwhile, you admonish others to keep close watch on your wrists and see that at no time do they become unbound. All this while you are keeping your hands in motion, and suddenly, the ribbon has passed right through the knotted handkerchief and is held free by the puzzled spectator.

Your process in the Ribbon Escape is as follows:

Because your wrists are not too tightly bound, you can bend your right fingers inward so that they come between your wrists and reach the ribbon. Usually, the ribbon can be quickly engaged with one finger such as the little finger.

Immediately, draw the center of the ribbon forward and out between the wrists telling the person to give you a little slack. Even though you worked your fingers through the handkerchief, your wrists stayed bound all the time.

Now slide the center of the ribbon over your left hand like a loop. Tell the person holding the string to tighten its ends gradually. This draws the center loop of the ribbon down the back of your left hand and under the girding handkerchief. As the ribbon stretches, it comes entirely clear of your wrists and you pull your hands away showing them still bound — a very startling climax.

This trick should be rehearsed to make it smooth and effective when it will become one of the most talked of items in your impromptu repertoire. Sometimes, while having a helper in prac-

ticing it, you can use that same person as an assistant when performing the trick publicly. Being familiar with the routine, such
an assistant will ease or tighten the string as required making the
ribbon's escape all the more rapid.

Another way to practice this at the start is to get into a room
by yourself, tie the ends of a rope to a stationary object, make a
loop out of a handkerchief, and place your hands into this. You
will at once see how to manipulate the rope.

LIFTING A HUMAN BEING WITH POWER FROM EYES
A Rare Trick of the Cingalese

A child is taken, tied up in a small net, and placed toward the
front part of the stage. A Cingalese comes in, bows, and slowly
walks toward the place where the child is lying on the floor tied
up in the net.

He stoops over, gazes intently at the child, and as he straightens
up the child's body is actually lifted from the floor and follows him
as he walks several steps backward.

He again stoops forward and allows the child to sink to the
floor.

To all appearances he has lifted the child from the floor with
power from his eyes.

The child and net are unprepared, but the Cingalese is prepared with a set of false eyes which he wears over his natural
eyes. These are made of silver and are painted to resemble the
human eye.

These artificial eyes have apertures which permit a perfect
range of vision and are held in place by being inserted underneath the eyelids.

A very strong piece of silk twine (reaching below the knees)
is fastened to each artificial eye, and a small strong hook is
secured to the lower end of each piece of silk twine. As the Cingalese bends over and gazes intently at the child he bends his knees
and secretly inserts the hooks into the net entwining the child.

After the hooks are made fast, he slowly straightens up and bends backwards and so causes the twine to rest upon his chest, thereby taking the actual strain from his eyes, and thus raises the child from the floor.

A vase is shown, some water is poured into it, and then the vase containing the water is set on a small table or stool. At command, the water starts to boil and increases until it boils violently.

Finally the Hindoo immerses his fingers into the water and shows the audience that it has been scalded. The water is then commanded to disappear and the vase is shown perfectly empty.

The vase is prepared by making a small hole in the bottom and attaching thereto a small sized pipe. While pouring in the water and until he sets the vase on table or stool, the Hindoo keeps his finger on the end of this pipe.

The table or stool is prepared by running a pipe through the center of the leg. The pipe in turn is attached to a long rubber tube which, covered with dirt, runs along the ground and terminates at a convenient point where a confederate can be concealed.

The Hindoo, when placing the vase on table or stool, is careful that the pipe of the vase is inserted into the hole on the table or stool so that the confederate can prevent the water from flowing out by blowing into the tube. When he blows very hard the water appears to boil.

To prove that the water does boil, the Hindoo places his finger into the vase and pretends to scald himself.

When the water is commanded to disappear, the concealed confederate stops blowing and allows the water to flow out through the pipe and tubing and when the vase is empty, it is shown to the audience.

THE SPELLING BEE CARD TRICK

A clever little trick which will be useful in parlors and small circles is to take thirteen cards and arrange them in such an order as to enable you to spell out the cards in sequence from 1 (ace) to the king by simply holding the 13 cards in your hand with face downward and removing one card from the top with each letter you spell.

Arrange the cards in the following sequence:

3-8-7-1-K-6-4-2-Q-J-10-9-5.

This arrangement face downward makes 3 the top card and the 5 the bottom card.

Commencing at the top, you remove one card with each letter you spell, but be careful not to disarrange the sequence of the cards as previouly prepared, viz: O-N-E, one; having removed one card with each letter, you turn over the fourth card when you pronounce the word "One," and it will be found to be the ace. This you place on the table as you have no further use for the card, and if it is returned to the pack it will break up your previously arranged sequence.

Next spell T-W-O, two, and the fourth card will be again turned up and discarded upon the table and will be found to be the two, or deuce card. Next, T-H-R-E-E, three is spelled and with the pronunciation of the word three the card is turned up, discarded upon the table and will be found to be the three. Continue in this way to spell F-O-U-R, four; F-I-V-E-, five; S-I-X, six; S-E-V-E-N, seven; E-I-G-H-T, eight; N-I-N-E, nine; T-E-N, ten; J-A-C-K, jack; Q-U-E-E-N, queen, and K-I-N-G, king.

The trick affords an excellent pastime and is very simple if you will only remember not to disturb the sequence of the cards and be sure not to place the card back into the pack when it has once been spelled and discarded.

Should you prefer to spell the Jack by its other name, K-N-A-V-E, the sequence is as follows:

Q-4-1-8-K-2-7-5-10-J-3-6-9.

It must be remembered that the card to be spelled must be turned up and discarded with the last letter named of the letter spelled, viz: O-N-E, as the E is named the card is turned up and will be found to be the ace; T-W-O, as the O is named the card is turned up and will be found to be the two; T-H-R-E-E as the

E is named the card is turned up and will be found to the the three, and so continue to spell each number, turning up the spelled card *with* the naming of each last letter and remembering not to break the prearranged sequence and not to return the spelled card to the pack.

The first method is the preferable one; still, both are given for the reader's benefit.

A MIND READING EFFECT

Lay two cards, coins, or any two small objects on a table. Instruct a member of the assemblage to place a hand on one of the objects while you are blindfolded and while your back is turned to the table, and ask him to raise the object in his hand to the level of his forehead. Think of it intently while he slowly counts to twenty. Then he is to lay it back on the table. You will turn around, gaze intently into his eyes, and announce the particular card, coin, or object he has selected and is at present thinking of.

When performing the trick, make the selected member of the assemblage place both hands on the table at the same time ere you commence the trick. Then instruct him to select the card, coin, or object while your back is turned, and hold it up on a level with his forehead. This causes the blood to flow from the hand and makes it appear whiter than the hand which has not been used and which remains at a low level on the table, retaining its natural color.

Naturally, when you turn around and look into the eyes of the committee, you manage to look for the paler hand and select the card, coin, or object located on the same side of the table as the paler hand.

COIN BALANCED ON SWORD

This is a good trick for a parlor and requires neither skill nor practice.

Place a small piece of shoemaker's wax on a dime and lay it upon your magic table. Next, borrow a half dollar from a member of your audience, return to your table, and remark that to prove that there is no preparation, you will place the coin on the table in full view of everybody and accompanying your words, you proceed to lay the coin upon the table right on top of the dime which has the piece of shoemaker's wax on it. This causes the two coins to be fastened together.

Now pick up the sword which you wish to use in the trick, show that it is not prepared, and place the two coins on it so that the groove between them rests on the edge of the sword. This makes it appear that the half dollar is being balanced on the edge of the sword. By slightly raising or depressing the point of the sword, you are able to make the coin move along the sword.

After the trick has been shown, detach the half dollar from the wax, hand it back to the person from whom it was borrowed, and hand the sword about to be examined.

A VANISH IN MID-AIR

The notes concerning this illusion state that the idea was described to Houdini by the famous magician, Chung Ling Soo, an American who gained great success in the guise of a Chinese wizard. Soo was none other than Billy Robinson, formerly stage manager for Herrmann the Great. He was the creator of many startling effects in magic. This mid-air vanish is typical of his ingenuity.

A board is resting on the stage or upon a raised platform. The magician introduces his assistant, who is placed upon the board and fastened to it by straps. The board is carried to the back of the stage where it is placed upon a metal framework or trestle which is specially designed to receive it. The board rests firmly in the metal frame which is tilted forward at an angle of forty-five degrees so that the entire audience can see the assistant.

The framework is within an open-fronted cabinet. It is well away from the sides, back, and top of the cabinet, which are made of plain cloth. There is no opportunity for the assistant to make a quick get-away. The magician stands at one side of the stage and aims a pistol at the cabinet. He fires a shot; there is a puff of smoke from the front of the cabinet. In a flash, the board falls to the stage. The man is gone. The skeleton framework is unoccupied. The board is picked up and carried forward. It is merely a thin slab of wood, its straps hanging loose. The assistant has escaped and disappeared — performing both wonders in the fraction of a second!

The explanation lies in both the board and the frame, while the cabinet plays a certain part in the mystery. The board is double. It is actually two boards held together by metal catches. The top board has straps that do not pass completely through it. Its under side is a thin, highly polished metal mirror. The lower board is a thin one which is fitted with straps on its bottom surface. The double board is not exhibited closely before the vanish.

ASSISTANT STRAPPED TO BOARD WHICH IS PLACED IN FRAME WITHIN CABINET.

The assistant is strapped to it. It is immediately tilted forward and carried to the framework. No one sees the bottom of the board.

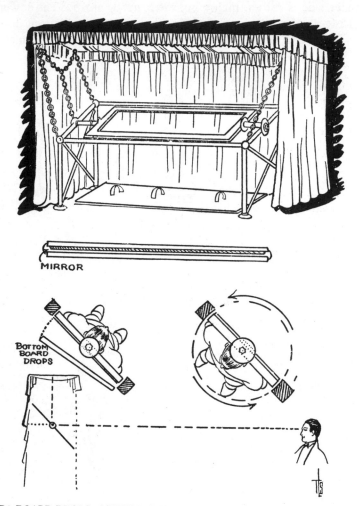

TOP: BOARD DROPS, ASSISTANT VANISHES. CENTER: DOUBLE BOARD, LOWER PORTION DROPS WHEN CATCH IS RELEASED. BOTTOM: LOWER BOARD FALLING, ASSISTANT BENEATH REVOLVING UPPER BOARD. NOTE THE SPECTATOR'S LINE OF VISION. MIRROR RE-FLECTS TOP OF CABINET.

The framework is a mechanical device. It is supported between two pivot rods—one at each end. These are arranged so that the operation of a simple releasing device will cause the entire frame to make a semirevolution, turning away from the audience. The same operation causes the loose lower board to fall from the upper one, which is securely in the frame.

When the magician fires his pistol, the machinery is set in motion. Coincident with the half-turn of the frame comes a puff of smoke and a bright light from the front of the cabinet. This prevents the spectators from observing exactly what happens. The most that can be seen is a slight motion of the frame. The lower board drops as the frame revolves. It strikes the stage. The upper board stops with its mirrored side upward. The polished surface reflects the top of the cabinet, which is identical in appearance to the back. The spectators can apparently see through the framework. It looks absolutely empty. The dropping of the dummy board is the subtle touch that renders the deception perfect.

The boards that are used should be wide and long. This prevents any view of the man beneath the mirrored board. The forty-five-degree angle is sufficient to keep him completely out of sight. The depth and height of the cabinet are properly arranged so that the reflection of the top will appear to be the background. The dummy straps on the lower board appear to be the actual straps which held the vanished man.

As the board is brought forward, a curtain falls, obscuring the presumably empty cabinet. This enables assistants to remove the mirrored board from the frame and to release the hidden man. The illusion should be presented on full stage, as the concluding number of a magical act. It is an excellent trick since the mechanical operation can be made simple and sure. With proper construction, this illusion should work with perfect precision, and its action is so fast that there is no chance of the spectators' realizing what takes place.

SAWING A WOMAN INTO TWINS

Houdini had many ideas for improvements of old illusions. One of the most sensational of modern stage tricks was the illusion of "sawing a woman in half," which was exhibited by many magicians with many variations. When Houdini started out with his full evening show, the sawing trick was no longer a novelty. He did not use it in his program. Nevertheless he, like many other magicians, gave considerable thought to the possibilities of presenting the illusion in a new guise.

His notes contain the details of a new variation of the sawing trick. This material gives the basic principles of the idea with many suggestions for actual working. The following description and explanation have been developed from the notes.

SAWING A WOMAN INTO TWINS. CUTTING THE CABINET.

The illusion begins with the exhibition of a long oblong box, which is resting on a large square platform. The platform is turned around to exhibit all sides of the box. The box has two doors in front and two doors on top. These are opened before the box is turned around.

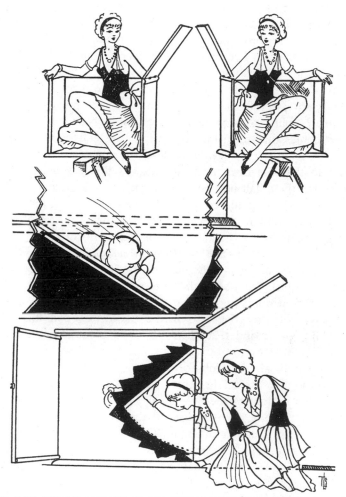

TOP: THE TWINS APPEAR FROM THE SEPARATED BOXES. BOTTOM: ESCAPE OF WOMAN INTO PLATFORM; TWINS COME FROM PLATFORM AND ENTER THROUGH THE BACK.

A large woman comes on the stage and takes a reclining position in the oblong box. The illusionist closes the doors, and the
assistants carry in two sawhorses which are set in front of the platform. Each front door of the box has sectional divisions, and these
are equipped with small curtains. The magician raises a curtain
near one end to speak to the woman. This proves to be the foot
end of the box so he lifts the curtain near the other end, revealing
the woman's head as well as her feet. This is done as the assistants pick up the box and place it upon the sawhorses.

The woman gives her consent to the performance. The illusionist closes the curtains and calls for a huge saw. He and an assistant saw the box in half. The two sections are turned so that the
cut ends are away from the spectators, and the halves are taken
completely apart. A woman has apparently been cut in half.

Now comes the surprising conclusion. Instead of restoring the
woman — as in the old sawing trick — the magician has the boxes
turned so that the open ends are toward the audience. As the
boxes turn, their half-lids open, and each box is seen to contain
a small girl dressed to resemble the woman who originally appeared. The woman has been sawed into twins!

The explanation is found chiefly in the platform on which the
box is first exhibited. The platform is nearly square. There is
considerable space behind the box. In the platform is a compartment which starts from beneath the box and continues to the back.
When the front doors and the top of the box are opened, the two
little girls, who are concealed in the platform, open lids above
their hiding-place and take their positions behind the box. All
this is concealed by the box and its doors. The action does not
take place until after the platform had been turned around.

When the girls are safely behind the box, the doors and lid are
closed. The bottom of the box is released. It goes downward at
the back of the box, being hinged at the front. The platform beneath it acts in a similar manner. This enables the large woman
to enter the platform. She moves out to the back; the bottom of
the box and the top of the platform come back into their normal
places, actuated by springs. These portions lock securely.

The back panels of the box are really secret doors. The small
girls open them inward and one enters each section of the box.

They close the secret doors behind them. The girl at the head end of the box lies with her knees doubled up; the girl at the foot end takes a sitting position with her feet extended.

By this time, the sawhorses are on the stage. Assistants raise the box. It is placed on the horses. The illusionist opens the curtains. He reveals the head of one girl and the feet of the other. This leads the audience to believe that the woman is still in the box. After the curtains are lowered, the sawing commences. The saw follows a regular path. In fact, the box is really two separate sections which are temporarily joined by thin boards. There is no danger to the girls as the saw goes between them.

When the sawing is completed, the open ends of the box are turned away so that each girl can be ready in a normal sitting position. Then the open ends are turned toward the audience. Acting on this cue, the girls raise the lids and make their appearance. They come front and do a dance while the sections of the box are shown by the assistants, placed on the platform, and wheeled away.

This illusion has excellent possibilities. It adds an element of comedy to the trick. The finish is surprising. It requires considerable speed in the changing of positions in order to produce its full effectiveness.

The box — as has been mentioned — is really two sections temporarily joined. This means that the box is not destroyed with each performance. It can be easily repaired by using new strips of wood between the sections.

Houdini's notes suggest means of bringing the girls behind the box from the wings instead of the platform, but such a plan would not be as practicable as the use of the special platform with the girls concealed at the outset. The only quick way to dispose of the large woman is in the platform; and since the platform is to be utilized for that purpose, the concealment of the small girls there is the better plan.

THE TRANSFORMATION CABINET

The purpose of this illusion is to cause the transformation of the performer, who changes into another person while isolated in an open-front cabinet six feet above the stage. The cabinet is simply a box, with no opportunity for concealment, as it is hardly large enough to contain the performer.

The magician climbs a ladder and sits in the cabinet facing the audience. The assistants arrange two ladders, one on each side of the cabinet. They bring on a large cloth and spread it on the stage. Each takes a corner of the cloth as it lies directly below the cabinet. They mount the ladder step by step until the bottom of the cloth is above the stage. The magician is concealed from view, but there is no chance of his escape. The spectators can see above, below, and on all sides. The pole on which the cabinet is mounted is by far too small to accommodate a living person.

After a few moments, the assistants slowly descend the ladders. The top of the cabinet comes in view, then the front. Instead of the performer, another person is seen — in the illustration, a girl.

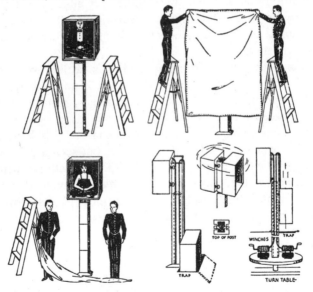

CHANGE OF THE PERFORMER FOR ASSISTANT. THE DIAGRAMS GIVE THE CONSTRUCTION OF THE POST AND MECHANISM BENEATH STAGE.

The assistants reach the stage. They spread out the cloth. The ladder is put in front of the cabinet and the new arrival descends to the stage.

The secret of this illusion involves various mechanical details, which are illustrated in the diagrams. It should first be noted that the cabinet is not mounted on the top of the pole. It is suspended from the front of the pole. The audience does not know exactly what holds it there. The pole is hollow and a cable comes up from beneath the stage and out of the top of the pole. It holds the cabinet.

There is also a second cabinet — a replica of the first. This is beneath the stage. It is attached to the bottom of the pole which runs beneath the stage, the base that the audience sees being merely a dummy. A second cable runs up through the center of the hollow pole, over the top, and down the back through the stage. It connects with the second cabinet.

As soon as the assistants spread the large cloth and prepare to ascend the ladders, a trap door opens behind the pole and the man below stage turns a winch that raises the duplicate cabinet. It comes up behind the cloth, traveling at the same rate of speed as the assistants. When the cloth has covered the cabinet that contains the magician, the duplicate cabinet is in place behind the original.

We must now consider the construction of the pole. It is nothing but a hollow shell below the cabinet. Inside it is a round metal pole, also hollow. The cables pass through this pole. The top part of the square pole — that is, the portion behind the cabinet — is also metal and is permanently attached to the round pole. The round pole is mounted on a turntable below stage. On this table are the winches that control the pulleys.

As soon as the rear cabinet is in place, the table is turned. The inner round pole and the upper portion of the square pole revolve as one piece bringing the duplicate cabinet to the rear and the original cabinet to the front.

The assistants are then ready to lower the cloth. The winch that controls the performer's cabinet is released. His cabinet travels downward behind the cloth. The trap door was closed as soon as the duplicate cabinet had cleared it. Now it opens when the cloth touches the stage. The magician and his cabinet pass through the trap, the trap closes, and the work is done.

The back of the shell pole and both the front and the back of the revolving square portion are grooved. Behind each cabinet are little wheels that fit into the grooves. These enable the cabinets to run smoothly up and down the pole. The turntable is located some five feet below the level of the stage so as to allow room for the cabinet and the operators who work below stage.

Each cabinet should be fronted with a thin gauge blind. This is pulled down by the performer after he is in place. When the second cabinet is revealed, the blind is not raised until the assistants have lowered the cloth. The purpose of the blind is to keep the spectators from seeing exactly who is in the cabinet although a form is visible through the gauze. This keeps attention on the cabinet, particularly at the conclusion of the illusion. If the girl should be fully revealed the instant that the cloth came below the cabinet, people would be searching for clues before the trick was completed.

The illustrations show the effect as well as the explanation. The gauze curtains are not illustrated. They must be considered as an additional item that adds to the effect. The pole is marked into ornamental sections so that no suspicion will be attached to the actual break which is necessary just below the level of the cabinet.

THE FLIGHT OF VENUS

This illusion is of special interest as it is one which Houdini planned for many years: the vanishing of a girl placed on a sheet of plate glass. Houdini mentioned this effect to the author on several occasions. An illusion involving a sheet of plate glass and a girl was described in a magical publication which appeared shortly after Houdini's death, but it was not the illusion to which Houdini referred. He specified that in his illusion, no stage traps were necessary; and the trick that was published required a trap.

The author was pleased to find a description of the plate-glass illusion, with its explanation, among Houdini's notes. There is no certainty, however, that this was the final form to which Houdini had developed the idea. The illusion, as explained, is certainly unique. Its practicability could only be demonstrated by actual experiment. Houdini spoke of the illusion as though it were completely designed and merely awaiting actual construction. It is probable that he made further plans for it after writing the brief explanation which appears in his notes. Yet there is no proof that he departed from the fundamental principle that he originally decided to use.

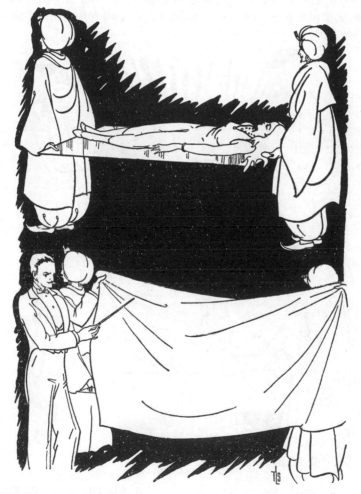

TOP: THE GIRL IS PLACED ON A SHEET OF GLASS. BOTTOM: THE GIRL IS COVERED WITH A CLOTH.

As the audience sees it, two Hindu assistants are standing on the stage when the curtain rises. They are facing the side of the stage. Between them they hold a sheet of plate glass. The magician introduces a girl clad in a scanty costume. She assumes a reclining position upon the sheet of plate glass. The magician and an assistant cover her with a large cloth. While the cloth completely hides the girl and the glass, it at no time touches the stage. There is absolutely no opportunity for the girl to escape by means of a trap. The men are standing well forward and there are no wings near by.

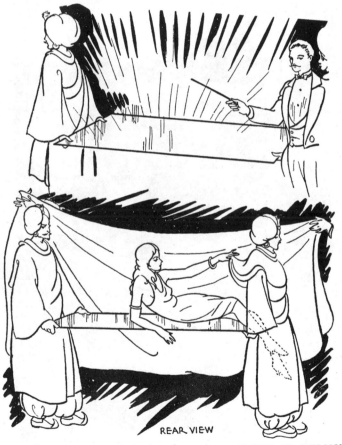

REAR VIEW

TOP: THE GIRL DISAPPEARS WHEN THE CLOTH IS REMOVED.
BOTTOM: HOW THE GIRL ENTERS THE DUMMY FIGURE.

A few moments after the cloth has been placed upon the girl, the magician whisks it away. The girl has vanished. The sheet of glass is transparent. She has apparently disappeared into thin air. The assistants carry the glass from the stage.

Now for the explanation. The foremost Hindu is a dummy figure. The figure is hollow and is considerably larger than the girl. As soon as the girl is covered by the cloth, she moves forward and enters the dummy figure. The form has no back. The opening is covered by a coat which is cut down the middle and held taut with strips of elastic. The girl's tight-fitting costume enables her to enter the figure without difficulty.

When the cloth is removed, the girl is gone. She walks off inside the figure, carrying the front end of the glass. In doing so, she turns toward the back of the stage to keep the spectators from observing the figure too closely.

There are certain important details which must be considered in connection with the illusion. As described, with two assistants, it is doubtful whether the dummy figure could remain upright and support the end of the glass. The illusion has been described and illustrated with two assistants — one a dummy — in order to clarify the idea. The notes, however, suggest the use of four assistants dressed as Hindus. The advantages of such an arrangement are obvious. With one man at each of the three corners of a large sheet of glass, the dummy figure could be stationed at the far corner at the front. A man would be between the figure and the audience, obscuring a close view of the dummy. Furthermore, the man at the front of the glass could support all the weight so that the dummy figure would bear none of the strain and would actually be supported by the glass itself. This arrangement greatly increases the practical possibilities of the idea. With four men holding the glass, there would be less suspicion on the part of keen observers.

To make the illusion most effective, the cloth should contain a wire frame resembling the form of the woman. Her entrance into the dummy figure is effected while the cloth is being held in front of the glass. With the wire frame, the cloth can be placed upon the glass and left there, apparently covering the girl. In the vanish, the cloth is swept away and crushed, the light frame collapsing with it. There is no possibility of the girl's being in the cloth. The clear glass, well above the stage alone remains.

Correct construction of the dummy figure, proper lighting conditions, and precise routine are essential factors in this illusion. Much of its success depends upon the ability of the performer who presents it.

THE GIANT BALL OF WOOL

Certain successful stage illusions have been adapted from smaller tricks while on some occasions, the principles of stage illusions have been applied to a smaller scale. This illusion is an outgrowth of a famous old trick — the production of a missing article in the center of a ball of wool.

In this instance, the missing article is a girl who has vanished in some mysterious way. Suspended on a trapeze is a solid ball of heavy wool. The end of the wool is attached to a huge reel. An assistant unwinds the wool, the ball revolving as he does so.

When the wool is nearly unwound, the lady makes her appearance. She pushes aside the remaining strands and emerges from the ball of wool, dropping to the stage to receive the applause of the audience.

This effect is obtained by very simple means. The girl is in the ball of wool from the outset. She is made up as the double of the girl who previously disappeared. The diagrams show the construction of the apparatus. There are two spheres connected to the trapeze, both attached to pivot rods. The outer sphere is made of thin wire which is covered with the wool. This sphere revolves when the wool is unwound.

The inner sphere does not revolve. Each pivot rod is hollow and contains a central axis which is stationary. The inner sphere is a strong framework of metal open at the front. It is covered with a thin layer of wool. It has a platform at the bottom, upon which the lady rests.

She is put in this place before the presentation of the illusion. The strands at the back of the ball of wool are parted to allow the woman to obtain air. When the time arrives to unwind the ball of wool, she closes the loose strands in the back.

The ball is unrolled. When it reaches the thin wire sphere, the assistant stops and the woman spreads the strands in both the inner and the outer spheres, thus making her way into view of

tho audience. It is unnecessary to unwind the ball of wool after
the woman appears. Hence the illusion is concluded before either
the thin wire frame or the center sphere has been completely
revealed.

This illusion offers a highly effective conclusion to a series of
disappearances as the ball of wool can be on the stage for some
time before it is used. The trick will prove of interest to the
audience and it has sufficient elements of mystery to make it
worthy of presentation.

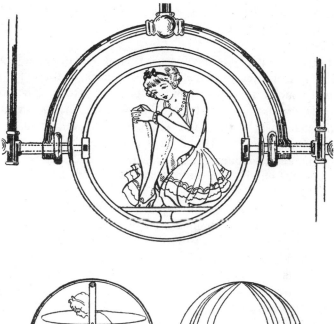

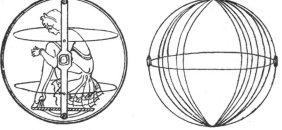

CONSTRUCTION OF APPARATUS SHOWING INNER BALL WHICH DOES
NOT REVOLVE. NOTE WIRE COVERING THAT HOLDS WOOL THROUGH
WHICH THE GIRL FORCES HER WAY.

A VANISH FROM A LADDER

The disappearance of a girl from the top of a ladder is not a new idea in stage illusions; but in the form described in Houdini's notes, it includes certain details that add greatly to the effectiveness of the trick. The ladder that is used is broad and heavy with large rungs. It is held upright by two assistants who support it near the rear of the stage in front of a low, ornamental picket fence.

The girl climbs the ladder and sits on the top rung, facing the audience. She raises a cloth and drapes it over her head and shoulders. Then the ladder begins to topple. The assistants have trouble holding it. They lift it and carry it toward the front of the stage. The cloth falls to the floor. There is a scream — the girl is gone! The assistants carry the ladder to the footlights and take it from the stage.

The secret lies partly in the construction of the ladder and partly in the ornamental picket fence. Along the back of the fence is a cloth that matches the background of the stage setting. There is a space between the fence and the back curtain. The ladder has a special rung which is the same distance above the stage as the top of the picket fence. This rung is merely a shell, open in the back. It contains a roller blind, the same color as the back drop. The end of the blind has projecting rods which extend to the sides of the ladder.

When the girl climbs the ladder, she naturally places her hands upon the sides. In this manner, she draws up the blind as she climbs. The blind stretches from the special rung to the top rung where the girl hooks the loose end to two special catches behind the back of the ladder. The movement of the blind is hidden by the girl's body. When she seats herself upon the top rung, the spectators still believe that they see between the upper rungs of the ladder.

With the cloth in front of her, the girl draws two sets of wire rods from the posts of the ladder. These are fitted with springs, and they form a mechanical holder for the cloth. The girl is free to slip from behind the cloth. She drops in back of the ladder, behind the picket fence. The roller blind and the cloth behind the pickets hide her departure.

When the girl is safely away, the assistants begin to let the ladder sway. They grip the ladder near the top and release the catch which holds the blind. It springs down behind the rung as the ladder is carried forward. Another release on the part of the assistants causes strong springs to draw the telescopic rods into the legs of the ladder. The cloth falls to the floor. The girl screams

THE GIRL CLIMBS A LADDER. SHE RAISES A CLOTH.

from behind the picket fence. She is gone and the evanishment seems unexplainable.

The ladder may be shown near the footlights before and after the exhibition, which gives this illusion a most convincing effect.

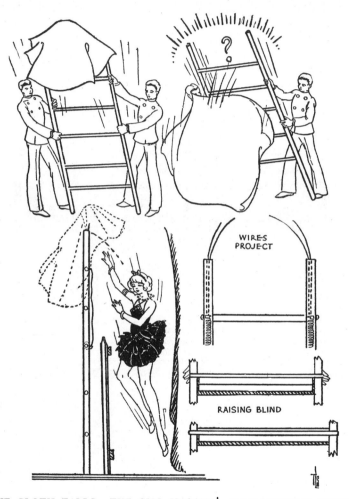

WIRES
PROJECT

RAISING BLIND

THE CLOTH FALLS. THE GIRL IS GONE! EXPLANATORY DIAGRAMS SHOW "GETAWAY". NOTE ARRANGEMENT OF PROJECTING WIRES FROM TOP OF POST. THESE HOLD THE CLOTH. ALSO OPERATION OF BLIND THAT MATCHES THE SCENERY.

WALKING THROUGH A BRICK WALL

The mysterious feat of walking through a brick wall was not one of Houdini's originations, but it has become closely identified with his name, for he introduced the illusion to the American stage and presented it with remarkable success. It was an ideal feat for Houdini to perform, for it can be classed both as a magical illusion and as an escape trick; and Houdini's popular reputation was certain to be an attraction for so sensational a mystery.

The wall was built of brick on an iron framework some twelve feet in length. The framework was mounted on rollers so that it could be moved about the stage and in its final position, it stood with one end toward the audience. A committee was invited on to the stage. The inspection proved conclusively that the wall was just what it appeared to be — a solid structure of brick; in fact, the wall could be built in the presence of the audience, if desired. The stage also bore minute inspection. It was covered with a large carpet of plain design and of heavy material, precluding all possibility of any openings. To make everything more convincing, a large cloth, inspected by the committee, was spread over the carpet.

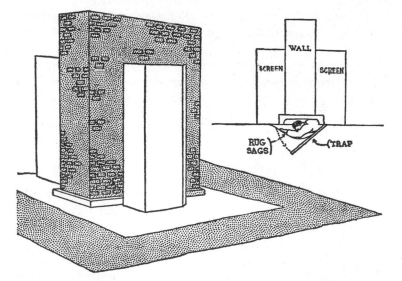

WALKING THROUGH A BRICK WALL. ONE OF HOUDINI'S MOST FAMOUS MYSTERIES.

Then the brick wall was set in the center of the stage, and two threefold screens were placed against it, one on each side of the wall.

Houdini went behind one of the screens while the committee members stood on all sides watching the wall from every angle. Houdini raised his hands above the screen for a moment, then drew them within the screen. The seconds clicked by, and suddenly the screen on the other side of the wall was moved away, and there stood the performer! When the first screen was taken down, it proved to be empty. Thus Houdini apparently passed through a solid brick wall, some eight feet in height, under the most exacting conditions. This effect seemed miraculous as it was apparently impossible for the performer to go through, over, around, or beneath the wall. Under it would have seemed most logical, but with only five or six inches of space and the carpet and cloth preventing use of a trapdoor, that method of passage seemed unusable. Yet Houdini went *underneath* the wall.

A large trapdoor was set in the center of the stage. When the screens were in position, the door was opened from below. Both the cloth and the carpet, which were large in area, sagged with the weight of the performer's body allowing sufficient space for him to work his way through, the cloth yielding as he progressed. The passage accomplished, the trap was closed, and no clew remained.

Even with people standing on the cloth, the "give" in the center was quite unnoticeable, and the passage from one side of the wall to the other was quickly accomplished by a man of Houdini's agility.

A SECOND-SIGHT ACT

The following material constitutes one of the most important items among Houdini's notes. It consists of a series of telepathic effects that enable two persons to present a most baffling entertainment. While the principles are not new, and some of the actual effects have been shown as individual items, the complete routine with all of its variations forms a complete act in itself. Smoothly and carefully presented, the effect will prove phenomenal.

Photograph of Houdini during the later years of his career.

Black Trunk Marked **M-5** continued
Center Tray
Two Fish Bowl Covers
The Four Clock Board
Giant Card Star
Bottom
Large Sucker Water Bowl
One Ventrilocal Figure
One Contact Mat
One Large Clock Complete with top
Top of Fish Bowls and covers
One Bamboo trick

1 RED TRUNK MARKED **"M-3"**
Tray
Five Fish Bowls and 3 spares.
Six batteries, shoes, wire, dictaphone
Three dozen playing cards
Bottom
Three big fish bowls
One spare Rose Bush Bowl.
One Fish Bowl Stand
Six Bananas
One Decanter with hole
Spirit Cabinet glass.(tumbler)
One Glass Pitcher
Dye Bottles.
One Contact Mat.
Noah's Ark.
One Skull.
Arm and Leg Cuts.

1 RED TRUNK MARKED **"M-1"**
Bottom
Tubes of 3 langkhx Lamps
Tubes of Rose Bushes
Tubes of three fish bowls
Tubes of Bird Cage
Tube of "D come B?"
One Wood-ring.
Four Mahatma Plumes.
Iron Bases,
"Do the Dead Come Back? Bier."
Lamp Bases
Feet of Clock Trick.
Lines of "Do the Dead come back?."

A single page from Houdini's long inventory of the list of props required with his full show giving a slight idea of how heavily illusionists traveled during magic's golden age.

The usual second-sight act involves the transmission of thoughts from one person to another. The performers are usually a man and a woman, the man passing through the audience and receiving articles which the woman names while seated on the stage. Such acts are learned only after long and patient practice.

The second-sight act about to be discussed is of a different nature. It is of the type known to the profession as a "test"; namely, a concentrated exhibition performed before a small and discriminating audience. It was designed as a routine to follow the usual second-sight act, but there is no reason why it should not be presented as an act in itself. This is particularly true because the act is not difficult. It does require keenness and practice, but two intelligent persons should be able to perform it with every variation after two or three preliminary trials.

Readers versed in magic will recognize the underlying principles of this act because most of them have seen effects in which a magician names the time on a watch or tells the denomination of a playing-card after such objects have been laid on the table during his absence. But few have ever seen an act of this sort worked up to a high-class state, involving so many tests that no repetition of one effect is necessary, and embellished with such unusual details that it carries all the effectiveness of a second-sight performance. This act does all that.

The performer, in introducing the act, discourses on the subject of telepathy. He states that he and his assistant can perform all the most remarkable tests that involve figures, cards, and black-board writing while they are in separate rooms and not within hearing distance of one another. One committee conducts the woman from the room while the man prepares to transmit the thoughts of those who remain.

A watch is set at any hour and minute. It is laid face down on the table. A number is written on a card, which is sealed in a small envelope and placed upon the table. A line is selected from the page of a book. Initials are written between two hinged slates which are then locked and placed upon the table.

The woman returns. It is best to have a blackboard available. She stands before the blackboard and writes answers to everything, performing the most complicated tests with ease and precision. The act is highly effective for platform performers and when it is done as a conclusion to a short second-sight act, its effect is naturally increased.

The basis of the trick depends upon a mental arrangement in which the table is divided into imaginary sections. This system is known to both the performer and his assistant. The table should measure about two by three feet although a square card table may be used. Upon the table is an ornamental mat, with curved edges, as shown. The mat should measure about twelve by sixteen inches. Laid crosswise, the mat is easily divided into twelve mentally noted squares, each four inches square. While the mat is useful, it is not absolutely essential after the system has been thoroughly understood. Any rectangular mat will do; marks on the table will suffice; or, in the most advanced form, the mat itself may be visualized without actually being used. However, an ordinary mat will not arouse suspicion, since it appears to be a mere ornament.

The twelve squares are numbered, four to a row. When both performers can recognize any field instantly, they are ready to proceed with their preliminary tests. These will be described individually, with all the necessary modifications of the fundamental principle.

THE WATCH TEST

This test is not difficult to learn; yet, it is performed with such exactitude — even to the very minute indicated by the hands of the watch — that it will prove puzzling to the wisest observer.

When the watch has been set at a definite time, and the performer has pretended to transmit that time to his assistant, the performer lays the watch upon the table, face down, but in a manner that indicates the exact time registered.

The hour is shown by means of the mat. There are twelve imaginary numbered squares. The performer puts the watch in the square that corresponds to the hour. Square one indicates one o'clock, and so on. The stem of the watch is the indicator that gives the position of the minute hand in reference to the numbers that appear upon the face of the watch. For instance, taking the

top of the mat as twelve o'clock, the performer can indicate
the number two (ten minutes after the hour) by pointing the stem
toward the spot where number two would appear if the watch itself
were surrounded by a dial. There is no difficulty whatever in indicating these imaginary numbers. If the time on the watch should
be thirty minutes after two, the watch would be placed in number
two square on the mat, with the stem of the watch pointing straight
down toward the spot where the number six would be on the
imaginary dial.

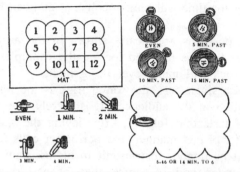

TWELVE IMAGINARY PORTIONS OF THE MAT. POSITIONS OF WATCH,
STEM, AND PLACEMENT ON MAT.

The committee usually chooses some minute in between the
fives and the performer is ready for this. Suppose the time is 5:18.
He sets it to indicate 5:15, ignoring the three extra minutes for the
moment, but he then indicates those additional minutes by a ring
which surrounds the stem of the watch. To indicate one additional minute, he points the ring upward at right angles to the
stem of the watch. To indicate two additional minutes, he bends
the ring back so that it lies flat against the upper side of the stem.
To show three additional minutes, he bends the ring so that it
points downward at right angles to the stem. For four additional
minutes, the ring is bent all the way beneath the stem. If the ring
projects straight outward in its normal position, no minutes are
added.

Thus for 5:15, the ring would be straight out; for 5:16, straight
up; for 5:17, back against the upper side of the stem; for 5:18,
straight down; for 5:19, back beneath the stem.

Once the system is understood, the performer can handle the watch without clumsiness. Upon receiving the watch, he notes the time and immediately decides on the square upon which it belongs, the position to which the stem must point, and how the ring should be set. While looking at the watch, he observes his location, puts the ring in its correct position, and immediately sets the watch face down upon the table.

This may be done with any pocket watch that may be offered by the committee, although it is a good idea to use a watch that is not running, for the time will remain constant and can be checked after the test.

The various positions are clearly shown in the accompanying diagrams, hence there is no need for lengthy examples. A study of the illustrations will make everything plain.

Presented as a single test, the watch trick is too apt to excite the close attention of the audience. It is merely one step in the entire series of tests that follow. After laying the watch on the table in a matter-of-fact manner, the performer calls for the next impression that he intends to transmit to his assistant.

It must be understood, of course, that the performer does not use the particular time that happens to be registered by a watch. He allows the spectators to set the watch at any time they may choose. It is quite natural for him to take the watch and look at it for a considerable number of seconds, since he is supposed to be engaged in concentration.

THE FIGURE TEST TO 10,000

In this test, the performer invites the committee to choose any number up to 10,000. For instance, the number 3,862 is selected. This number is written on a card. The performer looks at the card and studies the number. He may either lay the card face down on the table, or he may place it in an envelope and seal it there. That is a matter of choice. The essential details are the indication of the number.

There are four figures to be considered. In the instance given, those figures are 3, 8, 6, and 2. The performer indicates the first figure (3) by the square on which he lays the card (or envelope). He indicates the second figure (8) by the pointing of the card. This involves an imaginary dial surrounding the card and corresponding to the numbers on the face of a clock. If the card is used alone, it should be a business card with the number written on the blank side. Hence the name on the card serves as a pointer when read in its proper manner. If the envelope is used, one end is slightly marked so that the assistant will recognize it. In this way the envelope is useful. The performer has it ready in case some one chooses to use a blank card instead of a business card.

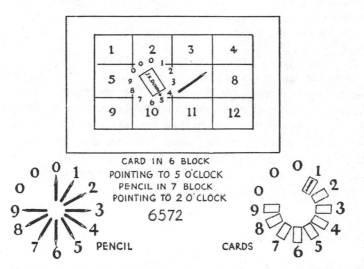

FIGURES INDICATED BY CARD PLACEMENT, CARD POINTING, PENCIL PLACEMENT, AND PENCIL POINTING.

Having put the card on the table, the performer is through with the pencil for the time, so he lays it on the table also. In this manner he indicates the third and fourth figures. The square on which he lays the pencil indicates the third figure (6), and the spot on the imaginary dial to which the pencil points tells the fourth figure (2).

In using the figure test, number ten serves as the figure 0. The spaces or pointers eleven and twelve are not utilized. Thus it is possible to indicate such numbers as 53 by simply placing the card to show 0 and pointing it to show 0. The performer can also extend this test, allowing any number up to 12,000. He does this by utilizing the ten and eleven squares on the mat. The twelve square indicates the figure 0 in this instance. This plan must be prearranged beforehand with the assistant.

The diagrams show the working of this test; it is an easy matter to indicate other numbers once the principle is recognized. As in the watch test, the performer should avoid all hesitancy, placing the card and pencil upon the table in an indifferent manner.

THE PLAYING-CARD TEST

Another test is performed with a pack of cards. This is best when two selected cards are used. The spectators choose two cards from the pack and show them to the performer. He places the two cards together and sets them on the table. He also replaces the pack of cards upon the table. The fact that the two chosen cards are squared together is a subtle touch. They indicate the name of but one card. It is the pack itself, so carelessly replaced, that declares the second chosen card.

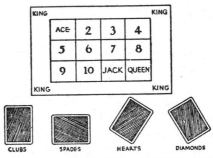

DIVISIONS OF MAT AND TABLE FOR PLAYING CARD TEST. ALSO
POINTING POSITIONS OF CARDS.

The rule for indicating cards is simply numerical, running from one to twelve. Ace is one, then the cards go in rotation, Jack being eleven and queen twelve. The squares on the mat are used as indicators. If a king is chosen, the pack is laid on the table near a corner — not on the mat at all.

An alternate plan to indicate a king is to lay the cards on any square but to spread them slightly; with two cards, they overlap a bit; with the entire pack, the cards are slightly fanned. This is not as good as the corner placement.

To indicate suit as well as value, the performer sets the cards in one of four positions. For clubs, the pack is laid so it points straight up and down. For spades, the pack points across. Hearts is indicated by a position of upper right to lower left, diagonally In indicating diamonds, the pack should point diagonally from upper left to lower right.

The joker is eliminated. It is preferable to use a borrowed pack; the two selected cards may be placed in an envelope, if desired, to prove indirectly that there are no marks on the chosen cards, though this possibility should not be mentioned in the performer's talk. It is also possible to indicate a third chosen card in a subtle manner by having the pack of cards in a case before the demonstration. To select three cards, the pack is taken from the case; the three cards are drawn, noted by the performer, and laid together or inserted in an envelope. To save time, the pack is not replaced in the case; the cards, the pack, and the case are placed on the table, and the position of the case tells the third selected card.

THE SLATE TEST

In its most effective form, the slate test is performed with a pair of slates that are fitted with a lock. A person writes his initials between the slates. Then the slates are locked.

Here we have letters instead of figures, hence another system must be employed; but it is easy to remember, as it is based on the numbered squares of the mat.

The performer merely counts through the alphabet. The twelve letters, A, B, C, D, E, F, G, H, I, J, K, L, correspond to the numbers from one to twelve. Continuing, the letters M, N, O, P, Q, R, S, T, U, V, W, X also correspond to the number from one to twelve. The slates are placed on the correct square to indicate the first initial. If the letter is in the first set, the slates are pointed up and down. If it is in the second set, the slates are pointed across.

The second initial is indicated with the chalk. The performer puts it in the proper square; first set of letters, chalk pointing upward; second set, pointing across. The third initial is indicated by the key to the locked slates. It is placed and pointed like the chalk. Should there be no third initial, the performer gives the key to a spectator to hold. In case the letters Y or Z appear, they are indicated by placing the slates, chalk, or key to the left or right of the mat. Left indicates Y; right indicates Z.

The slates should be quite small. If the performer wishes to restrict himself to two initials, he can use a single slate, placing it with the writing downward. The slate tells one initial, the chalk the other.

In lieu of locked slates, two ordinary slates may be used and bound together by heavy rubber bands, one in each direction. A third rubber band is available in case one should break. This band is used instead of the key to indicate the third initial.

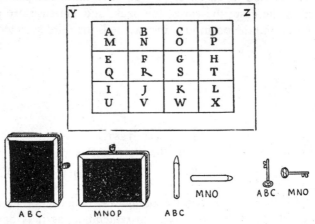

DOUBLE LETTER SYSTEM USED IN SLATE TEST. NOTE SLATES, CHALK, AND KEY.

THE BOOK TEST

This is the most advanced of all the tests. The performer uses a small, thick book. The committee opens the book and selects a line or word on any page. The performer notes the line or word, closes the book, and puts it on the table. The assistant, entering, picks up the book later on and opens it to find the line or word. A word is preferable to a line if a dictionary is used.

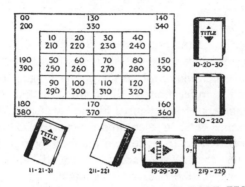

NUMERICAL INDICATIONS USED IN BOOK TEST.

Here we have the mat divided into tens; not units. Square 1 is 10; square 2, 20; and so on. After 120, the tens continue around the table outside of the mat. 130 lies directly above the mat; 140, upper right corner; 150, right of the mat; 160, lower right corner, etc. Thus 200 is the upper left corner of the table.

Beginning again, the squares of the mat have the values 210, 220, and so on; the points that lie outside the mat run 330, 340, up to 400. The book that is used should have fewer than four hundred pages. Hence the upper left corner of the table is not needed as a 400 indicator. Instead, it is given the value of 0.

To indicate any ten below two hundred, the book is placed on the correct spot with its title side in view. To indicate any ten above two hundred, the book is placed with its title downward. Inasmuch as the chosen page will probably be a unit, the book is turned to indicate the units by utilizing the plan of the imaginary clock dial surrounding the book. If the top of the book points to one o'clock, the page number ends in one; two o'clock, two; three o'clock, three; ten o'clock, zero.

When the assistant enters, she notes the book and in coming to the test, picks up the book, opens to the correct page and finds the line. The performer uses a simple system to indicate the line. In reading the line (or word) to himself, he marks it with his thumbnail. If the whole line is used, he makes the mark beside it. If a single word is used, he marks beneath it. With a dictionary, the performer simply marks at the side of the word.

THE COLORED-PENCIL TEST

This is a very ingenious test that may be used in addition to the others or which may replace the ordinary figure test. In order to understand it, refer first to the figure test and its method of indicating numbers of two figures by means of a card or a pencil.

The performer uses three colored pencils: red, blue, and green. The committee is told to write two numbers of four figures each, one above the other. These are to be added below a line. The addition is done on the back of a calling-card. The first number is written in one color, the second in another, the third in another; and the committee has absolute choice of the order in which the colors are to be used, for example, green for the first number, red for the second, blue for the total.

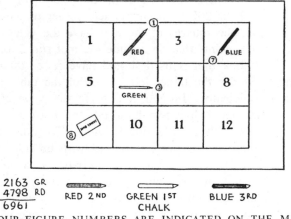

TWO FOUR-FIGURE NUMBERS ARE INDICATED ON THE MAT. THE CHALK POSITIONS SHOW THE ORDER OF THE NUMBERS.

There are also three pieces of chalk that correspond in color to the pencils used. The assistant writes with the chalk on the blackboard and duplicates both selected numbers and the total in the exact colors of the writing on the card.

The three pencils and the card are used to indicate the numbers alone. The red pencil shows the first two figures of the first number; the green pencil shows the last two figures of the first number. The blue pencil shows the first two figures of the second number; the card shows the last two figures of the second number. The total is not indicated. The assistant simply adds that after writing the two numbers on the blackboard. The order of the colors is indicated by the pieces of chalk. The three pieces are laid in a row, either on the edge of the table or on the base of the blackboard. The center chalk (green, for instance) represents the first number; the chalk on the left (red), the second number; the chalk on the right (blue), the total.

This is merely an elaboration of the figure test and the accompanying illustrations give examples.

PRESENTATION OF THE ACT

The act may be varied to suit the particular occasion, but the following presentation covers many important points that will make it most effective. The articles that are to be used are lying on the table. After the assistant has left the room, the performer begins the tests. He should start with the slates and the book, utilizing the smaller articles later. This is because both the slates and the book are large objects. They completely cover any square upon which they are placed. Should the cards or pencils require the same square as the slates or the book, the small articles may be placed upon the larger ones.

The blackboard is standing beside the table. The assistant, upon entering, immediately observes an article such as the watch, and going to the blackboard, draws a picture of a large clock dial upon which she registers the time exactly. She asks if that is correct, and the watch is turned up so that she can have proof that she

was right. That gives her the opportunity to detect the next item
— the playing-cards, for instance. She pretends to be under-
going great concentration and spends most of her time working
at the blackboard.

With the book test, she picks up the book and runs through
the pages in a thoughtful manner. She stops at different pages
and still keeps on a meditative search after she has discovered the
marked word. She lays the book on the table and after thinking
at the blackboard, writes the chosen word.

The performer either retires or goes to the background as soon
as his assistant enters the room. The impression is that he has sent
certain thoughts to the woman, but that she is also depending
upon the helpful concentration of the committee. After each test
she replaces any article that she has picked up, putting it on the
table in the same careless manner adopted by the performer.

Without the blackboard, the woman can name certain thoughts
aloud. She can also use a large slate for her writing. The vital
part of this performance is effective presentation. The idea of
two minds thinking as one must be stressed to the utmost.

Some performers may choose to do the simpler tests only, considering the entire table as divided into twelve squares. This is
a good plan in first presenting the act, as it simplifies the work
and makes a short, effective routine. But the more involved tests
should not be neglected, as they surpass the simpler ones and will
bewilder persons who think they have an inkling of the method.

There are certain impromptu tests that can be shown very effec-
tively. The performer may ask for a match box, a cigarette case, a
card case, or some similar object. Receiving a match box, he counts
the number of matches it contains, closes the box with the matches
in it, and lays the box on the table. The woman sees the box
and notes that it has been put in simple numerical position, its
square indicating the first figure, the way it points, the second
figure. She names the number of matches in the box as an addition to her regular routine.,

While the routine given here — with the additional impromptu
tests — is a wonderful act in itself, many additions and variations
will occur to individuals after they have performed the act them-

selves. They will discover methods of increasing the effectiveness of the act and should not hesitate to make any improvement which they feel sure is of value.

The author recommends this entire act as an excellent and practical demonstration of mental magic. It is one of those deceptions that can be learned and performed by two persons previously unversed in magical methods.

HOUDINI ON MISCELLANEOUS
MYSTERY

The material itself in this section explains the reason for its inclusion.

Chosen from a considerable quantity of Houdini's writings, it deals with off-trail subjects that reveal the range of Houdini's own interests and enthusiasm.

This in turn gives a better index to Houdini as a personality than would any amount of general observation or speculative appraisal.

Houdini's article on "Addressing An Audience", for example, gives a graphic impression of his own style of showmanship, amplified by a description of some of his personal experiences.

The material on cryptography, though it covers the subject only generally, shows the extent of Houdini's excursions into fields other than magic, but which he regarded as having some kindred quality.

These are but indicative of the many sides of Houdini's career and his constant thirst for knowledge that pertained to any phase of mystery. Such traces are also found in many of his dissertations on magic and magicians where he frequently delves into historical facts regarding the subjects or personalities under discussion.

WBG

ADDRESSING AN AUDIENCE
An Editorial by Houdini

The great trouble with magicians is the fact that they believe when they have bought a certain trick or piece of apparatus, and know the method of procedure, that they are full-fledged mystifiers.

The fact really is, it is not the trick itself, nor is it the mere handling of it. A successful presentation depends on the address in connection with the presentation. It is historically recorded that Demosthenes, having an impediment in his speech, placed pebbles into his mouth and spoke to the rolling waves. During nearly all my lifetime, I have had occasion to address large audiences, and a pertinent fact comes to my mind. In October, 1900, at the Berlin Winter Garden, which is really a type of a railroad station, I was the only one that could be heard all over the house.

At the New York Hippodrome where I performed for two successive seasons, my voice carried to all parts of that vast audience. As a matter of fact, I was told that I could be heard out in the lobby. The acoustic properties were wonderful in the Hippodrome, but there is something about a man's personality that is lost in a huge place; just as the man who is accustomed to speaking in a small circle is lost when he gets on the stage, and vice versa.

I have no objection to giving to magicians the secret of my manner of address and what I regard as the right speaking voice. Incidentally, once upon a time my grammar was corrected by a newspaper man. It was during my first trip on the Orpheum Circuit, and strange to say, our beloved Dean Harry Kellar had a similar experience. Alan Dale, in one of his criticisms, corrected him in the same manner. Mr. Kellar's remark was:—"When I done this trick," etc. In the criticism Alan Dale said, "I *did,* Mr. Kellar, I *did*, Mr. Kellar, I *did*, Mr. Kellar." Kellar informed me that he took the hint and went under training. I do not believe that Alan Dale knows to this day how grateful Kellar was for the criticism.

When an artist, even a magician, is corrected by a critic, he should not be dismayed, nor should he look upon it as wasted. He should consider it a friendly favor and look upon it as I have always looked upon criticism.

Constructive criticism is wonderfully helpful. Imagine having a great big newspaper man watch the performance and then write a criticism free of charge. Why, it is a wonderfully beneficial thing as I look at it. If you were to engage a critic to correct your performance, he would charge hundreds of dollars; so, instead of letting the criticism go to waste, or becoming antagonistic, the newspaper man's correction of your performance should be gratefully accepted.

When I had an engagement at a large place where I was afraid my voice would not carry, I would actually go into training for that place. I would run around the block early in the morning at a dog trot and get my lungs in good condition, for it is a fact that in my work, I required wonderful lungs to use in my physical manifestations before an audience. I would also take long walks, away from habitation, and address an imaginary audience.

I remember in Moscow, Russia, 1903, I went to the race track and delivered my speech with all the gestures to my imaginary audience, and in the course of my remarks I said, "I defy the police department of the world to hold me — I challenge any police official to handcuff me," and strange as it may appear, one of the spy detectives, or secret service men, overheard me. In about twenty minutes, as I was roaming around the race track, I was surrounded by policemen thinking that I was a madman and when I gave them an explanation, they just roared with laughter. Thereupon, I used them as my audience, and they made corrections regarding my speech, for which I was thankful.

In 1900, on my first trip to England, I had the good fortune to meet quite a number of the "legitimate" stars. Among others, I met Herman Vezin, the understudy of Sir Henry Irving. I was at that time called the "Syllable Accenting American" because I would spell my words, figuratively, that they should carry to the gallery. I never spoke to the first row.

My method of addressing an audience as result of experience was as follows:

I would walk down to the footlights, actually put one foot over the electric globes as if I were going to spring among the people, and then hurl my voice saying, "L a d i e s a n d G e n t l e - m e n ."

I was told by a number of men that in the Boston Polyclinic and various other schools, they would illustrate my method, and then the class would go to Keith's Theatre to hear my enunciation and manner of delivery.

When you can make the men in the gallery hear each syllable, the audience in front, or downstairs, is also most effectually served.

When you introduce an experiment, apply yourself seriously. Don't think that because you perform a trick well or the apparatus is detection proof from the viewpoint of an ordinary audience, that you have conquered the world of mystery and that you reign supreme. Work with determination that you intend to make them *believe* what you say. Say it as if you mean it, and believe it yourself. If you *believe* your own claim to miracle doing and are sincere in your work, you are bound to succeed.

The reason magicians do not forge to the front more than they now do, is that they content themselves with mere doing and imagine they have the act complete; that all they have to do is to lay the apparatus on the table and go from one trick to the other. The experiment and apparatus are both of secondary consideration. Your determination to improve the seriousness of your endeavors means success, and if you are a natural comedian (I do not mean a buffoon or something which does not become your personality), you may easily inject a tinge of humor into your work. But do not strain that point; it should come naturally and with ease or left alone.

Herrmann's method with an audience was: As soon as he appeared to their gaze, he bowed and smiled, and bowed and smiled all the way to the footlights as if he were tickled to death to have the honor of appearing before them, and the effect on his audience was salutary, and he won their sympathy forthwith.

Dean Harry Kellar's method was to walk in just the same as he would into a house party, welcoming all. He knew he was presenting a line of feats that the majority present might have known, but he handled each number beautifully, and he knew that the audience loved to see him do it. Therefore, everything he presented inspired the audience to a feeling of kindliness toward him, and an appreciation of his work.

The first flight of an airplane in Australia was accomplished by Houdini in his own Voisin biplane on March 16, 1910, awakening Australians to the possibilities of air invasion, specifically from Japan, according to articles appearing in Australian journals soon after Houdini's flight. *From the John J. McManus Collection.*

Houdini's book-plate, used in many of the volumes composing his extensive library.

If you want to be a success, make up your mind that your address to the audience will be the important item of your performance.

HELPFUL HINTS FOR YOUNG MAGICIANS UNDER EIGHTY

In winning your audience, remember that "Manners make fortunes," so don't be impertinent.

*   *   *

An old trick well done is far better than a new trick with no effect.

*   *   *

Never tell the audience how good you are; they will soon find that out for themselves.

*   *   *

Nothing can give greater delight to the gentler sex than to have some flowers handed to them which you have produced from a hat or paper cone.

*   *   *

Rabbit tricks are positive successes.

*   *   *

Never work to fool a magician; always work to your audience. You may think your trick is old, but it is always new to members of your audience.

*   *   *

An old trick in a new dress is always a pleasant change.

*   *   *

When practicing a new trick, try it in front of a looking glass, accompanying your moves with your entire patter.

*   *   *

Don't drag your tricks, but work as quickly as you can, bearing in mind the Latin proverb, "Make haste slowly."

*   *   *

When your audience is far distant from you, pantomime work will be well appreciated.

*   *   *

Well chosen remarks on topics of the day are always in order.

*   *   *

The newspapers generally commented more on Heller's wit than on his magic.

*   *   *

Always have a short sentence ready in case a trick should go wrong. One magician, who has the misfortune to blunder often, says, "Ladies and gentlemen, mistakes will happen, and that is one of them."

*   *   *

Walk right out on the stage, and tell your tale to your audience, and perhaps many will believe it.

*   *   *

It is far more difficult to give a trial show to a house full of seats and one manager than to a packed house and no manager.

BOBBY

Bobby, the Only Handcuff King dog in the world, my fox terrier who performed at the Annual Dinner of the Society of American Magicians, died Sunday, December 15th, 1918, of heart failure.

Bobby was carefully trained to escape from ropes, handcuffs (I had small sizes made for him), straitjackets, and was a wonderful card dog, but especially was he known to English dog trainers as the greatest somersault dog that ever lived, not even barring Dynamite, the once famous American Black and Tan.

Bobby was the household pet for eight years and unusually sagacious and affectionate.

The boys in the neighborhood, in Flatbush as well as here in New York, would ring our bell and ask Mrs. Houdini, "Please let Bobby play ball with us."

My cue for Bob when his trick was finished was "Good boy, Bobby." "Good boy" and he would signal his delight with quivering all over his body and wildly wigwagging his tail.

He positively understood my talking signals, for most of them were words like "Come on", "Right", and "Wrong".

    With eyes upraised, his master's looks to scan,
    The joy, the solace, and the aid of man;
    The rich man's guardian, and the poor man's friend,
    The only creature faithful to the end.

Now that Bobby is gone, good faithful Bobby, all I can say to him is "Good Boy, Bobby, Good Boy and Good-Bye."

CYPHER WRITING, OR THE ART OF CRYPTOGRAPHY

My first introduction to the world of cryptography occurred about twenty years ago when, not having enough money to wire home for my return fare, I was stranded with a small touring company in Chetopa, Kansas. I wished to leave that beautiful city as fast as the inventions of mankind would permit me. But alas! I lacked sufficient money with which to buy a postage stamp, let alone railroad fare, so I went to the telegraph office to send a message "collect at the other end". After a long conversation with one of the clerks or operators, he accepted my wire, and I sat down to wait for an answer from "Home, Sweet, Home".

While I was waiting, an old man walked into the office and handed in a message, paid for it, and left the office. No sooner was he gone than the operator called me to him and said, "Here, you magician, tell me what this means."

I shall never forget the message; it was of such a nature that it is almost impossible to forget it. The operator looked at me with a smile and said that he would send the message and then allow me to study it while I waited for my answer.

I was in that office at least five hours, and to that wait I am indebted for my ability today to read almost any cipher or secret writing that is handed to me. I have made quite a study of this art, and often it has been the means of giving me a friendly warning or clever hint to look out for myself.

The message that I studied in that grim telegraph station was written as follows:

"XNTQLZCXHM FOKDZRDQDS TQMZRJGDQ SNEN QFHUDE ZSGDQ."

I managed, after some worry, to solve the message, and very few things in after life gave me as much pleasure as did the unraveling of that code. I noticed that by putting one letter for another, I eventually spelled the entire message, which read as follows: "Your ma dying; please return; ask her to forgive. Father."

The telegraph operator seemed to think that this was a great feat, and even while we talked about it the answer arrived:
"BZTFGSDWOQ DRRZQQHUDMNN MXNTQKHSSKD ZKHBD."

Which reads: "Caught express; arrive noon. Your little Alice." This is a very simple cipher, and all there is to it is to alter the alphabet, and instead of writing the letter required, simply write the letter in front of it. For instance, if writing the word "yes", according to your code, you will have to write "XDR". Note: It is necessary to use "Z" for the letter "A".

This was my debut as a cypher-ist. Since then I have picked up the newspapers and have never failed to read any and all cyphers printed in the personal columns. Sometimes, I have in a joking manner answered their cypher and signed myself "Roger Bacon", as he was the first I know of to make use of this method of varying the alphabet.

A brief narrative of cryptography may not be out of place. The word cryptography is derived from the Greek. There seem to be two words used, *kryptos* and *graphein*, the first meaning "something that is concealed or hidden"; the second meaning, in plain English, "to write". Both together naturally mean to be able to communicate with others in a secret manner which to the uninitiated means nothing, but to the initiated, has all kinds of meaning.

Our second sight artists were the first to utilize the code or cipher for exhibitions. They had secret signs, movements, and questions in which they conveyed their answers or information to the medium. Horse, dog, and animal trainers train their troupes with signs that to the public are almost imperceptible. I know of several cases where the animal is so well trained that no man has ever been able to catch the trainer in their movements. Mazeppa, an American horse, while in England, was supposed to be a wonderful mathematician, and it was published that the horse was once known to have studied arithmetic. Maguire, the trainer, was formerly an expert accountant and had several peculiar signs for his horse that he could give either behind the animal or at the side. From what I can learn, a horse has wonderful eyesight; he can see in back of himself quite a distance. I don't mean looking backward, but from the position of his eyes, he manages to see quite a good deal of what is going on behind him.

Der Kluge Hans, a horse trained in Germany by some very well known gentlemen, fooled the learned professors a long time, and it was only through a certain Baumeister, who was a friend of Herr Dir---- of the Circus in Berlin, that the horse was exposed. This man had the horse trained in such an acute manner that his method was never discovered. He must have had his groom in the secret, for the horse would answer all questions correctly, but I think the groom gave Der Kluge Hans the signals. It created the biggest sensation that has ever taken place in Germany in the animal world.

This is how the trick was exposed: Baumeister came to the exhibition and wanted the horse to tell him the time. Now as it was claimed that the horse could tell it himself, the owner would look to see if the horse was correct. But this time, the owner was not allowed to look at the watch, nor was any one else, and Der Kluge Hans stood there Der Dumme Hans. This led to an argument, and Baumeister was asked in a manner more forcible than elegant, to vacate the building, which he did. The incident proved the Waterloo of the horse as well as the owner.

Dogs are trained to obey at the snapping of the finger nails one against the other, and I have an old bill where a goose and pig play a game of cards together, and the goose always beats the pig.

SCYTALA LACONIAS

But I wander from my subject. Roger Bacon thought so much of cryptography that he classed it under the name of cyphers as a part of grammar. The Lacedemonians, according to Plutarch, had a method in which a round stick is made use of. John Baptiste Porta (1658) also described this method, so I will show the reader just what there is in it. This method is sometimes attributed to Archimedes but as to that, I am in no position to argue one way or the other. For this system, you must obtain two round sticks, one being in your possession and the other in the possession of the person to whom you wish to send your message. A long and narrow strip of paper, say ticker tape, must be wrapped or rolled spirally across your stick or cylinder. Now write your message right across the strips as is shown in the accompanying illustration. When unrolled, the slips of paper seem to signify nothing. These wooden sticks are known as Scytala Laconias.

SCYTALA LACONIAS CYPHER.

CHECKER BOARD CIPHER

The method of using numbered squares is sometimes called the checker board system, and with this method, you can arrange almost any code in the world, using any article, places, or characters, as you simply use the checker board as your guide, and arrange everything accordingly.

It is possible to hold a conversation by knocks on the walls of cells, but in America, where they seldom have solid walls in prisons or station houses, it is sometimes used by holding up figures and spelling out the words, although the deaf and dumb alphabet is far better, but harder to learn. I mean by that, it can't be·learned the first lesson while with a chart, this checker board is a very easy matter. Criminals have their own hieroglyphics, in fact you will find secret signs and marks in almost every path of life.

Although you can find a great many ways and means of deciphering secret codes, the most reliable rules and those that will enable you to read any of the common cyphers used in the English language, are as follows: First find out which letter, number, or character is used most frequently, which you can set down as being one of the vowels. The letter "e" is used more than any other letter. The vowel used the least is the letter "u". You can also place "y" with your vowels as that letter will be certain of being used many times and often will denote the end of a word.

In the words of three letters, there are most commonly two consonants, such as: the, and, not, but, yet, for, why, all, you, she, his, her, our, who, may, can, did, was, are, has, had, let, one, two, six, ten, etc.

The most common words of four letters are: this, that, then, with, when, from, here, some, most, none, they, them, whom, mine, your, must, will, have, been, were, four, five, nine, etc.

The most usual words of five letters are: there, these, those, which, while, since, their, shall, might, could, would, ought, three, seven, eight, etc.

Words of two or more syllables frequently begin with two consonants or with a prefix, that is, a vowel joined with one or two consonants. The most common double consonants are: bl, br, dr, fl, fr, gl, ph, pl, sh, sp, st, th, tr, wh, wr, etc., and the most common prefixes are: com, con, de, dif, ex, im, in, int, mis, par, pre, pro, re, sub, sup, un, etc. The two consonants most frequently used at the ends of long words are: ck, ld, lf, mn, nd, ng, rl, rm, rn, rp, rt, sm, st, xt, etc., while the commonest terminations are: ed, en, et, es, er, ing, ly, son, sion, tion, able, ence, ent, ment, full, less, ness, etc.

The vowels that are used most frequently together are "ea" and "ou". The most common consonant at the ends of words is "s", and next in use will be "r" and "t".

Any time two similar characters come together, they are most likely to be the consonants "f", "l", or "s", or the vowels "e" or "o". The letter that preceeds or follows two similar characters is either a vowel or "l", "m", "n", or "r". In deciphering, begin with the words that consist of a single letter, which will be either "a", "i" or "o". Then take the words of two letters, one of which will be a vowel. Of these words, the most frequent are: an, to, be, by, of, on, or, no, so, as, at, if, in, it, he, me, my, us, we, and am.

In making use of a cypher, it must be understood that the longer the message is, the easier it is to decipher. And the message should be written without any space with all the letters close together. This will make it much more difficult to decipher.

To give you an idea of how important the letter "e" is in all writings, the following inscription over the Decalogue in a country church runs as follows:

PRSRVYPRFCTMNVRKPTHSPRCPTSTN.

It is stated that this was not read in over two hundred years, but if you will insert the letter "e" in a good many spaces, you will be able to read, "Preserve, ye perfect men; ever keep these precepts ten."

Merchants use words of ten letters for their trade or secret marks, but they are very simple to read. All you have to do is to get the worth of their prices for a few of their articles, and before you have 6 figures, you can read the rest as easily as the merchant or clerks themselves. Some of the words that I have known to be in actual use are French lady, with lucky, fish-market, etc.

It is as well to say here that the methods shown in my articles are not by any means a complete compilation. I have only col-lected some of the best methods and trust that it will repay the reader to study one or the other, as you can never tell when it may come in handy to give your friend or assistant some secret sign or gesture which your enemy will not understand. Some future day, I shall publish all the silent codes that I have met and those that are being made use of by second sight artists, but for the present moment, I trust this effort will suffice.

JOAQUIN MARIA ARGAMASILLA
THE SPANIARD WITH X-RAY EYES

This phenomenal mystifier essayed to perform or accomplish the impossible; he makes claim to a power of supernormal vision, X-Ray eyes and a penetrating brain; however, his claim to super-natural power was acknowledged as being limited, seemingly not familiar with the English language. He is always accompanied by his promoter who serves in capacity of interpreter.

This promoter presented Argamasilla as a youth of nineteen, his appearance and mannerism indicates a more mature personality As credentials, this young man brought letters purporting to have been written by the Nobel prize winner, Prof. Richet, and from Prof. Geley; likewise, from noted scientists of Spain who attested the fact that Argamasilla, unqualifiedly, came through all tests and that he had proved conclusively to their satisfaction *that he could read through metal.*

It was claimed the Spaniard, with his X-Ray eyes, could penetrate metal *provided it was unpainted.* Giving precedence to gold — and in sequence, silver, copper, zinc, tin and iron. His most popular test was the reading through the hunting case of a watch, the hands of which having been set at random just before the watch was placed in his hands; and that is just what, seemingly, he did, to the amazement of scientific onlookers — and this youth's handling of the watch was so innocently done as to ward off suspicion.

As in the case, always, with the first presentation of such unnatural things, a weird, uncanny impression is made on the mind of the lay investigator; having been thrown off guard by the art of misdirection he is susceptible to the superstitious element lurking in the minds of the assembled gathering — there is infection to existing superstition, particularly so when logical deduction seems foreign to the production.

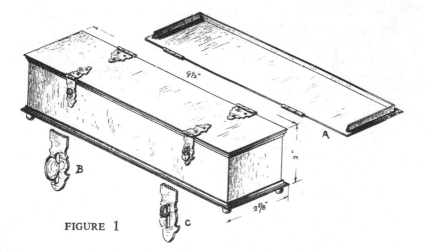

FIGURE 1

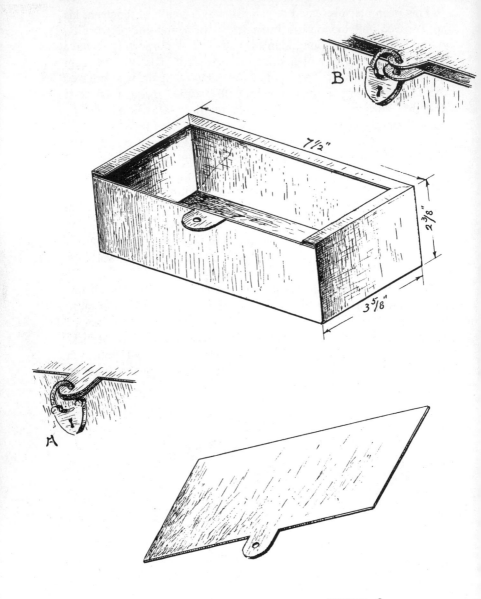

FIGURE 2

Aside from reading through the closed hunting case of a watch this Spaniard lays claim to visually penetrating metal when in the form of a box. It is true the box must be of convenient form and unpainted. Argamasilla carries two types of boxes, one made of solid silver, represented by illustration, Fig. 1, the top or lid of which is hinged to back wall and secured at front by two hinged hasps, but it will be noticed that one of these hasps is engaged by a *turn buckle,* "B," while the other one is fitted to a projecting *staple* "C," to accommodate a small padlock. The underside of lid "A" is provided with a flange at the two ends and along the entire length of the front edge, and this flange serves to intensify the mystery, as it apparently renders surreptitious opening, revealing a view of interior, impossible.

The other type of box is represented by Fig. 2, three walls of which are crowned with horizontal flanges in conjunction with lug strips on each end wall under flanges, constitutes a runway for a sliding lid.

The front wall is minus such flange, but, centrally situated, it has a flange lug bent at right angles and projecting upward. The sliding lid has a similar lug and both are pierced to accommodate a small padlock.

This box is of sheet iron, or *steel,* and since the visual performance is supposed to take place as result of penetration through the metallic lid, to demonstrate economically, the one box is made to serve the purpose with lids of copper, zinc, tin and iron.

The watch; any hunting case watch borrowed from a spectator serves the purpose. There is no special preparation to make; it is only necessary that the hands be so shifted as to disguise the correct time and to prove the genuineness of the reading. So, the Spaniard's method of procedure is simply to ask for a hunting case watch, with request that the setting of the hands be done optionally with the holder; while this is being done, he proceeds to blindfold his own eyes with his own handkerchief which has been already prepared by folding, and as this lies across his left hand he adjusts two wads of cotton batting, ostensibly, pads for each eye, and at once applies the bandage to his eyes and ties it at back of his head. He is now ready to receive the watch in right hand, face up but case closed. He disclaims power to look through the works of a watch, therefore, logically requires the face to be on the uppermost side. He receives the watch, holds it gingerly in a horizontal position between the index finger and thumb for a moment or two. He then raises the hand with watch between the same fingers, to such position that watch is vertical and at a height about to his chin. After a moment he lowers the hand with a sweep, and in so doing lowers the watch to a horizontal position in the palm of hand with the stem head resting against the ball or root of thumb, and hinge of case against ring and second fingers, simultaneously he exerts sufficient pressure by ball of thumb to spring case open which is covered and guarded by the flexed fingers. The watch case is opened but a trifle, perhaps one-half to three-quarters of an inch, and a quick glance is all sufficient for the reading, and this is made possible, as watch is held so low that a downward glance on line of cheeks, beneath handkerchief, gives a perfect line of vision, this is facilitated by the cotton pads previously referred to, which when applied, rest on the brows, rather than directly over the eyes, also by "knitting the brow" and raising again, rides the handkerchief up and opens a line of vision, in which case the watch is seen with the greatest ease.

I have seen this man place his left hand to his forehead and by so doing almost imperceptibly raise the handkerchief to improve his downward line of vision.

A glance having been gotten at watch, and time noted, pressure by ball of thumb at same time, fingers press lid closed, by this combined movement the watch is noiselessly closed, and this accomplished, the watch is again raised vertically before the eyes and manoeuvered back and forth as though endeavoring to get it to a certain focus. As the watch is raised to the last position, it is caused to lie flat on the open palm that it may be visibly observed to be closed. This whole manoeuver is so natural that suspicion is warded off and the back of hand toward observers forms a perfect screen when watch case is open.

This last manoeuver is simply acting, and during time consumed by it the Spaniard makes mental calculation for the *lapse* of time, and so, seemingly tells the time as he sees (?) it just a moment before it is opened for comparison. For example, if the exact time is twenty-two minutes to ten at the moment he actually sees the face of watch, he stalls by manoeuvering and at the psychological moment declares the time as twenty minutes to ten, and though he might be thirty seconds out of the way, it is not of sufficient importance to note.

A personal trial of this experiment will convince the reader of the ease with which it can be accomplished.

I have had several sittings with Argamasilla, and at one of them I handed him a watch which was itself tricky to open, consequently, he failed to tell the time by that watch. At another time, at the Newspaper Feature Syndicate office, 241 West 58th Street, I had opportunity for standing at his extreme left side and from that position *I positively saw him open and close the watch.* Of course, he did not know of my vantage point, because of his blindfold, as I looked over his left shoulder.

It is a rule with this man, to stand back in a corner close to a window, for the beneficial play of light, also that no one of the

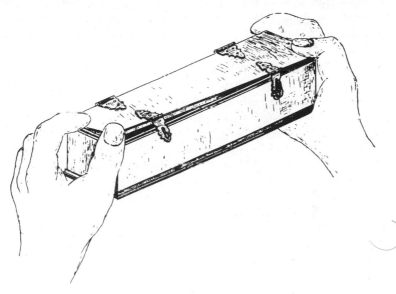

FIGURE 3

observers may get behind him, but my favorable opportunity clinched my suspicion.

This man is a very clever manipulator, and he acts his part in such manner as to insure misdirection.

Since witnessing his performance I have presented the watch trick and so far no one has been able to detect the movement unless knowing, before-hand, the trick of opening and closing the watch.

The handling of the boxes varies considerably from that of the watch — but that too, will be made clear by accompanying illustrations.

Giving first, attention to the silver box: A printed card or small slip of paper with writing, placed in box, lid closed and locked with one small padlock and the second hasp secured by the turn buckle. The operator holds the closed box by a hand clinching each end and in his manoeuvering twisting and slightly swinging the box from side to side, he manages to drop the left hand and by aid of the thumb lifts up the lid at the left corner, see Figure 3. Just before raising lid and during manipulation he manages to release turn buckle so hasp slips free.

The right hand is so placed as to expose that end of box, at times by merely balancing box on finger ends. A firmer grip when required, is obtained as shown in Figure 3. In course of manoeuvering, the card is brought to a favorable position for reading by successive joltings of box, the left end being lowered and turned away from observers. The fact that box is opened is unobserved by them.

The view shown in Figure 3, is as seen by the operator himself. The audience, or observers, see the back of box and its end only as held or poised on fingers of right hand. The box is also held at such an angle that the observers do not get a view of top of it.

It should be noted that Argamasilla always chooses a position with light behind himself, and such that observers are always *in front*, facing him. He very adroitly guards against observers being at his side or behind himself.

The box with sliding lid is handled differently, necessarily so, because of its particular form of construction. The casual observer on first examination, being unfamiliar with the mode of handling is unprepared for a critical examination, consequently he does not notice that the metal of lid is quite flexible, and that the running

grooves at ends of box are so free as to afford sufficient play by
raising the lid — just a trifle, but *"every little helps."*

The runner flanges around three edges of lid, and projecting
lugs for attaching a padlock, would seem proof positive against
possibility of trick, but the innocent observer has failed to note the
fact that the bow, or shackle is elongated a trifle, perpendicularly.
It looks innocent enough when seen in its normal position (Fig.
2-A), but that innocence is soon dissipated when viewed as shown
at "B." This opening is made possible by the fact that the front
edge of the lid projects a fraction of an inch beyond the front wall
of box, which affords a purchase for the left thumb without resorting to pressure on the lugs. The flexibility of metal and slight play
in runners makes the opening possible. "B", Fig. 2, is slightly
erroneous in drawing, the horizontal edge could slant slightly downward both ways from the lug converging at the ends of box where
held by the running grooves.

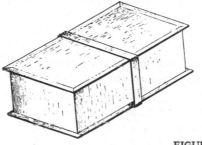

FIGURE 4

The box is held practically the same as the silver box, reading
of the card is made possible by variable deflection of both light
rays and visual beam, and by proper manipulation of angles the
eye has a range of practically the full bottom of box from front to
back walls; the card being kept in left hand corner of box. By
turning the box upside-down it is an easy matter to slide the card
out of box, enough for reading, and even at that it can be ob-
scured from observation by the on-looker by the angularity in
position of holding box.

Fig. 4, represents a Park & Tilford Nut and Fruit box made of tin; its lid has vertical flanges to fit into box on all but hinge side, and in lieu of a lock, the lid is held in place by an elastic band. This box is covered on all sides with colors from black to gold, the mass of color being black. Nevertheless ,and notwithstanding the ban Argamasilla puts on painted metal, he did accept this box for a test, and safely so, because a casual examination shows the lid

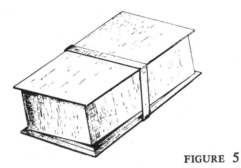

FIGURE 5

securely hinged, but the means of holding lid closed is so *elastic,* that the manipulation made necessary became identical with that for the silver box; however, Argamasilla took precaution to turn box upside down to facilitate reading as shown in Figure 5. Under these conditions the possibility of reading is made perfectly clear by Fig. 6 and by Fig. 7, which represent the silver box minus trimmings, drawing slightly exaggerated as to distance opened.

FIGURE 6   FIGURE 7

By successive joltings of box the card is sometimes brought to a vertical position against back of box, Figure 7.

Figures 8 and 9 are boxes made of tin, unpainted, for testing Argamasilla's power for reading through metal. The square box was wired with two strands of copper wire soldered to bottom of box and twisted on top. The round box was simply bolted shut by a clamp bolt passing through the vertical axis of box, soldered on underside of bottom, and lid locked in place by a thumb nut, and insomuchas there was no possible flexibility, to the lid of either box, Argamasilla failed by refusal to make a test in both instances, as undoubtedly, he would have done with all the other boxes, if subterfuges and trick appliances had not been resorted to.

FIGURE 8

FIGURE 9

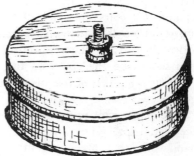

CHING LING FOO'S PAPER TRICK

Magicians have long connected Ching Ling Foo, the genuine Chinese magician, with the torn and restored paper trick. The trick now under discussion is a different paper trick entirely. It was performed by Harry Kellar and attributed by him to Ching Ling Foo. Kellar passed the secret along to Houdini.

The magician has a glass bowl which contains water. It is resting on a stand. Beside the bowl are sheets of tissue paper of different colors. The magician sets the stand to one side. He picks

up the sheets of paper and tears them into strips, constantly showing his hands empty. He lets some of the paper strips fall to the
floor. Finally, he gathers them all together and drops them into
the bowl of water. He shows his hands empty, takes out the wet
strips of paper and squeezes them. He holds the strips in his left
hand. He starts to draw them forth. They come out in the form
of a long strip of paper, composed of various colors. There are
many yards of the dry paper.

Now for the subtle secret. The restored paper is in the form
of a tight roll. The outside is pasted together. In the center is a
whisk of straw, which is attached to the end of the paper at the
center of the coil. This roll is previously dipped in melted parafine. The roll must be very tight so that the parafine will not
penetrate but will merely form a protective film. The prepared
roll of paper is placed on the floor behind the stand which supports the glass bowl.

The magician, walks to the stand and shows his hands empty.
He places his foot over the coil of paper so that it rests beneath
his instep. He sets the stand to the side and shows his hands
empty. He tears up strips of tissue paper. He lets some of the
strips fall to the floor. When he leans forward to pick up the
strips, he sweeps them toward his foot. He steps back a trifle
and scoops up the coil with the loose strips of paper. He wads
the coil with the strips of paper when he places them in the
glass bowl.

The paper coil remains dry. It is taken from the bowl with
the wet strips. They are squeezed and are retained in the right
hand when they are apparently transferred to the left. Only the
coil of paper goes into the left hand. The magician pulls the straw
in the center of the coil. The paper begins to unwind. It comes
out in a long strip. Meanwhile the magician disposes of the torn
pieces. He can do this as his hand sweeps downward, by dropping
the wet papers on a small shelf behind the stand. He can wait
until the coil is unwound, then drop the wet papers behind the
stand. Or he can give the massed coil of dry paper to an assistant,
handing him the wet papers under cover of the dry.

The really subtle part of this trick is the obtaining of the coil of paper. It is done in a natural manner and in a most unexpected way. Both the stand and the magician's body are free from suspicion. The paper strips must be taken from the floor, and the magician uses that movement as a perfect excuse for getting his coil. Houdini's notes state that Kellar kept the coil under his right foot.

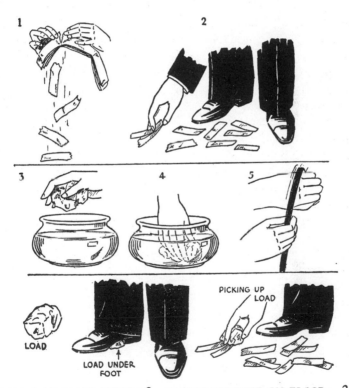

1. STRIPS OF PAPER TORN. 2. PAPERS DROPPED ON FLOOR. . 3-4. SOAKING PAPERS IN BOWL. 5. PRODUCTION OF DRY COIL. BOTTOM: HOW "LOAD" IS OBTAINED.

 HOUDINI ON THE RIGHT WAY
TO DO WRONG

During his early career, Houdini authored various articles on
subjects relevant to fraud and deception rather than magic. One
group of these appeared in a pamphlet which has since become a
collector's item and which carried the provocative title: "The Right
Way To Do Wrong."

This booklet was an exposé of crooks and their methods. Un-
questionably it created quite a stir at the time when it appeared.
In fact, there are rumors to the effect that petty crooks snatched
up all available copies rather than have their ways laid bare to
the public and that this accounts for the pamphlet's rarity today.

There is some truth to that claim, although its exaggeration is
equally likely. However, Houdini's comments represent an interesting cross-section of the picaresque aspects of the American
scene as it existed in the early 1900's. Even the dated descriptions and the language used carry the flavor of the period, recom-
mending it all the more to those who are interested in the subjects
that the booklet covers.

As a sidelight on Houdini's own career, "The Right Way To
Do Wrong" emphasizes how thoroughly he studied all ways and
means of trickery, whether fair or crooked, in an effort to improve
his own status as a mystifier. It also shows how conscious he
was of his duty, as a public service, to expose all frauds that came
within his ken.

In his own work, particularly the jail breaking phase, Houdini
recognized that any adverse publicity might lead to the erroneous
impression that he was at odds with the law. This was one reason
why he was so jealous toward imitators and rivals who might
in some way upset the delicate status of the escape artist's
profession.

So there is reason to believe that Houdini's publication of "The Right Way To Do Wrong" was a preventive measure, or at least an anticipation of the day when some doubt might be directed toward his own integrity. His ability at such a time to produce copies of a pamphlet in which he had denounced questionable characters would certainly have stood him in good stead in the upholding of his name.

Whatever the ultimate purpose or value of this almost forgotten booklet, the material itself is of unusual interest, and that is why a selection of its more intriguing chapters has been included in this volume.

WBG

CHEATING UNCLE SAM

Under this heading, I shall group such crimes as counterfeiting and the kindred crimes of forgery and raising notes, as well as smuggling. It is a serious matter to get into trouble with the Federal government. The criminal is pursued relentlessly, and the sentence, when conviction follows the almost certain arrest, is always a heavy one. For these reasons, such crimes are usually attempted only by the boldest and most skillful criminals or by those whose positions of trust in the government employ afford them special opportunities.

The three greatest crimes against any government (outside, of course, of actual treason) are counterfeiting its money, gold, silver, or bills; evading its custom laws, and smuggling. Counterfeiting, which offers enormous rewards if successful, is frequently attempted — indeed, scarcely a month passes that does not see the appearance of some new and dangerous counterfeit of some United States bill. Notice is at once sent to all the banks by the authorities and often published in the newspapers, so that the public at large may be warned against the spurious bill in circulation.

Many years ago, when the art of engraving and plate making was in its infancy, the paper money in circulation was much more crude than today. Then it was comparatively easy for the counterfeiter to engrave just as good a bill as the government could produce, but now the matter is much more difficult, owing to the delicate and intricate work of the lathe and tool work and the special fibre paper upon which it is printed. The conditions of caution surrounding the government printing works make it almost impossible for an original plate to be stolen. The paper is made especially for this purpose and under strictest government supervision. In designing, lettering, and engraving the bills, only artists of the foremost professional standing are employed. Every bank note or greenback is truly a work of art, so that an exact counterfeit — one that will deceive even an ordinary business man accustomed to handling money — is each year more and more difficult to produce.

The counterfeits of silver and gold coins are mostly of two kinds — either moulded or stamped with a die. The die-made counterfeits are usually much more difficult to detect if the metal employed has anywhere near the right weight, ring, and color. Electroplating is employed by counterfeiters with some success. One dangerous counterfeit now in circulation is a compound of antimony and lead heavily electroplated with silver. In this way the gold ten-dollar piece of 1858 and the gold five-dollar pieces of 1847, 1848, 1862, and 1869 have been counterfeited with a platinum coin heavily gold plated. The most sucessful, and therefore the most dangerous, of all counterfeits are those composed of actual gold and silver but with a mixture of metal. The actual value of the gold in the counterfeit five-dollar gold pieces dated 1881 and 1882 has been determined by assay to be $4.43. [This was in 1906 — *Ed.*]

Genuine gold and silver coins are often tampered with. These schemes are known as "sweating", "plugging", and "filling". For instance, a hundred gold ten-dollar pieces subject to an acid bath would lose perhaps $35 or $40 of their gold and remain unchanged in appearance. The coins are put into circulation again, and the gold which has been "sweated" off of them is easily extracted from the acid bath and sold. Coins are also robbed of precious metal by drilling a hole, the cavity being filled with an alloy and the filling covered with a light gold wash. "Filling" a coin is sawing it through the edge in two parts, scraping out the gold, and putting the two parts together again filled with some baser metal.

Thomas Ballard was the first counterfeiter to reproduce government fibre paper successfully, which he did in 1870. The next year he and his gang were captured but escaped from jail and found a hiding-place from which they continued to issue dangerous counterfeits. In 1873, his counterfeit $500 treasury note alarmed banks and government officials. Ballard was finally captured in his lair in Buffalo just as he was about to produce a counterfeit $5 bill of a Canadian bank. This bill, he boasted, was to have corrupted all Canada.

John Peter McCartney was the counterfeiter who successfully removed all the ink from genuine $1 bills so that he could secure government paper on which to print counterfeit bills of much higher denominations. He made a fortune, so it is said, but was brought to book at last.

To a counterfeiter named "One-eyed Thompson" is given the credit for being the first to transform bills of small denominations to larger by cutting and pasting. He also had an ingenious trick of cutting up $10 or $100 bills into strips and making eleven counterfeit bills of the same denomination.

A German by the name of Charles Ulrich won the distinction of having produced the most dangerous Bank of England notes ever made.

Langdon W. Moore, one time expert bank robber, forger, and counterfeiter, who has now reformed and is leading an honest life, has written an interesting autobiography in which he tells of his own experience in raising notes, counterfeiting, and getting the counterfeits in circulation. At one time, another gang of counterfeiters declared war on him. He sent a spy into the enemy's camp, learned where they were going to put out their next batch of "queer", and then proceeded to carry out a plan for outwitting them.

Postage stamp counterfeits are common enough but mostly practiced to impose on the collectors of rare stamps; for instance, a certain issue of Hawaiian stamps are very valuable as there are not supposed to be more than half a dozen or so in existence. When one is found, it sells for thousands of dollars. One of the most daring stamp counterfeiters "planted" about twenty forgeries of this rare stamp into collections of wealthy philatelists and realized many thousands of dollars.

Another daring gang introduced a beautifully engraved stamp into Paris by posing as the "King of Sodang" and his suite — Sodang being an island that existed only in the imagination of the clever swindler. A stamp dealer was the principal victim and paid the "king" a large sum of money for a number of the stamps of this fictitious kingdom.

Speaking of stamps recalls a method of secret writing which defied detection. The plan was to put a fake letter inside the envelope but to write the real message in microscopic characters in the upper right-hand corner, and over this to paste the stamp. The correspondent who was, of course, in the secret, would simply soak off the stamp.

This trick is often made use of by convicts who wish to send a secret message to their friends on the outside.

MESSAGE UNDER POSTAGE STAMP.

Cancelled postage stamps are frequently washed and sold or used again. I have in my possession a receipt given me by a Russian convict which will do this perfectly, removing every trace of the cancellation mark but leaving the stamp perfect. Such a secret is too dangerous, however, for general publication.

On the continent, I have known of a clever dodge being practiced which reaches the same result. Before the letter is mailed, the stamp is covered with a transparent paste. When the letter is received, the correspondent can simply wash off the stamp with water, and, of course, the cancellation marks with it. The penalty for this crime is so severe and the reward so small that not even hardened criminals are willing to risk the attempt.

A clever gang of smugglers adopted this ruse in order to get their trunks through the custom-house free. They had counterfeit labels made, such as an inspector places upon a trunk. Passing among the trunks where the inspectors were at work, they would slyly poke the "inspected" labels on all their own trunks. Each official seeing the labels would suppose some other official had actually inspected the trunks and so would pass on to others.

Instances might be multiplied, but all goes to show that dishonesty, whether to your fellow men or to the government, is the worst of all policies in the end.

TRICKS OF BUNCO MEN

Something for nothing has ever tempted the simple and unsophisticated; indeed, it is a trait of human nature upon which the swindler everywhere, and in all ages, has relied for his profit.

The term "bunco" comes from an old English game of chance in which a checkered cloth covered with numbers and stars is covered with a hood called a "bunco". The game was to throw dice which counted up to a certain concealed number. The man who knew the game was called the "bunco man", or the banker, and later, when this form of swindle became notorious, the term was corrupted into "bunco". Today, the word is used to denote almost any swindle where the victim is made to believe he is to receive a large sum of money or valuables and then gets nothing at all.

The real Simon Pure Bunco Game, as practiced in the United States some years ago by Tom O'Brien, the King of Bunco Men, was played as follows: The victim, some wealthy farmer usually, was lured to a room at a hotel and a game was proposed. A confederate took the part of another player. A pack of forty-eight cards in eight sets, each set numbered from one to six was produced, shuffled, and dealt out, eight cards to each player. The total sum of the numbers in each hand was then compared with the number carrying a prize on the chart. If it corresponded, the hand won the prize.

The cards were gravely counted and compared. The dealer then said to the confederate and the dupe, "Gentlemen, you have drawn the grand conditional advertising prize. You're entitled to $10,000 apiece on condition that you prove yourself worth $50,000 and promise to advertise our battery whether you win or lose. You will have to put up $10,000 apiece against the prize; then you draw once more. If you draw a star number, you get only the $10,000 prize and your money back. If you draw any other number, you get its prize added to your own money and the big prize."

The confederate says he is worth more than $50,000 and declares his intention of going and getting the $10,000 stake. The dupe is also persuaded to put up the cash, and both winners go away to get the money. They return, and the money is put up. Four cards are dealt each. The total of each hand is twenty-eight. "Why, gentlemen," says the bunco man in apparent surprise, "twenty-eight is the 'State number', the total blank! You have lost all."

The confederate pretends to be very much broken up, commiserates with his "fellow victim", and gets him out of the room as soon as he can. In a few moments, he gives the farmer the slip, joins his partner, and they escape from town as quickly as possible.

Such is the principle of the bunco game, and it is worked under many guises with cards, dice, at the pool or billiard table — our poolroom bunco is known as "selling the lemon", as bets are made on the yellow ball — but always with the idea of making the victim believe he is going to get something for nothing.

A variation of the bunco game, often played in the farming districts, is for a well-dressed, plausible man to drive up to a well-to-do farmer's home and inquire if he knows of a good farm for sale. If he does, he is invited to drive with the stranger to take a look at it and give his advice. The farmer finds his new acquaintance bright and entertaining. The property is reached, and the sharper, with apparent satisfaction, inspects the land and buildings and closes a bargain without much haggling. In the course of the conversation, the man from the city flashes a big roll of bank notes of high denominations and the farmer is duly impressed.

As they drive homeward, a confederate will appear who stops the carriage to make some inquiry. The three enter into conversation, and good-natured chaffing leads up to a proposal of some game of cards or bet. The farmer is induced to take a hand, the first swindler offering to put up his half of the stake. When the two "partners" — the farmer and the first swindler — have won a large sum, the loser asks for proof of their ability to make good their stake. The first swindler produces the cash, and the farmer drives with him to the next town to draw his money out of the bank to make good his claim.

Now comes the rapid denouement. The first swindler asks the farmer to oblige him by taking charge of all the money, including the money with which he is to buy the farm, until he can return and close the bargain. The country man, naturally pleased at this confidence, is induced to put his own money in the same convenient tin box which the stranger has ready. At that point, the stranger and the farmer part. The former, to parts unknown; the latter, with his precious tin box under his arm. When he gets home, he finds, instead of money, that the box is filled only with heavy folded paper to give it the same weight. A rapid shift has been made before his eyes without his detecting it; his money is gone, and two adroit scoundrels are far away.

Among the most famous (or infamous) bunco men of this country are Tom O'Brien, mentioned above, William Raymond, "Doc" Mincheon, George Post, William Barrocks, Lewis Ludlow, and Clay Wilson. O'Brien is serving a life sentence for murder, but Post is supposed to be still at his old tricks.

Jacob Sindheim, alias "Al" Wise, has a star game. His lay is to persuade a gullible person that he has a secret process by means of which genuine gold coins can be "sweated" or robbed

An excellent likeness of Houdini, as he appeared during the later years of his career.

Houdini with his "two sweethearts", his mother and his wife. Houdini's love and devotion toward his family formed striking evidence of the finer side of his aggressive and challenging nature.

From the John J. McManus Collection.

of a portion of their gold by a certain solution without impairing their appearance. Several times, he has induced speculative indiviuals without conscience to construct tanks in the basements of their houses and to put in from $10,000 to $20,000 in gold pieces for treatment. Twenty days are to be required for the process. Before that time, he removes all the gold, which needless to say has not lost a grain of its weight, and makes his escape. The victim, after getting tired of waiting, opens the tank to find a liberal deposit of paving-stones instead of gold coins. Then he wakes up.

If men did not try and get something for nothing, they might often be able to retain what they have.

One of the latest dodges of a bunco nature is a bogus express company which caters to those who never receive packages by express, but who want to. In a large room above its showy office, a force of skilled workmen is employed manufacturing bundles and filling them with old bricks and newspapers.

The express company, having made up a convincing looking parcel, sends out a postcard to its prospective victim on which it says:

Mr. E. Z. Mark Steiner, 398 Jay Street:
Please furnish us with your address as there is a package addressed to you at our office.

COMEANDGO EXPRESS CO.

The fact that the express company has written to him at his address to ask him what his address is does not strike the victim as strange. The "company" does it in order that it may get in writing a request from Mr. Steiner to deliver the package, thus making him its debtor to the extent of the "express charges", usually $2.

THIEVES AND THEIR TRICKS

A thief is one who appropriates any kind of property or money to his own use wtihout the consent of the owner. As distinguished from a burglar, a thief does not break into a house or enter in the night time, but takes his plunder wherever he can find it. A thief may gain entrance into a house and steal a valuable diamond, but he uses his sharp wits to pass the door instead of the burglar's jimmy and skeleton keys.

There are thieves of various kinds, from the common sneak thief and shoplifter to the expert pickpocket and clever swindler who sometimes makes hauls amounting to many thousands of dollars. The use of the word "thief", however, is generally confined to such classes of criminals as shoplifters, pickpockets, and the like. Overcoat thieves ply their trade in the residential sections of the city. They will sometimes ring the front doorbell and ask for the master or mistress of the house, giving some plausible pretext and usually the name of the party living there. While the servant has gone to tell the mistress about the caller, he quietly picks up what garments are in sight on the hat-rack and makes off with them.

The Venetian blind thief got his name from the practice of the English thieves of making the pretense that they had come to repair the blinds of the house. A thief will call at the door claiming to be a mechanic to look over the house for necessary repairs, and in his rounds will gather up any valuable article that he can lay his hands on. This class of rascal even impersonates the plumber or gas inspector with equally successful results.

Thieves at church are a very common occurrence. A case was related in London not long ago about a chapel that had been furnished with one hundred new Bibles. They were first used at the afternoon service, and when the congregation gathered for evening, they had all disappeared.

A very common experience of church officers is to find that books disappear gradually; not only books, but hassocks and cushions are taken from houses of worship. Petty robberies from the collection box are not infrequent. In some localities, the custom of covering one's hand, so that other worshipper may not see the amount given, gives the thief his opportunity, for in the rapid passing of the plate, it is easy for the skillful professional thief to put in a penny and at the same moment to take out a dollar. This is sometimes done by a sticky substance put on a single finger. Umbrella thieves and pickpockets also ply their trade in churches as well as in other places of public gathering.

How can you detect a church thief is a question I have often asked detectives. There seems to be no real answer, but, as a general rule, it is just as well to look out for your property as carefully when you are in church as when you are out.

Thieves as Wedding Guests. There is scarcely a fashionable wedding, where the contracting parties are wealthy, that does not suffer from the presence of wedding thieves. For this reason, the more expensive items of jewelry are often imitated in paste before they are put on exhibition among the gifts while the originals are sent to the bank. The wedding-gift lifter works his game as follows: Disguised as a tradesman or assistant, he gains the confidence of the servants, gets a description of the diamond tiara, or other article of great value, of which he has then made a duplicate, set with imitation diamonds. He will even go as far as to pay $15 to $100 for a good imitation article. Armed with this and perfectly dressed, he makes his way among the party of guests and finds it no risk adroitly to change the counterfeit for the genuine jewel.

Trick of the Van Thief. Vans that are covered entirely with tarpaulin or canvas and have a loose back present opportunities to the van thief. A favorite trick is for the thief to wheel a hand cart covered with sacking, under which a confederate lies concealed, behind one of the vans. The confederate quickly puts the upper part of his body inside the van, his feet remaining in the cart. Being concealed from view by the loose tarpaulin, he seizes

THE VAN THIEF AT WORK.

a package and drops back with it into the cart, which is pushed off at once. A wet day is preferred for this trick as then not so many people are about, and the driver is apt to be holding his head down as a protection from the rain, in consequence of which, he will not look behind.

The Trick Satchel Thieves. It is when the dark days come around that the railway station thief most safely conducts his operations. The summer tourist he loves not, for his luggage contains few valuables, and there is then too much light about. A dull afternoon and well-to-do people getting off the train are what the platform prowler asks for. And here is shown as a warning, if need be, an artful appliance that station thieves have used of late. It looks like an ordinary portmanteau; and so it is, with a difference. It is a specially made portmanteau, the bottom of which closes up when pressure is applied. Thus, as shown in the illustration, when the "trick" portmanteau is placed over a smaller one that lies upon the platform, the larger one comes down as a cover over it. By a movement of the thumb of the hand that holds the portmanteau handle, powerful springs are released which tightly grasp the portmanteau that is inside, and it can thus be carried away completely enveloped.

THE TRICK SATCHEL.

If, therefore, you see a suspicious looking character hanging about, don't set him down as a genuine passenger just because he has a bag.

Diamond in a Chew of Gum. One of the cleverest and most unscrupulous diamond thieves I ever heard of perfected a scheme for daylight robbery of unmounted gems which for a time simply defied detective of London and Paris. The game was played as follows:

A lady, well dressed and looking like a respectable and wealthy matron who might be the wife of a banker or large merchant, enters a jewelry store and asks to see some unmounted diamonds. The clerk shows her the stones, and while she is looking at them, a second lady equally respectable in appearance enters and approaches the same counter. She seems to be interested in diamonds. Suddenly, one of the most valuable gems is missing. The proprietor is summoned, the detectives rush in, and an officer is called. The women, who have declared their innocence, are carefully searched, but the diamond has absolutely disappeared. Eventually, both of the women are released, but the diamond is never recovered.

The way the trick was played was this:

One of the women (both of whom are members of the gang) deftly conceals the diamond in a piece of chewing gum and sticks it on the under side of the front edge of the counter. There it remains safely hidden away while the frantic search is going on. A third member of the gang slips in afterward with the crowd of curious and removes the gum containing the diamond and makes off with it.

PICKPOCKETS AT WORK

Among the most interesting classes of thieves is the pickpocket, whose clever subterfuges and skill of hand have been so often exploited in novel and story-book. Your professional pickpocket is naturally a rover and travels the country over, attending large gatherings. Of professional pickpockets, there are numerous types, each adapted to the class of "work" in which he engages.

It is the usual opinion that a pickpocket is a forbidding and suspicious looking fellow, but a glance at the rogues' gallery in any police headquarters will show you that they look much like ordinary individuals and are of more than average intelligence. The pickpocket is usually very well dressed and of prepossessing appearance. Those who seek to make only large hauls are entertaining talkers and easy in manner. They are generally self-possessed and, while dexterous, are very cautious in their operations.

It is needless to say that women make the most patient as well as the most dangerous pickpockets. It is simply amazing how quickly an expert pickpocket with a delicate touch, seemingly accidental, will locate the resting place of a well filled purse or any other article of value which he chooses to abstract. When once they discover it, they follow their intended victims until the proper opportunity comes. A common pickpocket trick is for the operator to carry a shawl or overcoat carelessly over the left arm and to take a seat on the right side of the person he intends to rob in a streetcar or other vehicle.

Sometimes, a small and very sharp knife is used to cut the side of the dress or trousers of the victim so that the purse may be abstracted without going into the pocket directly. Others of this light-fingered gentry wear light overcoats with large pockets removed. They will endeavor to stand near a person, preferably a woman, who is paying her fare and has displayed a well filled purse. The pickpocket then carelessly throws his coat over her dress, and by inserting his hand through the outside opening of his own pocket, quietly proceeds to abstract her purse. Pickpockets work alone, in pairs, or in what is called a mob. Most female pickpockets seem to prefer to work alone, sometimes, however, working in conjunction with a man thief to whom they pass their plunder and thus make detection impossible if they are suspected and searched.

The mob is a gang of expert pickpockets under the direction of a leader who has had experience and knows all the tricks. Their usual game it to frequent some crowded platform or a railway station and raise a row in which two men seem to engage in a scuffle or quarrel and come to blows. Others rush in attempting to separate them, and the attention of the whole crowd of people is for the moment directed strongly that way. At the same moment, other single light fingered members of the same gang crowd in with the citizens who are being jostled and abstract their pocketbooks and watches without any trouble. Recently, a gang has successfully worked in several of the subway stations in Boston, and the same gang has successfuly plied this vocation in New York, Chicago, and Philadelphia.

The false-arm game, or the "third mit", as it is known to the professional pickpocket, is said to be little employed in this country now. A loose cape overcoat is worn, in one of the sleeves of which a false arm and hand are fixed. Thus a detective who may be watching the pickpocket will apparently see both of his hands in view while in reality, the light skillful fingers of the operator's left hand are going through the pockets of the man beside whom he is standing. This dodge is very much employed by shoplifters on the continent.

One of the many fertile dodges by which a pickpocket escapes detection is known as the "horse-dodge". The thief arranges it so as to meet his victim by the side of a horse standing at the curbstone. He has previously located the watch or purse he wishes to lift, and with a quick blow, he knocks the victim's hat over his eyes, grabs the pocketbook or watch or whatever else he is after, and immediately darts under the horse and hides himself in the traffic on the other side. By the time the victim has got the use of his eyes and is able to look around, the thief has entirely disappeared. He would not be apt to look in the right direction at any rate.

In the outskirts of London, among the small shops, a rather unusual trick has been played frequently upon unsuspecting shopkeepers. Two men in earnest argument over some matter enter a small grocery store and approach the proprietor who is behind his till. One man says to the proprietor, "My friend and I have gotten into an argument over a peculiar matter which we believe you can settle for us. I have bet him that my hat," taking off an old-fashioned stove-pipe hat, "will hold more than four quarts of molasses while he contends that it will hold hardly three quarts. We are willing to buy the molasses if you will fill this hat and prove the question to decide the bet." The shopkeeper good-humoredly agrees and brings the hat brimful with sticky molasses, at which one of the thieves slaps it over the shopkeeper's head, and before he can extricate himself and call help, they have robbed the till and disappeared.

HUMBUGS

A humbug, or a hoax, is often comparatively harmless in its nature — more in the way of a high practical joke upon the public. Long ago, P. T. Barnum, the great American showman declared: "The American people want to be humbugged." I believe he was right, and certainly his great success in the show business would seem to point to the same conclusion. In my own particular work, I find that there is so much that is marvellous and wonderful that can be accomplished by perfectly natural means that I have no need to have recourse to humbugging the public. In my case, at least, truth is stranger than fiction.

At the present day, a firm in New York makes a business of manufacturing fakes such as double-bodied babies, mermaids, and fake mummies. Dr. L. D. Weiss, of New York, discovered that he could detect a fake mummy from an original by placing it under his X-ray machine.

Another clever hoax which created much amusement at the time was contrived by some English students years ago and perpetrated at a county fair. On a vacant lot near the fair, a large tent was erected, and a huge placard announced that "The Great Wusser" was on exhibition within — admission free! It was supposed that some payment or purchase would be required inside, but it was not so. The crowd, eager for free amusement, was formed into a long "queue", and the people — admitted only one at a time — were escorted through a maze of hurdles into a darkened compartment of the tent before a curtain. There they were entreated not to irritate or disturb the "animal" in any way, and the curtain went up, disclosing a sorry and spavined looking donkey.

"This is The Great Wusser," explained the showman, and when the bewildered spectator asked what it meant, he was told that, "though you may have seen as bad a donkey, you certainly never saw a wusser!" Then, when the victim of the hoax became indignant, he was besought to "keep it quiet" and take his revenge by allowing the remainder of the crowd to be hoaxed. This request showed a deep knowledge of human nature, for the victim always complied, and many went among the crowd to spread the most astonishing accounts of the "Great Wusser" and waited to see their comrades taken in. Eventually, however, rioting arose, and the jesters, being arrested for creating a disturbance, had to pay over $100 in fines and damages.

But humbugs are not all so harmless. An adroit rascal was caught not so long ago in London who was posing as an American bishop. He was certainly a great humbug, for he looked the part of the "bishop" to perfection. It seems that he called in his carriage, mind, you, at a well known jewelers and asked to see some bracelets, mentioning that he was returning to America and wished to take a present to his wife. "Nothing very expensive," he said, "I could not afford that — but something about seventy or eighty pounds.". Eventually, he agreed to take a bracelet that cost one hundred pounds. He said he would pay for it with a hundred pound note he had with him at the moment, but he would wait while they sent it to the bank to ascertain that it was all right. He should really prefer doing this. They sent it to the bank and received an answer that it was perfectly correct.

Having paid for his bracelet, the bishop took it and was just about to step into his carriage when a policeman tapped him on the shoulder and said, "Hello Jim! You're up to your old tricks again, are you? You just come along with me," and he took him back into the shop.

The jeweler said there was some mistake, that the gentleman was an American bishop, that he had bought a bracelet, and that he paid for it with an excellent note.

"Just let me look at the note, will you?" said the policeman. He looked at it and said, "Yes, it's just as I thought. This note is one of a particularly clever batch of forgeries which are very difficult to detect, and the man is no more a bishop than you are. We will go off to the police station at once. I will take the note and go on with the prisoner in advance, and you must send your salesman to me and meet us and bear witness." So the policeman took the bishop and the bracelet and the note, but when the jeweler's man reached the police station, they had not arrived, and they have never been heard of since!

Harry Houdini

SELECTIVE BIBLIOGRAPHY

Cannell, J. C. *The Secrets of Houdini.* Hutchinson & Co. Ltd., London. (Second impression) 1932.

Dunninger, Joseph. *Houdini's Spirit Exposés from Houdini's Own Manuscripts, Records and Photographs and Dunninger's Psychical Investigations,* edited by Joseph H. Kraus. Experimenter Publishing Co., Inc. New York. 1928.

Ernst, Bernard M. L. and Hereward Carrington. *Houdini and Conan Doyle. The Story of a Strange Friendship.* Albert and Charles Boni, Inc. New York. 1932.

Frikell, Samri. *(Pseud.* Fulton Oursler). *Spirit Mediums Exposed. With special chapters, affidavits, and letters by the world-famed HOUDINI.* New Metropolitan Fiction, Inc. New York. 1930.

Gibson, Walter B. *Houdini's Escapes.* Blue Ribbon Books, Inc. New York. 1930.

——————. *Houdini's Magic.* Blue Ribbon Books, Inc. New York. 1932.

Hardeen, Theo. *Houdini, His Life and Work in Prose and Pictures, Prepared from HOUDINI'S own PICTURES AND CLIPPINGS.* New York.

Hardeen, Theo. *Life and History of Hardeen. 20 Years of an Eventful Career on the Stage. Fully illustrated. Containing Numerous Tricks and Secrets especially compiled by Hardeen.*

Houdini, Harry. (Editor and contributing author). "The Conjurers' Monthly Magazine." Vols. I and II. New York. Sept. 1906 to Aug. 1908. Some material from this publication later incorporated in *The Unmasking of Robert-Houdin, q.v.* and *Handcuff Secrets, q.v.*

——————. (Editor). *Elliott's Last Legacy* by Dr. James William Elliott. Adams Press Print. New York. 1923.

——————. *Handcuff Secrets.* George Routledge and Sons Ltd. London. 1909.

——————. *Houdini Exposes the tricks used by the Boston Medium "Margery" to win the $2500 prize offered by the Scientific American. Also a complete exposure of Argamasilla The famous Spaniard who baffled noted Scientists of Europe and America, with his claim to X-ray Vision.* Adams Press Publishers. New York. 1924.

279

_____. *Houdini's Book of Magic.* Whitman Publishing Co. Racine, Wisconsin. 1927.

_____. *Houdini's Paper Magic.* E. P. Dutton & Co. New York. 1922.

_____. *Life, History and Handcuff Secrets of Houdini.* Several editions and printings.

_____. *Magical Rope Ties and Escapes.* Will Goldston, Ltd. London. 1921.

_____. *A Magician Among the Spirits.* Harper and Bros. New York. 1924.

_____. *Mein Training, meine Tricks.* Leipzig. 1909.

_____. *Miracle Mongers and Their Methods.* E. P. Dutton. New York. 1920.

_____. (Editor, 1917-1926). *M.U.M.* Official monthly publication of the Society of American Magicians, of which Houdini was President from 1917 to the time of his death in 1926. The periodical contains many contributions by Houdini. New York.

_____. (Editor). *Red Magic.* Supplement of the *New York World.* Nos. 1-22. New York. 1924-1925.

_____. *The Right Way To Do Wrong.* Boston. 1906.

_____. *Souvenir Program. Coast to Coast Tour. Season 1926-27.*

_____. *The Unmasking of Robert-Houdin.* New York. 1908.

Kellock, Harold. *Houdini. His Life Story. From the Recollections and Documents of Beatrice Houdini.* Harcourt, Brace & Co. New York. 1928.

Murchison, Carl. (Edited by). *The Case For and Against Psychical Belief.* Clark University. Worcester, Mass. 1927.

Osgood, Whitman. *The Adventurous Life of a Versatile Artist. Houdini.* Several editions and printings.

Rinn, Joseph F. *Sixty Years of Psychical Research. Houdini and I among the Spiritualists.* The Truth Seeker Co., Inc. New York. 1950.

Williams, Beryl and Samuel Epstein. *The Great Houdini. Magician Extraordinary.* Julian Messner, Inc. New York. 1950.

CATALOGUE OF DOVER BOOKS

Books Explaining Science and Mathematics

WHAT IS SCIENCE?, N. Campbell. The role of experiment and measurement, the function of mathematics, the nature of scientific laws, the difference between laws and theories, the limitations of science, and many similarly provocative topics are treated clearly and without technicalities by an eminent scientist. "Still an excellent introduction to scientific philosophy," H. Margenau in PHYSICS TODAY. "A first-rate primer . . . deserves a wide audience," SCIENTIFIC AMERICAN. 192pp. 5⅜ x 8.   S43 Paperbound **$1.25**

THE NATURE OF PHYSICAL THEORY, P. W. Bridgman. A Nobel Laureate's clear, non-technical lectures on difficulties and paradoxes connected with frontier research on the physical sciences. Concerned with such central concepts as thought, logic, mathematics, relativity, probability, wave mechanics, etc. he analyzes the contributions of such men as Newton, Einstein, Bohr, Heisenberg, and many others. "Lucid and entertaining . . . recommended to anyone who wants to get some insight into current philosophies of science," THE NEW PHILOSOPHY. Index. xi + 138pp. 5⅜ x 8.   S33 Paperbound **$1.25**

EXPERIMENT AND THEORY IN PHYSICS, Max Born. A Nobel Laureate examines the nature of experiment and theory in theoretical physics and analyzes the advances made by the great physicists of our day: Heisenberg, Einstein, Bohr, Planck, Dirac, and others. The actual process of creation is detailed step-by-step by one who participated. A fine examination of the scientific method at work. 44pp. 5⅜ x 8.   S308 Paperbound **75¢**

THE PSYCHOLOGY OF INVENTION IN THE MATHEMATICAL FIELD, J. Hadamard. The reports of such men as Descartes, Pascal, Einstein, Poincaré, and others are considered in this investigation of the method of idea-creation in mathematics and other sciences and the thinking process in general. How do ideas originate? What is the role of the unconscious? What is Poincaré's forgetting hypothesis? are some of the fascinating questions treated. A penetrating analysis of Einstein's thought processes concludes the book. xiii + 145pp. 5⅜ x 8.   T107 Paperbound **$1.25**

THE NATURE OF LIGHT AND COLOUR IN THE OPEN AIR, M. Minnaert. Why are shadows sometimes blue, sometimes green, or other colors depending on the light and surroundings? What causes mirages? Why do multiple suns and moons appear in the sky? Professor Minnaert explains these unusual phenomena and hundreds of others in simple, easy-to-understand terms based on optical laws and the properties of light and color. No mathematics is required but artists, scientists, students, and everyone fascinated by these "tricks" of nature will find thousands of useful and amazing pieces of information. Hundreds of observational experiments are suggested which require no special equipment. 200 illustrations; 42 photos. xvi + 362pp. 5⅜ x 8.   T196 Paperbound **$2.00**

THE UNIVERSE OF LIGHT, W. Bragg. Sir William Bragg, Nobel Laureate and great modern physicist, is also well known for his powers of clear exposition. Here he analyzes all aspects of light for the layman: lenses, reflection, refraction, the optics of vision, x-rays, the photoelectric effect, etc. He tells you what causes the color of spectra, rainbows, and soap bubbles, how magic mirrors work, and much more. Dozens of simple experiments are described. Preface. Index. 199 line drawings and photographs, including 2 full-page color plates. x + 283pp. 5⅜ x 8.   T538 Paperbound **$1.85**

SOAP-BUBBLES: THEIR COLOURS AND THE FORCES THAT MOULD THEM, C. V. Boys. For continuing popularity and validity as scientific primer, few books can match this volume of easily-followed experiments, explanations. Lucid exposition of complexities of liquid films, surface tension and related phenomena, bubbles' reaction to heat, motion, music, magnetic fields. Experiments with capillary attraction, soap bubbles on frames, composite bubbles, liquid cylinders and jets, bubbles other than soap, etc. Wonderful introduction to scientific method, natural laws that have many ramifications in areas of modern physics. Only complete edition in print. New Introduction by S. Z. Lewin, New York University. 83 illustrations; 1 full-page color plate. xii + 190pp. 5⅜ x 8½.   T542 Paperbound **95¢**

THE STORY OF X-RAYS FROM RONTGEN TO ISOTOPES, A. R. Bleich, M.D. This book, by a member of the American College of Radiology, gives the scientific explanation of x-rays, their applications in medicine, industry and art, and their danger (and that of atmospheric radiation) to the individual and the species. You learn how radiation therapy is applied against cancer, how x-rays diagnose heart disease and other ailments, how they are used to examine mummies for information on diseases of early societies, and industrial materials for hidden weaknesses. 54 illustrations show x-rays of flowers, bones, stomach, gears with flaws, etc. 1st publication. Index. xix + 186pp. 5⅜ x 8.
T622 Paperbound **$1.35**

SPINNING TOPS AND GYROSCOPIC MOTION, John Perry. A classic elementary text of the dynamics of rotation — the behavior and use of rotating bodies such as gyroscopes and tops. In simple, everyday English you are shown how quasi-rigidity is induced in discs of paper, smoke rings, chains, etc., by rapid motions; why a gyrostat falls and why a top rises; precession; how the earth's motion affects climate; and many other phenomena. Appendix on practical use of gyroscopes. 62 figures. 128pp. 5⅜ x 8.
T416 Paperbound **$1.00**

SNOW CRYSTALS, W. A. Bentley, M. J. Humphreys. For almost 50 years W. A. Bentley photographed snow flakes in his laboratory in Jericho, Vermont; in 1931 the American Meteorological Society gathered together the best of his work, some 2400 photographs of snow flakes, plus a few ice flowers, windowpane frosts, dew, frozen rain, and other ice formations. Pictures were selected for beauty and scientific value. A very valuable work to anyone in meteorology, cryology; most interesting to layman; extremely useful for artist who wants beautiful, crystalline designs. All copyright free. Unabridged reprint of 1931 edition. 2453 illustrations. 227pp. 8 x 10½.
T287 Paperbound **$3.00**

A DOVER SCIENCE SAMPLER, edited by George Barkin. A collection of brief, non-technical passages from 44 Dover Books Explaining Science for the enjoyment of the science-minded browser. Includes work of Bertrand Russell, Poincaré, Laplace, Max Born, Galileo, Newton; material on physics, mathematics, metallurgy, anatomy, astronomy, chemistry, etc. You will be fascinated by Martin Gardner's analysis of the sincere pseudo-scientist, Moritz's account of Newton's absentmindedness, Bernard's examples of human vivisection, etc. Illustrations from the Diderot Pictorial Encyclopedia and De Re Metallica. 64 pages.
FREE

THE STORY OF ATOMIC THEORY AND ATOMIC ENERGY, J. G. Feinberg. A broader approach to subject of nuclear energy and its cultural implications than any other similar source. Very readable, informal, completely non-technical text. Begins with first atomic theory, 600 B.C. and carries you through the work of Mendelejeff, Röntgen, Madame Curie, to Einstein's equation and the A-bomb. New chapter goes through thermonuclear fission, binding energy, other events up to 1959. Radioactive decay and radiation hazards, future benefits, work of Bohr, moderns, hundreds more topics. "Deserves special mention . . . not only authoritative but thoroughly popular in the best sense of the word," Saturday Review. Formerly, "The Atom Story." Expanded with new chapter. Three appendixes. Index. 34 illustrations. vii + 243pp. 5⅜ x 8.
T625 Paperbound **$1.60**

THE STRANGE STORY OF THE QUANTUM, AN ACCOUNT FOR THE GENERAL READER OF THE GROWTH OF IDEAS UNDERLYING OUR PRESENT ATOMIC KNOWLEDGE, B. Hoffmann. Presents lucidly and expertly, with barest amount of mathematics, the problems and theories which led to modern quantum physics. Dr. Hoffmann begins with the closing years of the 19th century, when certain trifling discrepancies were noticed, and with illuminating analogies and examples takes you through the brilliant concepts of Planck, Einstein, Pauli, Broglie, Bohr, Schroedinger, Heisenberg, Dirac, Sommerfeld, Feynman, etc. This edition includes a new, long postscript carrying the story through 1958. "Of the books attempting an account of the history and contents of our modern atomic physics which have come to my attention, this is the best," H. Margenau, Yale University, in "American Journal of Physics." 32 tables and line illustrations. Index. 275pp. 5⅜ x 8.
T518 Paperbound **$1.50**

SPACE AND TIME, E. Borel. Written by a versatile mathematician of world renown with his customary lucidity and precision, this introduction to relativity for the layman presents scores of examples, analogies, and illustrations that open up new ways of thinking about space and time. It covers abstract geometry and geographical maps, continuity and topology, the propagation of light, the special theory of relativity, the general theory of relativity, theoretical researches, and much more. Mathematical notes. 2 Indexes. 4 Appendices. 15 figures. xvi + 243pp. 5⅜ x 8.
T592 Paperbound **$1.45**

FROM EUCLID TO EDDINGTON: A STUDY OF THE CONCEPTIONS OF THE EXTERNAL WORLD, Sir Edmund Whittaker. A foremost British scientist traces the development of theories of natural philosophy from the western rediscovery of Euclid to Eddington, Einstein, Dirac, etc. The inadequacy of classical physics is contrasted with present day attempts to understand the physical world through relativity, non-Euclidean geometry, space curvature, wave mechanics, etc. 5 major divisions of examination: Space; Time and Movement; the Concepts of Classical Physics; the Concepts of Quantum Mechanics; the Eddington Universe. 212pp. 5⅜ x 8.
T491 Paperbound **$1.35**

Nature, Biology

NATURE RECREATION: Group Guidance for the Out-of-doors, William Gould Vinal. Intended for both the uninitiated nature instructor and the education student on the college level, this complete "how-to" program surveys the entire area of nature education for the young. Philosophy of nature recreation; requirements, responsibilities, important information for group leaders; nature games; suggested group projects; conducting meetings and getting discussions started; etc. Scores of immediately applicable teaching aids, plus completely updated sources of information, pamphlets, field guides, recordings, etc. Bibliography. 74 photographs. + 310pp. 5⅜ x 8½.   T1015 Paperbound **$1.75**

HOW TO KNOW THE WILD FLOWERS, Mrs. William Starr Dana. Classic nature book that has introduced thousands to wonders of American wild flowers. Color-season principle of organization is easy to use, even by those with no botanical training, and the genial, refreshing discussions of history, folklore, uses of over 1,000 native and escape flowers, foliage plants are informative as well as fun to read. Over 170 full-page plates, collected from several editions, may be colored in to make permanent records of finds. Revised to conform with 1950 edition of Gray's Manual of Botany. xlii + 438pp. 5⅜ x 8½.   T332 Paperbound **$2.00**

HOW TO KNOW THE FERNS, F. T. Parsons. Ferns, among our most lovely native plants, are all too little known. This classic of nature lore will enable the layman to identify almost any American fern he may come across. After an introduction on the structure and life of ferns, the 57 most important ferns are fully pictured and described (arranged upon a simple identification key). Index of Latin and English names. 61 illustrations and 42 full-page plates. xiv + 215pp. 5⅜ x 8.   T740 Paperbound **$1.35**

MANUAL OF THE TREES OF NORTH AMERICA, Charles Sprague Sargent. Still unsurpassed as most comprehensive, reliable study of North American tree characteristics, precise locations and distribution. By dean of American dendrologists. Every tree native to U.S., Canada, Alaska, 185 genera, 717 species, described in detail—leaves, flowers, fruit, winterbuds, bark, wood, growth habits etc. plus discussion of varieties and local variants, immaturity variations. Over 100 keys, including unusual 11-page analytical key to genera, aid in identification. 783 clear illustrations of flowers, fruit, leaves. An unmatched permanent reference work for all nature lovers. Second enlarged (1926) edition. Synopsis of families. Analytical key to genera. Glossary of technical terms. Index. 783 illustrations, 1 map. Two volumes. Total of 982pp. 5⅜ x 8.   T277 Vol. I Paperbound **$2.25**
T278 Vol. II Paperbound **$2.25**
The set **$4.50**

TREES OF THE EASTERN AND CENTRAL UNITED STATES AND CANADA, W. M. Harlow. A revised edition of a standard middle-level guide to native trees and important escapes. More than 140 trees are described in detail, and illustrated with more than 600 drawings and photographs. Supplementary keys will enable the careful reader to identify almost any tree he might encounter. xiii + 288pp. 5⅜ x 8.   T395 Paperbound **$1.35**

GUIDE TO SOUTHERN TREES, Ellwood S. Harrar and J. George Harrar. All the essential information about trees indigenous to the South, in an extremely handy format. Introductory essay on methods of tree classification and study, nomenclature, chief divisions of Southern trees, etc. Approximately 100 keys and synopses allow for swift, accurate identification of trees. Numerous excellent illustrations, non-technical text make this a useful book for teachers of biology or natural science, nature lovers, amateur naturalists. Revised 1962 edition. Index. Bibliography. Glossary of technical terms. 920 illustrations; 201 full-page plates. ix + 709pp. 4⅝ x 6⅜.   T945 Paperbound **$2.35**

FRUIT KEY AND TWIG KEY TO TREES AND SHRUBS, W. M. Harlow. Bound together in one volume for the first time, these handy and accurate keys to fruit and twig identification are the only guides of their sort with photographs (up to 3 times natural size). "Fruit Key": Key to over 120 different deciduous and evergreen fruits. 139 photographs and 11 line drawings. Synoptic summary of fruit types. Bibliography. 2 Indexes (common and scientific names). "Twig Key": Key to over 160 different twigs and buds. 173 photographs. Glossary of technical terms. Bibliography. 2 Indexes (common and scientific names). Two volumes bound as one. Total of xvii + 126pp. 5⅝ x 8⅜.   T511 Paperbound **$1.25**

INSECT LIFE AND INSECT NATURAL HISTORY, S. W. Frost. A work emphasizing habits, social life, and ecological relations of insects, rather than more academic aspects of classification and morphology. Prof. Frost's enthusiasm and knowledge are everywhere evident as he discusses insect associations and specialized habits like leaf-rolling, leaf-mining, and case-making, the gall insects, the boring insects, aquatic insects, etc. He examines all sorts of matters not usually covered in general works, such as: insects as human food, insect music and musicians, insect response to electric and radio waves, use of insects in art and literature. The admirably executed purpose of this book, which covers the middle ground between elementary treatment and scholarly monographs, is to excite the reader to observe for himself. Over 700 illustrations. Extensive bibliography. x + 524pp. 5⅜ x 8.   T517 Paperbound **$2.45**

COMMON SPIDERS OF THE UNITED STATES, J. H. Emerton. Here is a nature hobby you can pursue right in your own cellar! Only non-technical, but thorough, reliable guide to spiders for the layman. Over 200 spiders from all parts of the country, arranged by scientific classification, are identified by shape and color, number of eyes, habitat and range, habits, etc. Full text, 501 line drawings and photographs, and valuable introduction explain webs, poisons, threads, capturing and preserving spiders, etc. Index. New synoptic key by S. W. Frost. xxiv + 225pp. 5⅜ x 8.   T223 Paperbound **$1.45**

THE LIFE STORY OF THE FISH: HIS MANNERS AND MORALS, Brian Curtis. A comprehensive, non-technical survey of just about everything worth knowing about fish. Written for the aquarist, the angler, and the layman with an inquisitive mind, the text covers such topics as evolution, external covering and protective coloration, physics and physiology of vision, maintenance of equilibrium, function of the lateral line canal for auditory and temperature senses, nervous system, function of the air bladder, reproductive system and methods—courtship, mating, spawning, care of young—and many more. Also sections on game fish, the problems of conservation and a fascinating chapter on fish curiosities. "Clear, simple language . . . excellent judgment in choice of subjects . . . delightful sense of humor," New York Times. Revised (1949) edition. Index. Bibliography of 72 items. 6 full-page photographic plates. xii + 284pp. 5⅜ x 8.   T929 Paperbound **$1.65**

BATS, Glover Morrill Allen. The most comprehensive study of bats as a life-form by the world's foremost authority. A thorough summary of just-about everything known about this fascinating and mysterious flying mammal, including its unique location sense, hibernation and cycles, its habitats and distribution, its wing structure and flying habits, and its relationship to man in the long history of folklore and superstition. Written on a middle-level, the book can be profitably studied by a trained zoologist and thoroughly enjoyed by the layman. "An absorbing text with excellent illustrations. Bats should have more friends and fewer thoughtless detractors as a result of the publication of this volume," William Beebe, Books. Extensive bibliography. 57 photographs and illustrations. x + 368pp. 5⅜ x 8½.
T984 Paperbound **$2.00**

BIRDS AND THEIR ATTRIBUTES, Glover Morrill Allen. A fine general introduction to birds as living organisms, especially valuable because of emphasis on structure, physiology, habits, behavior. Discusses relationship of bird to man, early attempts at scientific ornithology, feathers and coloration, skeletal structure including bills, legs and feet, wings. Also food habits, evolution and present distribution, feeding and nest-building, still unsolved questions of migrations and location sense, many more similar topics. Final chapter on classification, nomenclature. A good popular-level summary for the biologist; a first-rate introduction for the layman. Reprint of 1925 edition. References and index. 51 illustrations. viii + 338pp. 5⅜ x 8½.   T957 Paperbound **$1.85**

LIFE HISTORIES OF NORTH AMERICAN BIRDS, Arthur Cleveland Bent. Bent's monumental series of books on North American birds, prepared and published under auspices of Smithsonian Institute, is the definitive coverage of the subject, the most-used single source of information. Now the entire set is to be made available by Dover in inexpensive editions. This encyclopedic collection of detailed, specific observations utilizes reports of hundredo of contemporary observers, writings of such naturalists as Audubon, Burroughs, William Brewster, as well as author's own extensive investigations. Contains literally everything known about life history of each bird considered: nesting, eggs, plumage, distribution and migration, voice, enemies, courtship, etc. These not over-technical works are musts for ornithologists, conservationists, amateur naturalists, anyone seriously interested in American birds.

BIRDS OF PREY. More than 100 subspecies of hawks, falcons, eagles, buzzards, condors and owls, from the common barn owl to the extinct caracara of Guadaloupe Island. 400 photographs. Two volume set. Index for each volume. Bibliographies of 403, 520 items. 197 full-page plates. Total of 907pp. 5⅜ x 8½.   Vol. I T931 Paperbound **$2.50**
                                                              Vol. II T932 Paperbound **$2.50**

WILD FOWL. Ducks, geese, swans, and tree ducks—73 different subspecies. Two volume set. Index for each volume. Bibliographies of 124, 144 items. 106 full-page plates. Total of 685pp. 5⅜ x 8½.   Vol. I T285 Paperbound **$2.50**
                                                              Vol. II T286 Paperbound **$2.50**

SHORE BIRDS. 81 varieties (sandpipers, woodcocks, plovers, snipes, phalaropes, curlews, oyster catchers, etc.). More than 200 photographs of eggs, nesting sites, adult and young of important species. Two volume set. Index for each volume. Bibliographies of 261, 188 items. 121 full-page plates. Total of 860pp. 5⅜ x 8½.   Vol. I T933 Paperbound **$2.35**
                                                              Vol. II T934 Paperbound **$2.35**

THE LIFE OF PASTEUR, R. Vallery-Radot. 13th edition of this definitive biography, cited in Encyclopaedia Britannica. Authoritative, scholarly, well-documented with contemporary quotes, observations; gives complete picture of Pasteur's personal life; especially thorough presentation of scientific activities with silkworms, fermentation, hydrophobia, inoculation, etc. Introduction by Sir William Osler. Index. 505pp. 5⅜ x 8.   T632 Paperbound **$2.00**

Puzzles, Mathematical Recreations

SYMBOLIC LOGIC and THE GAME OF LOGIC, Lewis Carroll. "Symbolic Logic" is not concerned with modern symbolic logic, but is instead a collection of over 380 problems posed with charm and imagination, using the syllogism, and a fascinating diagrammatic method of drawing conclusions. In "The Game of Logic" Carroll's whimsical imagination devises a logical game played with 2 diagrams and counters (included) to manipulate hundreds of tricky syllogisms. The final section, "Hit or Miss" is a lagniappe of 101 additional puzzles in the delightful Carroll manner. Until this reprint edition, both of these books were rarities costing up to $15 each. Symbolic Logic: Index. xxxi + 199pp. The Game of Logic: 96pp. 2 vols. bound as one. 5⅜ x 8. **T492 Paperbound $1.50**

PILLOW PROBLEMS and A TANGLED TALE, Lewis Carroll. One of the rarest of all Carroll's works, "Pillow Problems" contains 72 original math puzzles, all typically ingenious. Particularly fascinating are Carroll's answers which remain exactly as he thought them out, reflecting his actual mental process. The problems in "A Tangled Tale" are in story form, originally appearing as a monthly magazine serial. Carroll not only gives the solutions, but uses answers sent in by readers to discuss wrong approaches and misleading paths, and grades them for insight. Both of these books were rarities until this edition, "Pillow Problems" costing up to $25, and "A Tangled Tale" $15. Pillow Problems: Preface and Introduction by Lewis Carroll. xx + 109pp. A Tangled Tale: 6 illustrations. 152pp. Two vols. bound as one. 5⅜ x 8. **T493 Paperbound $1.50**

AMUSEMENTS IN MATHEMATICS, Henry Ernest Dudeney. The foremost British originator of mathematical puzzles is always intriguing, witty, and paradoxical in this classic, one of the largest collections of mathematical amusements. More than 430 puzzles, problems, and paradoxes. Mazes and games, problems on number manipulation, unicursal and other route problems, puzzles on measuring, weighing, packing, age, kinship, chessboards, joiners', crossing river, plane figure dissection, and many others. Solutions. More than 450 illustrations. vii + 258pp. 5⅜ x 8. **T473 Paperbound $1.25**

THE CANTERBURY PUZZLES, Henry Dudeney. Chaucer's pilgrims set one another problems in story form. Also Adventures of the Puzzle Club, the Strange Escape of the King's Jester, the Monks of Riddlewell, the Squire's Christmas Puzzle Party, and others. All puzzles are original, based on dissecting plane figures, arithmetic, algebra, elementary calculus and other branches of mathematics, and purely logical ingenuity. "The limit of ingenuity and intricacy," The Observer. Over 110 puzzles. Full Solutions. 150 illustrations. vii + 225pp. 5⅜ x 8. **T474 Paperbound $1.25**

MATHEMATICAL EXCURSIONS, H. A. Merrill. Even if you hardly remember your high school math, you'll enjoy the 90 stimulating problems contained in this book and you will come to understand a great many mathematical principles with surprisingly little effort. Many useful shortcuts and diversions not generally known are included: division by inspection, Russian peasant multiplication, memory systems for pi, building odd and even magic squares, square roots by geometry, dyadic systems, and many more. Solutions to difficult problems. 50 illustrations. 145pp. 5⅜ x 8. **T350 Paperbound $1.00**

MAGIC SQUARES AND CUBES, W. S. Andrews. Only book-length treatment in English, a thorough non-technical description and analysis. Here are nasik, overlapping, pandiagonal, serrated squares; magic circles, cubes, spheres, rhombuses. Try your hand at 4-dimensional magical figures! Much unusual folklore and tradition included. High school algebra is sufficient. 754 diagrams and illustrations. viii + 419pp. 5⅜ x 8. **T658 Paperbound $1.85**

CALIBAN'S PROBLEM BOOK: MATHEMATICAL, INFERENTIAL AND CRYPTOGRAPHIC PUZZLES, H. Phillips (Caliban), S. T. Shovelton, G. S. Marshall. 105 ingenious problems by the greatest living creator of puzzles based on logic and inference. Rigorous, modern, piquant; reflecting their author's unusual personality, these intermediate and advanced puzzles all involve the ability to reason clearly through complex situations; some call for mathematical knowledge, ranging from algebra to number theory. Solutions. xi + 180pp. 5⅜ x 8.
T736 Paperbound $1.25

MATHEMATICAL PUZZLES FOR BEGINNERS AND ENTHUSIASTS, G. Mott-Smith. 188 mathematical puzzles based on algebra, dissection of plane figures, permutations, and probability, that will test and improve your powers of inference and interpretation. The Odic Force, The Spider's Cousin, Ellipse Drawing, theory and strategy of card and board games like tit-tat-toe, go moku, salvo, and many others. 100 pages of detailed mathematical explanations. Appendix of primes, square roots, etc. 135 illustrations. 2nd revised edition. 248pp. 5⅜ x 8.
T198 Paperbound $1.00

MATHEMAGIC, MAGIC PUZZLES, AND GAMES WITH NUMBERS, R. V. Heath. More than 60 new puzzles and stunts based on the properties of numbers. Easy techniques for multiplying large numbers mentally, revealing hidden numbers magically, finding the date of any day in any year, and dozens more. Over 30 pages devoted to magic squares, triangles, cubes, circles, etc. Edited by J. S. Meyer. 76 illustrations. 128pp. 5⅜ x 8. **T110 Paperbound $1.00**

THE BOOK OF MODERN PUZZLES, G. L. Kaufman. A completely new series of puzzles as fascinating as crossword and deduction puzzles hut hased upon different principles and techniques. Simple 2-minute teasers, Word labyrinths, design and pattern puzzles, logic and observation puzzles — over 150 braincrackers. Answers to all problems. 116 illustrations. 192pp. 5⅜ x 8.
T143 Paperbound **$1.00**

NEW WORD PUZZLES, G. L. Kaufman. 100 ENTIRELY NEW puzzles based on words and their combinations that will delight crossword puzzle, Scrabble and Jotto fans. Chess words, based on the moves of the chess king; design-onyms, symmetrical designs made of synonyms; rhymed double-crostics; syllable sentences; addle letter anagrams; alphagrams; linkograms; and many others all brand new. Full solutions. Space to work problems. 196 figures. vi + 122pp. 5⅜ x 8.
T344 Paperbound **$1.00**

MAZES AND LABYRINTHS: A BOOK OF PUZZLES, W. Shepherd. Mazes, formerly associated with mystery and ritual, are still among the most intriguing of intellectual puzzles. This is a novel and different collection of 50 amusements that embody the principle of the maze: mazes in the classical tradition; 3-dimensional, ribbon, and Möbius-strip mazes; hidden messages; spatial arrangements; etc.—almost all built on amusing story situations. 84 illustrations. Essay on maze psychology. Solutions. xv + 122pp. 5⅜ x 8.
T731 Paperbound **$1.00**

MAGIC TRICKS & CARD TRICKS, W. Jonson. Two books bound as one. 52 tricks with cards, 37 tricks with coins, bills, eggs, smoke, ribbons, slates, etc. Details on presentation, misdirection, and routining will help you master such famous tricks as the Changing Card, Card in the Pocket, Four Aces, Coin Through the Hand, Bill in the Egg, Afghan Bands, and over 75 others. If you follow the lucid exposition and key diagrams carefully, you will finish these two books with an astonishing mastery of magic. 106 figures. 224pp. 5⅜ x 8. T909 Paperbound **$1.00**

PANORAMA OF MAGIC, Milbourne Christopher. A profusely illustrated history of stage magic, a unique selection of prints and engravings from the author's private collection of magic memorabilia, the largest of its kind. Apparatus, stage settings and costumes; ingenious ads distributed by the performers and satiric broadsides passed around in the streets ridiculing pompous showmen; programs; decorative souvenirs. The lively text, by one of America's foremost professional magicians, is full of anecdotes about almost legendary wizards: Dede, the Egyptian; Philadelphia, the wonder-worker; Robert-Houdin, "the father of modern magic;" Harry Houdini; scores more. Altogether a pleasure package for anyone interested in magic, stage setting and design, ethnology, psychology, or simply in unusual people. A Dover original. 295 illustrations; 8 in full color. Index. viii + 216pp. 8⅜ x 11¼.
T774 Paperbound **$2.25**

HOUDINI ON MAGIC, Harry Houdini. One of the greatest magicians of modern times explains his most prized secrets. How locks are picked, with illustrated picks and skeleton keys; how a girl is sawed into twins; how to walk through a brick wall — Houdini's explanations of 44 stage tricks with many diagrams. Also included is a fascinating discussion of great magicians of the past and the story of his fight against fraudulent mediums and spiritualists. Edited by W.B. Gibson and M.N. Young. Bibliography. 155 figures, photos. xv + 280pp. 5⅜ x 8.
T384 Paperbound **$1.35**

MATHEMATICS, MAGIC AND MYSTERY, Martin Gardner. Why do card tricks work? How do magicians perform astonishing mathematical feats? How is stage mind-reading possible? This is the first book length study explaining the application of probability, set theory, theory of numbers, topology, etc., to achieve many startling tricks. Non-technical, accurate, detailed! 115 sections discuss tricks with cards, dice, coins, knots, geometrical vanishing illusions, how a Curry square "demonstrates" that the sum of the parts may be greater than the whole, and dozens of others. No sleight of hand necessary! 135 illustrations. xii + 174pp. 5⅜ x 8.
T335 Paperbound **$1.00**

EASY-TO-DO ENTERTAINMENTS AND DIVERSIONS WITH COINS, CARDS, STRING, PAPER AND MATCHES, R. M. Abraham. Over 300 tricks, games and puzzles will provide young readers with absorbing fun. Sections on card games; paper-folding; tricks with coins, matches and pieces of string; games for the agile; toy-making from common household objects; mathematical recreations; and 50 miscellaneous pastimes. Anyone in charge of groups of youngsters, including hard-pressed parents, and in need of suggestions on how to keep children sensibly amused and quietly content will find this book indispensable. Clear, simple text, copious number of delightful line drawings and illustrative diagrams. Originally titled "Winter Nights Entertainments." Introduction by Lord Baden Powell. 329 illustrations. v + 186pp. 5⅜ x 8½.
T921 Paperbound **$1.00**

STRING FIGURES AND HOW TO MAKE THEM, Caroline Furness Jayne. 107 string figures plus variations selected from the best primitive and modern examples developed by Navajo, Apache, pygmies of Africa, Eskimo, in Europe, Australia, China, etc. The most readily understandable, easy-to-follow book in English on perennially popular recreation. Crystal-clear exposition; step-by-step diagrams. Everyone from kindergarten children to adults looking for unusual diversion will be endlessly amused. Index. Bibliography. Introduction by A. C. Haddon. 17 full-page plates. 960 illustrations. xxiii + 401pp. 5⅜ x 8½.
T152 Paperbound **$2.00**

Entertainments, Humor

ODDITIES AND CURIOSITIES OF WORDS AND LITERATURE, C. Bombaugh, edited by M. Gardner. The largest collection of idiosyncratic prose and poetry techniques in English, a legendary work in the curious and amusing bypaths of literary recreations and the play technique in literature—so important in modern works. Contains alphabetic poetry, acrostics, palindromes, scissors verse, centos, emblematic poetry, famous literary puns, hoaxes, notorious slips of the press, hilarious mistranslations, and much more. Revised and enlarged with modern material by Martin Gardner. 368pp. 5⅜ x 8. T759 Paperbound **$1.50**

A NONSENSE ANTHOLOGY, collected by Carolyn Wells. 245 of the best nonsense verses ever written, including nonsense puns, absurd arguments, mock epics and sagas, nonsense ballads, odes, "sick" verses, dog-Latin verses, French nonsense verses, songs. By Edward Lear, Lewis Carroll, Gelett Burgess, W. S. Gilbert, Hilaire Belloc, Peter Newell, Oliver Herford, etc., 83 writers in all plus over four score anonymous nonsense verses. A special section of limericks, plus famous nonsense such as Carroll's "Jabberwocky" and Lear's "The Jumblies" and much excellent verse virtually impossible to locate elsewhere. For 50 years considered the best anthology available. Index of first lines specially prepared for this edition. Introduction by Carolyn Wells. 3 indexes: Title, Author, First lines. xxxiii + 279pp. T499 Paperbound **$1.35**

THE BAD CHILD'S BOOK OF BEASTS, MORE BEASTS FOR WORSE CHILDREN, and A MORAL ALPHABET, H. Belloc. Hardly an anthology of humorous verse has appeared in the last 50 years without at least a couple of these famous nonsense verses. But one must see the entire volumes—with all the delightful original illustrations by Sir Basil Blackwood—to appreciate fully Belloc's charming and witty verses that play so subacidly on the platitudes of life and morals that beset his day—and ours. A great humor classic. Three books in one. Total of 157pp. 5⅜ x 8. T749 Paperbound **$1.00**

THE DEVIL'S DICTIONARY, Ambrose Bierce. Sardonic and irreverent barbs puncturing the pomposities and absurdities of American politics, business, religion, literature, and arts, by the country's greatest satirist in the classic tradition. Epigrammatic as Shaw, piercing as Swift, American as Mark Twain, Will Rogers, and Fred Allen, Bierce will always remain the favorite of a small coterie of enthusiasts, and of writers and speakers whom he supplies with "some of the most gorgeous witticisms of the English language" (H. L. Mencken). Over 1000 entries in alphabetical order. 144pp. 5⅜ x 8. T487 Paperbound **$1.00**

THE PURPLE COW AND OTHER NONSENSE, Gelett Burgess. The best of Burgess's early nonsense, selected from the first edition of the "Burgess Nonsense Book." Contains many of his most unusual and truly awe-inspiring pieces: 36 nonsense quatrains, the Poems of Patagonia, Alphabet of Famous Goops, and the other hilarious (and rare) adult nonsense that place him in the forefront of American humorists. All pieces are accompanied by the original Burgess illustrations. 123 illustrations. xiii + 113pp. 5⅜ x 8. T772 Paperbound **$1.00**

MY PIOUS FRIENDS AND DRUNKEN COMPANIONS and MORE PIOUS FRIENDS AND DRUNKEN COMPANIONS, Frank Shay. Folksingers, amateur and professional, and everyone who loves singing: here, available for the first time in 30 years, is this valued collection of 132 ballads, blues, vaudeville numbers, drinking songs, sea chanties, comedy songs. Songs of pre-Beatnik Bohemia; songs from all over America, England, France, Australia; the great songs of the Naughty Nineties and early twentieth-century America. Over a third with music. Woodcuts by John Held, Jr. convey perfectly the brash insouciance of an era of rollicking unabashed song. 12 illustrations by John Held, Jr. Two indexes (Titles and First lines and Choruses). Introductions by the author. Two volumes bound as one. Total of xvi + 235pp. 5⅜ x 8½. T946 Paperbound **$1.25**

HOW TO TELL THE BIRDS FROM THE FLOWERS, R. W. Wood. How not to confuse a carrot with a parrot, a grape with an ape, a puffin with nuffin. Delightful drawings, clever puns, absurd little poems point out far-fetched resemblances in nature. The author was a leading physicist. Introduction by Margaret Wood White. 106 illus. 60pp. 5⅜ x 8. T523 Paperbound **75¢**

PECK'S BAD BOY AND HIS PA, George W. Peck. The complete edition, containing both volumes, of one of the most widely read American humor books. The endless ingenious pranks played by bad boy "Hennery" on his pa and the grocery man, the outraged pomposity of Pa, the perpetual ridiculing of middle class institutions, are as entertaining today as they were in 1883. No pale sophistications or subtleties, but rather humor vigorous, raw, earthy, imaginative, and, as folk humor often is, sadistic. This peculiarly fascinating book is also valuable to historians and students of American culture as a portrait of an age. 100 original illustrations by True Williams. Introduction by E. F. Bleiler. 347pp. 5⅜ x 8. T497 Paperbound **$1.35**

THE HUMOROUS VERSE OF LEWIS CARROLL. Almost every poem Carroll ever wrote, the largest collection ever published, including much never published elsewhere: 150 parodies, burlesques, riddles, ballads, acrostics, etc., with 130 original illustrations by Tenniel, Carroll, and others. "Addicts will be grateful . . . there is nothing for the faithful to do but sit down and fall to the banquet," N. Y. Times. Index to first lines. xiv + 446pp. 5⅜ x 8.
T654 Paperbound **$2.00**

DIVERSIONS AND DIGRESSIONS OF LEWIS CARROLL. A major new treasure for Carroll fans! Rare privately published humor, fantasy, puzzles, and games by Carroll at his whimsical best, with a new vein of frank satire. Includes many new mathematical amusements and recreations, among them the fragmentary Part III of "Curiosa Mathematica." Contains "The Rectory Umbrella," "The New Belfry," "The Vision of the Three T's," and much more. New 32-page supplement of rare photographs taken by Carroll. x + 375pp. 5⅜ x 8.
T732 Paperbound **$1.65**

THE COMPLETE NONSENSE OF EDWARD LEAR. This is the only complete edition of this master of gentle madness available at a popular price. A BOOK OF NONSENSE, NONSENSE SONGS, MORE NONSENSE SONGS AND STORIES in their entirety with all the old favorites that have delighted children and adults for years. The Dong With A Luminous Nose, The Jumblies, The Owl and the Pussycat, and hundreds of other bits of wonderful nonsense. 214 limericks, 3 sets of Nonsense Botany, 5 Nonsense Alphabets, 546 drawings by Lear himself, and much more. 320pp. 5⅜ x 8.
T167 Paperbound **$1.00**

THE MELANCHOLY LUTE, The Humorous Verse of Franklin P. Adams ("FPA"). The author's own selection of light verse, drawn from thirty years of FPA's column, "The Conning Tower," syndicated all over the English-speaking world. Witty, perceptive, literate, these ninety-six poems range from parodies of other poets, Millay, Longfellow, Edgar Guest, Kipling, Masefield, etc., and free and hilarious translations of Horace and other Latin poets, to satiric comments on fabled American institutions—the New York Subways, preposterous ads, suburbanites, sensational journalism, etc. They reveal with vigor and clarity the humor, integrity and restraint of a wise and gentle American satirist. Introduction by Robert Hutchinson. vi + 122pp. 5⅜ x 8½.
T108 Paperbound **$1.00**

SINGULAR TRAVELS, CAMPAIGNS, AND ADVENTURES OF BARON MUNCHAUSEN, R. E. Raspe, with 90 illustrations by Gustave Doré. The first edition in over 150 years to reestablish the deeds of the Prince of Liars exactly as Raspe first recorded them in 1785—the genuine Baron Munchausen, one of the most popular personalities In English literature. Included also are the best of the many sequels, written by other hands. Introduction on Raspe by J. Carswell. Bibliography of early editions. xliv + 192pp. 5⅜ x 8.
T698 Paperbound **$1.00**

THE WIT AND HUMOR OF OSCAR WILDE, ed. by Alvin Redman. Wilde at his most brilliant, In 1000 epigrams exposing weaknesses and hypocrisies of "civilized" society. Divided into 49 categories—sin, wealth, women, America, etc.—to aid writers, speakers. Includes excerpts from his trials, books, plays, criticism. Formerly "The Epigrams of Oscar Wilde." Introduction by Vyvyan Holland, Wilde's only living son. Introductory essay by editor. 260pp. 5⅜ x 8.
T602 Paperbound **$1.00**

MAX AND MORITZ, Wilhelm Busch. Busch is one of the great humorists of all time, as well as the father of the modern comic strip. This volume, translated by H. A. Klein and other hands, contains the perennial favorite "Max and Moritz" (translated by C. T. Brooks), Plisch and Plum, Das Rabennest, Eispeter, and seven other whimsical, sardonic, jovial, diabolical cartoon and verse stories. Lively English translations parallel the original German. This work has delighted millions, since it first appeared in the 19th century, and is guaranteed to please almost anyone. Edited by H. A. Klein, wIth an afterword. x + 205pp. 5⅝ x 8½.
T181 Paperbound **$1.15**

HYPOCRITICAL HELENA, Wilhelm Busch. A companion volume to "Max and Moritz," with the title piece (Die Fromme Helena) and 10 other highly amusing cartoon and verse stories, all newly translated by H. A. Klein and M. C. Klein: Adventure on New Year's Eve (Abenteuer in der Neujahrsnacht), Hangover on the Morning after New Year's Eve (Der Katzenjammer am Neujahrsmorgen), etc. English and German in parallel columns. Hours of pleasure, also a fine language aid. x + 205pp. 5⅝ x 8½.
T184 Paperbound **$1.00**

THE BEAR THAT WASN'T, Frank Tashlin. What does it mean? Is it simply delightful wry humor, or a charming story of a bear who wakes up in the midst of a factory, or a satire on Big Business, or an existential cartoon-story of the human condition, or a symbolization of the struggle between conformity and the individual? New York Herald Tribune said of the first edition: ". . . a fable for grownups that will be fun for children. Sit down with the book and get your own bearings." Long an underground favorite with readers of all ages and opinions. v + 51pp. Illustrated. 5⅜ x 8½.
T939 Paperbound **75¢**

RUTHLESS RHYMES FOR HEARTLESS HOMES and MORE RUTHLESS RHYMES FOR HEARTLESS HOMES, Harry Graham ("Col. D. Streamer"). Two volumes of Little Willy and 48 other poetic disasters. A bright, new reprint of oft-quoted, never forgotten, devastating humor by a precursor of today's "sick" joke school. For connoisseurs of wicked, wacky humor and all who delight in the comedy of manners. Original drawings are a perfect complement. 61 illustrations. Index. vi + 69pp. Two vols. bound as one. 5⅜ x 8½.
T930 Paperbound **75¢**

Say It language phrase books

These handy phrase books (128 to 196 pages each) make grammatical drills unnecessary for an elementary knowledge of a spoken foreign language. Covering most matters of travel and everyday life each volume contains:

Over 1000 phrases and sentences in immediately useful forms — foreign language plus English.

Modern usage designed for Americans. Specific phrases like, "Give me small change," and "Please call a taxi."

Simplified phonetic transcription you will be able to read at sight.

The only completely indexed phrase books on the market.

Covers scores of important situations: — Greetings, restaurants, sightseeing, useful expressions, etc.

These books are prepared by native linguists who are professors at Columbia, N.Y.U., Fordham and other great universities. Use them independently or with any other book or record course. They provide a supplementary living element that most other courses lack. Individual volumes in:

Russian 75¢   Italian 75¢   Spanish 75¢   German 75¢
Hebrew 75¢   Danish 75¢   Japanese 75¢   Swedish 75¢
Dutch 75¢   Esperanto 75¢   Modern Greek 75¢   Portuguese 75¢
Norwegian 75¢   Polish 75¢   French 75¢   Yiddish 75¢
Turkish 75¢   English for German-speaking people 75¢
English for Italian-speaking people 75¢   English for Spanish-speaking people 75¢

Large clear type. 128-196 pages each. 3½ x 5¼. Sturdy paper binding.

Listen and Learn language records

LISTEN & LEARN is the only language record course designed especially to meet your travel and everyday needs. It is available in separate sets for FRENCH, SPANISH, GERMAN, JAPANESE, RUSSIAN, MODERN GREEK, PORTUGUESE, ITALIAN and HEBREW, and each set contains three 33⅓ rpm long-playing records—1½ hours of recorded speech by eminent native speakers who are professors at Columbia, New York University, Queens College.

Check the following special features found only in LISTEN & LEARN:

- **Dual-language recording. 812 selected phrases and sentences, over 3200 words,** spoken first in English, then in their foreign language equivalents. A suitable pause follows each foreign phrase, allowing you time to repeat the expression. You learn by unconscious assimilation.
- **128 to 206-page manual** contains everything on the records, plus a simple phonetic pronunciation guide.
- **Indexed for convenience. The only set on the market** that is completely indexed. No more puzzling over where to find the phrase you need. Just look in the rear of the manual.
- **Practical.** No time wasted on material you can find in any grammar. LISTEN & LEARN covers central core material with phrase approach. Ideal for the person with limited learning time.
- **Living, modern expressions,** not found in other courses. Hygienic products, modern equipment, shopping—expressions used every day, like "nylon" and "air-conditioned."
- **Limited objective.** Everything you learn, no matter where you stop, is immediately useful. You have to finish other courses, wade through grammar and vocabulary drill, before they help you.
- **High-fidelity recording.** LISTEN & LEARN records equal in clarity and surface-silence any record on the market costing up to $6.

"Excellent . . . the spoken records . . . impress me as being among the very best on the market," **Prof. Mario Pei,** Dept. of Romance Languages, Columbia University. "Inexpensive and well-done . . . it would make an ideal present," CHICAGO SUNDAY TRIBUNE. "More genuinely helpful than anything of its kind which I have previously encountered," **Sidney Clark,** well-known author of "ALL THE BEST" travel books.

UNCONDITIONAL GUARANTEE. Try LISTEN & LEARN, then return it within 10 days for full refund if you are not satisfied.

Each set contains three twelve-inch 33⅓ records, manual, and album.

SPANISH	the set $5.95	GERMAN	the set $5.95
FRENCH	the set $5.95	ITALIAN	the set $5.95
RUSSIAN	the set $5.95	JAPANESE	the set $5.95
PORTUGUESE	the set $5.95	MODERN GREEK	the set $5.95
MODERN HEBREW	the set $5.95		

Americana

THE EYES OF DISCOVERY, J. Bakeless. A vivid reconstruction of how unspoiled America appeared to the first white men. Authentic and enlightening accounts of Hudson's landing in New York, Coronado's trek through the Southwest; scores of explorers, settlers, trappers, soldiers. America's pristine flora, fauna, and Indians in every region and state in fresh and unusual new aspects. "A fascinating view of what the land was like before the first highway went through," Time. 68 contemporary illustrations, 39 newly added in this edition. Index. Bibliography. x + 500pp. 5⅜ x 8. T761 Paperbound **$2.00**

AUDUBON AND HIS JOURNALS, J. J. Audubon. A collection of fascinating accounts of Europe and America in the early 1800's through Audubon's own eyes. Includes the Missouri River Journals —an eventful trip through America's untouched heartland, the Labrador Journals, the European Journals, the famous "Episodes", and other rare Audubon material, including the descriptive chapters from the original letterpress edition of the "Ornithological Studies", omitted in all later editions. Indispensable for ornithologists, naturalists, and all lovers of Americana and adventure. 70-page biography by Audubon's granddaughter. 38 illustrations. Index. Total of 1106pp. 5⅜ x 8.
T675 Vol I Paperbound **$2.25**
T676 Vol II Paperbound **$2.25**
The set **$4.50**

TRAVELS OF WILLIAM BARTRAM, edited by Mark Van Doren. The first inexpensive illustrated edition of one of the 18th century's most delightful books is an excellent source of first-hand material on American geography, anthropology, and natural history. Many descriptions of early Indian tribes are our only source of information on them prior to the infiltration of the white man. "The mind of a scientist with the soul of a poet," John Livingston Lowes. 13 original illustrations and maps. Edited with an introduction by Mark Van Doren. 448pp. 5⅜ x 8. T13 Paperbound **$2.00**

GARRETS AND PRETENDERS: A HISTORY OF BOHEMIANISM IN AMERICA, A. Parry. The colorful and fantastic history of American Bohemianism from Poe to Kerouac. This is the only complete record of hoboes, cranks, starving poets, and suicides. Here are Pfaff, Whitman, Crane, Bierce, Pound, and many others. New chapters by the author and by H. T. Moore bring this thorough and well-documented history down to the Beatniks. "An excellent account," N. Y. Times. Scores of cartoons, drawings, and caricatures. Bibliography. Index. xxviii + 421pp. 5⅝ x 8⅜. T708 Paperbound **$1.95**

THE EXPLORATION OF THE COLORADO RIVER AND ITS CANYONS, J. W. Powell. The thrilling first-hand account of the expedition that filled in the last white space on the map of the United States. Rapids, famine, hostile Indians, and mutiny are among the perils encountered as the unknown Colorado Valley reveals its secrets. This is the only uncut version of Major Powell's classic of exploration that has been printed in the last 60 years. Includes later reflections and subsequent expedition. 250 illustrations, new map. 400pp. 5⅝ x 8⅜. T94 Paperbound **$2.25**

THE JOURNAL OF HENRY D. THOREAU, Edited by Bradford Torrey and Francis H. Allen. Henry Thoreau is not only one of the most important figures in American literature and social thought; his voluminous journals (from which his books emerged as selections and crystallizations) constitute both the longest, most sensitive record of personal internal development and a most penetrating description of a historical moment in American culture. This present set, which was first issued in fourteen volumes, contains Thoreau's entire journals from 1837 to 1862, with the exception of the lost years which were found only recently. We are reissuing it, complete and unabridged, with a new introduction by Walter Harding, Secretary of the Thoreau Society. Fourteen volumes reissued in two volumes. Foreword by Henry Seidel Canby. Total of 1888pp. 8⅜ x 12¼. T312-3 Two volume set, Clothbound **$20.00**

GAMES AND SONGS OF AMERICAN CHILDREN, collected by William Wells Newell. A remarkable collection of 190 games with songs that accompany many of them; cross references to show similarities, differences among them; variations; musical notation for 38 songs. Textual discussions show relations with folk-drama and other aspects of folk tradition. Grouped into categories for ready comparative study: Love-games, histories, playing at work, human life, bird and beast, mythology, guessing-games, etc. New introduction covers relations of songs and dances to timeless heritage of folklore, biographical sketch of Newell, other pertinent data. A good source of inspiration for those in charge of groups of children and a valuable reference for anthropologists, sociologists, psychiatrists. Introduction by Carl Withers. New indexes of first lines, games. 5⅜ x 8½. xii + 242pp. T354 Paperbound **$1.75**

Art, History of Art, Antiques, Graphic Arts, Handcrafts

ART STUDENTS' ANATOMY, E. J. Farris. Outstanding art anatomy that uses chiefly living objects for its illustrations. 71 photos of undraped men, women, children are accompanied by carefully labeled matching sketches to illustrate the skeletal system, articulations and movements, bony landmarks, the muscular system, skin, fasciae, fat, etc. 9 x-ray photos show movement of joints. Undraped models are shown in such actions as serving in tennis, drawing a bow in archery, playing football, dancing, preparing to spring and to dive. Also discussed and illustrated are proportions, age and sex differences, the anatomy of the smile, etc. 8 plates by the great early 18th century anatomic illustrator Siegfried Albinus are also included. Glossary. 158 figures, 7 in color. x + 159pp. 5⅝ x 8⅜.   T744 Paperbound **$1.50**

AN ATLAS OF ANATOMY FOR ARTISTS, F Schider. A new 3rd edition of this standard text enlarged by 52 new illustrations of hands, anatomical studies by Cloquet, and expressive life studies of the body by Barcsay. 189 clear, detailed plates offer you precise information of impeccable accuracy. 29 plates show all aspects of the skeleton, with closeups of special areas, while 54 full-page plates, mostly in two colors, give human musculature as seen from four different points of view, with cutaways for important portions of the body. 14 full-page plates provide photographs of hand forms, eyelids, female breasts, and indicate the location of muscles upon models. 59 additional plates show how great artists of the past utilized human anatomy. They reproduce sketches and finished work by such artists as Michelangelo, Leonardo da Vinci, Goya, and 15 others. This is a lifetime reference work which will be one of the most important books in any artist's library. "The standard reference tool," AMERICAN LIBRARY ASSOCIATION. "Excellent," AMERICAN ARTIST. Third enlarged edition. 189 plates, 647 illustrations. xxvi + 192pp. 7⅞ x 10⅝.   T241 Clothbound **$6.00**

AN ATLAS OF ANIMAL ANATOMY FOR ARTISTS, W. Ellenberger, H. Baum, H. Dittrich. The largest, richest animal anatomy for artists available in English. 99 detailed anatomical plates of such animals as the horse, dog, cat, lion, deer, seal, kangaroo, flying squirrel, cow, bull, goat, monkey, hare, and bat. Surface features are clearly indicated, while progressive beneath-the-skin pictures show musculature, tendons, and bone structure. Rest and action are exhibited in terms of musculature and skeletal structure and detailed cross-sections are given for heads and important features. The animals chosen are representative of specific families so that a study of these anatomies will provide knowledge of hundreds of related species. "Highly recommended as one of the very few books on the subject worthy of being used as an authoritative guide," DESIGN. "Gives a fundamental knowledge," AMERICAN ARTIST. Second revised, enlarged edition with new plates from Cuvier, Stubbs, etc. 288 illustrations. 153pp. 11⅜ x 9.   T82 Clothbound **$6.00**

THE HUMAN FIGURE IN MOTION, Eadweard Muybridge. The largest selection in print of Muybridge's famous high-speed action photos of the human figure in motion. 4789 photographs illustrate 162 different actions: men, women, children—mostly undraped—are shown walking, running, carrying various objects, sitting, lying down, climbing, throwing, arising, and performing over 150 other actions. Some actions are shown in as many as 150 photographs each. All in all there are more than 500 action strips in this enormous volume, series shots taken at shutter speeds of as high as 1/6000th of a second! These are not posed shots, but true stopped motion. They show bone and muscle in situations that the human eye is not fast enough to capture. Earlier, smaller editions of these prints have brought $40 and more on the out-of-print market. "A must for artists," ART IN FOCUS. "An unparalleled dictionary of action for all artists," AMERICAN ARTIST. 390 full-page plates, with 4789 photographs. Printed on heavy glossy stock. Reinforced binding with headbands. xxi + 390pp. 7⅞ x 10⅝.
T204 Clothbound **$10.00**

ANIMALS IN MOTION, Eadweard Muybridge. This is the largest collection of animal action photos in print. 34 different animals (horses, mules, oxen, goats, camels, pigs, cats, guanacos, lions, gnus, deer, monkeys, eagles—and 21 others) in 132 characteristic actions. The horse alone is shown in more than 40 different actions. All 3919 photographs are taken in series at speeds up to 1/6000th of a second. The secrets of leg motion, spinal patterns, head movements, strains and contortions shown nowhere else are captured. You will see exactly how a lion sets his foot down; how an elephant's knees are like a human's—and how they differ; the position of a kangaroo's legs in mid-leap; how an ostrich's head bobs; details of the flight of birds—and thousands of facets of motion only the fastest cameras can catch. Photographed from domestic animals and animals in the Philadelphia zoo, it contains neither semiposed artificial shots nor distorted telephoto shots taken under adverse conditions. Artists, biologists, decorators, cartoonists, will find this book indispensable for understanding animals in motion. "A really marvelous series of plates," NATURE (London). "The dry plate's most spectacular early use was by Eadweard Muybridge," LIFE. 3919 photographs; 380 full pages of plates. 440pp. Printed on heavy glossy paper. Deluxe binding with headbands. 7⅞ x 10⅝.   T203 Clothbound **$10.00**

CATALOGUE OF DOVER BOOKS

THE AUTOBIOGRAPHY OF AN IDEA, Louis Sullivan. The pioneer architect whom Frank Lloyd Wright called "the master" reveals an acute sensitivity to social forces and values in this passionately honest account. He records the crystallization of his opinions and theories, the growth of his organic theory of architecture that still influences American designers and architects, contemporary ideas, etc. This volume contains the first appearance of 34 full-page plates of his finest architecture. Unabridged reissue of 1924 edition. New introduction by R. M. Line. Index. xiv + 335pp. 5⅜ x 8. **T281 Paperbound $2.00**

THE DRAWINGS OF HEINRICH KLEY. The first uncut republication of both of Kley's devastating sketchbooks, which first appeared in pre-World War I Germany. One of the greatest cartoonists and social satirists of modern times, his exuberant and iconoclastic fantasy and his extraordinary technique place him in the great tradition of Bosch, Breughel, and Goya, while his subject matter has all the immediacy and tension of our century. 200 drawings. viii + 128pp. 7¾ x 10¾. **T24 Paperbound $1.85**

MORE DRAWINGS BY HEINRICH KLEY. All the sketches from Leut' Und Viecher (1912) and Sammel-Album (1923) not included in the previous Dover edition of Drawings. More of the bizarre, mercilessly iconoclastic sketches that shocked and amused on their original publication. Nothing was too sacred, no one too eminent for satirization by this imaginative, individual and accomplished master cartoonist. A total of 158 illustrations. Iv + 104pp. 7¾ x 10¾. **T41 Paperbound $1.85**

PINE FURNITURE OF EARLY NEW ENGLAND, R. H. Kettell. A rich understanding of one of America's most original folk arts that collectors of antiques, interior decorators, craftsmen, woodworkers, and everyone interested in American history and art will find fascinating and immensely useful. 413 illustrations of more than 300 chairs, benches, racks, beds, cupboards, mirrors, shelves, tables, and other furniture will show all the simple beauty and character of early New England furniture. 55 detailed drawings carefully analyze outstanding pieces. "With its rich store of illustrations, this book emphasizes the individuality and varied design of early American pine furniture. It should be welcomed," ANTIQUES. 413 illustrations and 55 working drawings. 475. 8 x 10¾. **T145 Clothbound $10.00**

THE HUMAN FIGURE, J. H. Vanderpoel. Every important artistic element of the human figure is pointed out in minutely detailed word descriptions in this classic text and illustrated as well in 430 pencil and charcoal drawings. Thus the text of this book directs your attention to all the characteristic features and subtle differences of the male and female (adults, children, and aged persons), as though a master artist were telling you what to look for at each stage. 2nd edition, revised and enlarged by George Bridgman. Foreword. 430 illustrations. 143pp. 6⅛ x 9¼. **T432 Paperbound $1.50**

LETTERING AND ALPHABETS, J. A. Cavanagh. This unabridged reissue of LETTERING offers a full discussion, analysis, illustration of 89 basic hand lettering styles — styles derived from Caslons, Bodonis, Garamonds, Gothic, Black Letter, Oriental, and many others. Upper and lower cases, numerals and common signs pictured. Hundreds of technical hints on make-up, construction, artistic validity, strokes, pens, brushes, white areas, etc. May be reproduced without permission! 89 complete alphabets; 72 lettered specimens. 121pp. 9¾ x 8. **T53 Paperbound $1.35**

STICKS AND STONES, Lewis Mumford. A survey of the forces that have conditioned American architecture and altered its forms. The author discusses the medieval tradition in early New England villages; the Renaissance influence which developed with the rise of the merchant class; the classical influence of Jefferson's time; the "Mechanicsvilles" of Poe's generation; the Brown Decades; the philosophy of the Imperial facade; and finally the modern machine age. "A truly remarkable book," SAT. REV. OF LITERATURE. 2nd revised edition. 21 illustrations. xvii + 228pp. 5⅜ x 8. **T202 Paperbound $1.65**

THE STANDARD BOOK OF QUILT MAKING AND COLLECTING, Marguerite Ickis. A complete easy-to-follow guide with all the information you need to make beautiful, useful quilts. How to plan, design, cut, sew, appliqué, avoid sewing problems, use rag bag, make borders, tuft, every other aspect. Over 100 traditional quilts shown, including over 40 full-size patterns. At-home hobby for fun, profit. Index. 483 illus. 1 color plate. 287pp. 6¾ x 9½. **T582 Paperbound $2.00**

THE BOOK OF SIGNS, Rudolf Koch. Formerly $20 to $25 on the out-of-print market, now only $1.00 in this unabridged new edition! 493 symbols from ancient manuscripts, medieval cathedrals, coins, catacombs, pottery, etc. Crosses, monograms of Roman emperors, astrological, chemical, botanical, runes, housemarks, and 7 other categories. Invaluable for handicraft workers, illustrators, scholars, etc., this material may be reproduced without permission. 493 illustrations by Fritz Kredel. 104pp. 6½ x 9¼. **T162 Paperbound $1.00**

PRIMITIVE ART, Franz Boas. This authoritative and exhaustive work by a great American anthropologist covers the entire gamut of primitive art. Pottery, leatherwork, metal work, stone work, wood, basketry, are treated in detail. Theories of primitive art, historical depth in art history, technical virtuosity, unconscious levels of patterning, symbolism, styles, literature, music, dance, etc. A must book for the interested layman, the anthropologist, artist, handicrafter (hundreds of unusual motifs), and the historian. Over 900 illustrations (50 ceramic vessels, 12 totem poles, etc.). 376pp. 5⅜ x 8. **T25 Paperbound $2.00**

Fiction

THE LAND THAT TIME FORGOT and THE MOON MAID, Edgar Rice Burroughs. In the opinion of many, Burroughs' best work. The first concerns a strange island where evolution is individual rather than phylogenetic. Speechless anthropoids develop into intelligent human beings within a single generation. The second projects the reader far into the future and describes the first voyage to the Moon (in the year 2025), the conquest of the Earth by the Moon, and years of violence and adventure as the enslaved Earthmen try to regain possession of their planet. "An imaginative tour de force that keeps the reader keyed up and expectant," NEW YORK TIMES. Complete, unabridged text of the original two novels (three parts in each). 5 illustrations by J. Allen St. John. vi + 552pp. 5⅜ x 8½.
T1020 Clothbound **$3.75**
T358 Paperbound **$2.00**

AT THE EARTH'S CORE, PELLUCIDAR, TANAR OF PELLUCIDAR: THREE SCIENCE FICTION NOVELS BY EDGAR RICE BURROUGHS. Complete, unabridged texts of the first three Pellucidar novels. Tales of derring-do by the famous master of science fiction. The locale for these three related stories is the inner surface of the hollow Earth where we discover the world of Pellucidar, complete with all types of bizarre, menacing creatures, strange peoples, and alluring maidens—guaranteed to delight all Burroughs fans and a wide circle of adventure lovers. Illustrated by J. Allen St. John and P. F. Berdanier. vi + 433pp. 5⅜ x 8½.
T1051 Paperbound **$2.00**

THREE MARTIAN NOVELS, Edgar Rice Burroughs. Contains: Thuvia, Maid of Mars; The Chessmen of Mars; and The Master Mind of Mars. High adventure set in an imaginative and intricate conception of the Red Planet. Mars is peopled with an intelligent, heroic human race which lives in densely populated cities and with fierce barbarians who inhabit dead sea bottoms. Other exciting creatures abound amidst an inventive framework of Martian history and geography. Complete unabridged reprintings of the first edition. 16 illustrations by J. Allen St. John. vi + 499pp. 5⅜ x 8½.
T39 Paperbound **$1.85**

TO THE SUN? and OFF ON A COMET!, Jules Verne. Complete texts of two of the most imaginative flights into fancy in world literature display the high adventure that have kept Verne's novels read for nearly a century. Only unabridged edition of the best translation, by Edward Roth. Large, easily readable type. 50 illustrations selected from first editions. 462pp. 5⅜ x 8.
T634 Paperbound **$1.75**

FROM THE EARTH TO THE MOON and ALL AROUND THE MOON, Jules Verne. Complete editions of two of Verne's most successful novels, in finest Edward Roth translations, now available after many years out of print. Verne's visions of submarines, airplanes, television, rockets, interplanetary travel; of scientific and not-so-scientific beliefs; of peculiarities of Americans; all delight and engross us today as much as when they first appeared. Large, easily readable type. 42 illus. from first French edition. 476pp. 5⅜ x 8.
T633 Paperbound **$1.75**

THREE PROPHETIC NOVELS BY H. G. WELLS, edited by E. F. Bleiler. Complete texts of "When the Sleeper Wakes" (1st book printing in 50 years), "A Story of the Days to Come," "The Time Machine" (1st complete printing in book form). Exciting adventures in the future are as enjoyable today as 50 years ago when first printed. Predict TV, movies, intercontinental airplanes, prefabricated houses, air-conditioned cities, etc. First important author to foresee problems of mind control, technological dictatorships. "Absolute best of imaginative fiction," N. Y. Times. Introduction. 335pp. 5⅜ x 8.
T605 Paperbound **$1.50**

SEVEN SCIENCE FICTION NOVELS, H. G. Wells. Full unabridged texts of 7 science-fiction novels of the master. Ranging from biology, physics, chemistry, astronomy to sociology and other studies, Mr. Wells extrapolates whole worlds of strange and intriguing character. "One will have to go far to match this for entertainment, excitement, and sheer pleasure . . . ," NEW YORK TIMES. Contents: The Time Machine, The Island of Dr. Moreau, First Men in the Moon, The Invisible Man, The War of the Worlds, The Food of the Gods, In the Days of the Comet. 1015pp. 5⅜ x 8.
T264 Clothbound **$4.50**

28 SCIENCE FICTION STORIES OF H. G. WELLS. Two full unabridged novels, MEN LIKE GODS and STAR BEGOTTEN, plus 26 short stories by the master science-fiction writer of all time. Stories of space, time, invention, exploration, future adventure—an indispensable part of the library of everyone interested in science and adventure. PARTIAL CONTENTS: Men Like Gods, The Country of the Blind, In the Abyss, The Crystal Egg, The Man Who Could Work Miracles, A Story of the Days to Come, The Valley of Spiders, and 21 more! 928pp. 5⅜ x 8.
T265 Clothbound **$4.50**

THE WAR IN THE AIR, IN THE DAYS OF THE COMET, THE FOOD OF THE GODS: THREE SCIENCE FICTION NOVELS BY H. G. WELLS. Three exciting Wells offerings bearing on vital social and philosophical issues of his and our own day. Here are tales of air power, strategic bombing, East vs. West, the potential miracles of science, the potential disasters from outer space, the relationship between scientific advancement and moral progress, etc. First reprinting of "War in the Air" in almost 50 years. An excellent sampling of Wells at his storytelling best. Complete, unabridged reprintings. 16 illustrations. 645pp. 5⅜ x 8½.
T1135 Paperbound **$2.00**

Music

A GENERAL HISTORY OF MUSIC, Charles Burney. A detailed coverage of music from the Greeks up to 1789, with full information on all types of music: sacred and secular, vocal and instrumental, operatic and symphonic. Theory, notation, forms, instruments, innovators, composers, performers, typical and important works, and much more in an easy, entertaining style. Burney covered much of Europe and spoke with hundreds of authorities and composers so that this work is more than a compilation of records . . . it is a living work of careful and first-hand scholarship. Its account of thoroughbass (18th century) Italian music is probably still the best introduction on the subject. A recent NEW YORK TIMES review said, "Surprisingly few of Burney's statements have been invalidated by modern research . . . still of great value." Edited and corrected by Frank Mercer. 35 figures. Indices. 1915pp. 5⅜ x 8. 2 volumes.   T36 The Set, Clothbound **$12.50**

A DICTIONARY OF HYMNOLOGY, John Julian. This exhaustive and scholarly work has become known as an invaluable source of hundreds of thousands of important and often difficult to obtain facts on the history and use of hymns in the western world. Everyone interested in hymns will be fascinated by the accounts of famous hymns and hymn writers and amazed by the amount of practical information he will find. More than 30,000 entries on individual hymns, giving authorship, date and circumstances of composition, publication, textual variations, translations, denominational and ritual usage, etc. Biographies of more than 9,000 hymn writers, and essays on important topics such as Christmas carols and children's hymns, and much other unusual and valuable information. A 200 page double-columned index of first lines — the largest in print. Total of 1786 pages in two reinforced clothbound volumes. 6¼ x 9¼.
The set, T333 Clothbound **$17.50**

MUSIC IN MEDIEVAL BRITAIN, F. Ll. Harrison. The most thorough, up-to-date, and accurate treatment of the subject ever published, beautifully illustrated. Complete account of institutions and choirs; carols, masses, and motets; liturgy and plainsong; and polyphonic music from the Norman Conquest to the Reformation. Discusses the various schools of music and their reciprocal influences; the origin and development of new ritual forms; development and use of instruments; and new evidence on many problems of the period. Reproductions of scores, over 200 excerpts from medieval melodies. Rules of harmony and dissonance; influence of Continental styles; great composers (Dunstable, Cornysh, Fairfax, etc.); and much more. Register and index of more than 400 musicians. Index of titles. General index. 225-item bibliography. 6 Appendices. xix + 491pp. 5⅝ x 8¾.   T705 Clothbound **$10.00**

THE MUSIC OF SPAIN, Gilbert Chase. Only book in English to give concise, comprehensive account of Iberian music; new Chapter covers music since 1941. Victoria, Albéniz, Cabezón, Pedrell, Turina, hundreds of other composers; popular and folk music; the Gypsies; the guitar, dance, theatre, opera, with only extensive discussion in English of the Zarzuela; virtuosi such as Casals; much more. "Distinguished . . . readable," Saturday Review. 400-item bibliography. Index. 27 photos. 383pp. 5⅜ x 8.   T549 Paperbound **$2.00**

ON STUDYING SINGING, Sergius Kagen. An intelligent method of voice-training, which leads you around pitfalls that waste your time, money, and effort. Exposes rigid, mechanical systems, baseless theories, deleterious exercises. "Logical, clear, convincing . . . dead right," Virgil Thomson, N.Y. Herald Tribune. "I recommend this volume highly," Maggie Teyte, Saturday Review. 119pp. 5⅜ x 8.   T622 Paperbound **$1.25**

Prices subject to change without notice.

Dover publishes books on art, music, philosophy, literature, languages, history, social sciences, psychology, handcrafts, orientalia, puzzles and entertainments, chess, pets and gardens, books explaining science, intermediate and higher mathematics, mathematical physics, engineering, biological sciences, earth sciences, classics of science, etc. Write to:

Dept. catrr.
Dover Publications, Inc.
180 Varick Street, N.Y. 14, N.Y.